CW00496578

AIR FRYER
COOKBOOK

650 Delicious Recipes for family and busy people. Your favourite meals for every day.

Beginners & Advanced Users

NAOMI LANE

Table *of* Content

Beef, Lamb and Pork 33

Fish and Seafood 53

Bread 94

Pizza 99

Pasta 105

Desserts 109

Introduction

Are you always looking for easier and more modern ways to cook the best meals for you and all your family? Are you constantly searching for useful kitchen appliances that will make cooking in the kitchen more fun?

Well, you don't need to search anymore! This book will take you through the best kitchen appliance available on the market, the air fryer! Air fryers are simply the best kitchen tool for so many reasons. Would you like to know more about air fryers?

If yes, please read on!

As the proud owner of a new air fryer, you are probably wondering where to start. You may be looking for tips on how to use your new appliance or for new recipes. I was once in the same place you are now. By sharing my own journey with the air fryer, I hope to help guide and inform your new adventure with air fryer cooking.

Back in 2016, I received my first air fryer as a gift. At the time, I was homeschooling my children, and they were taking part in oodles of after-school activities. Our days were packed, and I was faced with the challenge of getting dinner on the table in record time. While grabbing fast food would have been an easy choice, I chose to cook with the air fryer, because we were trying to teach our children the importance of family meals and making healthy choices.

I had a rough start using the air fryer. Air fryers weren't that popular yet, so there wasn't much guidance out there. The recipes I was able to find didn't always work out. As aresult, I made a few horrible meals or, as my kids would say, inedible. I had months of trial and error. I would often make a recipe in the oven and in the air fryer, and I would — more often than not- throw away the air fried food. The chefs on the informercials made it look so easy.

I took this as a challenge. Soon, I was mastering the art of the air fryer and enjoying it. I began sharing my tried-and-true recipes with my friends in an online Facebook group, and I loved trying and sharing theirs, too.

My first recipe, which I worked days and days on, was very simple: cinnamon rolls. I was convinced that if you could cook in the air fryer, you should also be able to bake in the air fryer. I had never been much of a baker, but I have now baked hundreds of cakes, muffins, brownies, and cookies using my air fryer.

You also need to know that air fryers are special and revolutionary kitchen appliances that cook your food using the circulation of hot air. This tool uses a special technology called rapid air technology. Therefore, all the food you cook in these fryers is succulent on the inside and perfectly cooked on the outside.

The next thing you need to know about air fryers is that they allow you to cook, bake, steam, and roast pretty much everything you can imagine. Last but not least, you should know that air fryers help you cook your meals in a much healthier way.

So many people all over the world just fell in love with this great and amazing tool and now it's your turn to become one of them. 18This book is dedicated to each UK citizen that wants to expand the cooking smells that come out of the kitchen, and at the same time make meals that will fulfil not only the stomach but the soul as well.

The good news is that there are all kinds of food that you can air-fry. I have prepared a wide variety of different recipes with colourful pictures for you. If you have already bought this fantastic appliance, I will share how you can use it, how to clean it, its conversion and all the other details you should know about it.

Other than that, you will discover many tricks and tips that can make your cooking with an air fryer feel like a new experience. On the other hand, if you still haven't purchased an air fryer yet, I am sure this book of recipes will change your way of thinking.

This cookbook has been put together as a simple and understandable guide for you as you explore the uses of an air fryer. It is my goal that you will be able to make some delicious, drool-worthy but healthy meals while cooking with as little heat as possible. I put in the effort to ensure that the ingredients used are very easy to find and the directions very easy to follow.

With this, I wish you all the best making dishes that will create lasting memories for you and your loved ones.

Why You Should Use an Air Fryer?

As the name suggests, air fryers cook using convection heating. they circulate hot air around food. This gives a crispy, crunchy coating without the need to deep fry.

Look at air fried food and you'll see evidence of the Maillard reaction, which is a chemical effect produced between amino acids and reducing sugars that browns food and gives it a distinctive taste. In other words, an air fryer will provide the taste and texture of fried food, without you having to immerse your dinner in oil.

The Convection Concept

The concept of an air fryer is very similar to a convection oven that uses forced, heated, and circulated air to cook food faster, neatly and ever so completely. It also ensures the ingredients are cooked more evenly and the process is shorter compared to traditional gas or electric ovens.

A Timely Example

There's no preheating necessary when using an air fryer. Think of it this way: If you're looking to cook some frozen chips, for example, you'll need to preheat a regular oven to a blazing 200 degrees (or more) which usually takes around 10 minutes before baking them for an additional 18-20 minutes. In an air fryer, they only take 10 minutes from start to finish in order to completely cook frozen fries to crispy perfection.

Kid-Friendly

Given today's modern technology, many parents allow younger children to use the microwave oven since it doesn't really conduct much in the way of direct heat to potentially burn little fingers.

Health Benefits
Reduce the amount of acrylamide in food

Deep-fried foods contain high amounts of acrylamide—a substance formed when carbohydrates are heated to high temperatures—which has been linked to heart disease. The Department of Health and Human Services also classifies acrylamide as a"reasonably anticipated to be a human carcinogen" based on animal studies that have found it can lead to cancer. However, results from human studies are mixed and more research is needed, according to the National Cancer Institute.

The good news is air fryers appear to produce lower amounts of acrylamide. In fact, one 2015 study published in the Journal of Food Science found that air-fried potatoes had 90% less acrylamide compared to deep-fried versions.

Cut back on calories

Another benefit of air fryers is that they slash calories, since they require significantly less oil. For example. air fried foods may only need one teaspoon of oil, which adds a mere 40 calories. In contrast, just one tablespoon of oil absorbed into foods during deep frying adds about 120 calories. Therefore, swapping deep-fried foods for air-fried ones may help with weight management.

Do not produce some toxic compounds found in deep-fried food

Cutting back on oil frying has other health benefits as well. For instance, when oil is reused for deep frying (as is often the case at restaurants), the quality degrades, depleting food of antioxidants and producing harmful chemicals called reactive oxygen species, as per one 2015 study. Consuming foods with fewer antioxidants and more of these harmful byproducts compromise the body's antioxidant defense system, thus increasing the risk of disease. It also might cause blood vessel inflammation (which reduces blood flow) and high blood pressure.

Using air fryers can promote weight loss

A higher intake of fried foods has direct links with higher obesity risk. This is because deep fried foods tend to be high in fat and calories.

Switching from deep-fried foods to air-fried foods and reducing regular intake of unhealthful oils can promote weight loss.

Function Of Air Fryer

The top section of an air fryer holds a heating mechanism and fan. You place the food in a fryer-style basket and when you turn it on, hot air rushes down and around the food. This rapid circulation makes the food crisp—much like deep-frying, but without the oil.

Tips & Tricks

An air fryer can be a great addition to your kitchen, and not just because it's a healthier alternative to a deep fryer. It can also save time spent cooking and cleaning. However, here are some of my health-focused tips to keep in mind when using an air fryer:

Read the instructions: Most air fryers require you to leave at least five inches of space above the exhaust vent—otherwise, they become a fire hazard.

Use minimal amounts of oil: I recommend tossing or brushing food with about one to two teaspoons of oil per serving. Not only can too much oil up the calorie and fat content, but it can also cause smoking which makes food taste bad and impacts your health by producing free radicals that can harm cells.

Avoid aerosol sprays: Aerosol cooking oils can potentially break down the air fryer's non-stick basket, releasing toxic fumes.

Pair with other cooking methods: While air fryers are great, switch up your cooking methods throughout the week via sauté, slow cooking, and steaming. This will further reduce your exposure to chemicals like acrylamide. It also ensures you enjoy a wider variety of foods—not just those compatible with air fryers—which increases the spectrum of nutrients you consume.

Best Oils to Use

- Avocado oil
- Ghee
- Extra Light Olive Oil
- Olive Oil
- Soybean Oil
- Coconut Oil
- Peanut Oil
- Vegetable Oil
- ExtraVirgin Olive Oil
- Butter

Suggested Additional Equipment

- Silicone Mats
- 5.3 to 5.8 accessory kit for larger air fryers
- Baking Paper Sheets
- Silicone Pots

- Baking Tins
- Cake Tins
- Barrel Pans
- Skewers and rack
- Silicone Trivet
- Silicone Tongs
- Tortilla Stand for Tacos

How To Clean the Air Fryer?

Step 1: Gather Your Supplies

Before you start cleaning your air fryer, first gather all of the necessary tools and supplies.

Step 2: Let Your Air Fryer Cool Down

Unplug your air fryer and let it cool for a minimum of 30 minutes. Once cooled, take all of the removable parts out of the appliance (basket, tray, pan).

Step 3: Clean the Removable Parts

Wash the removable parts in warm soapy water. If you notice there's some baked-on grease or charred food on the parts, let them soak in hot soapy water for about 10 to 15 minutes, after which you can scrub them using anonabrasive sponge. For any hard-to-wash parts of the fryer or super-stubborn food residue that won't come off, you can make a cleaning paste of baking soda and water. Scrub the paste onto the residue with a soft-bristle brush and wipe clean.

Step 4: Clean the Interior

Wipe down the interior of your air fryer using a damp microfiber cloth or nonabrasive sponge with a splash of washing up liquid on it. Then wipe any soap residue off with a clean damp cloth.

Step 5: Check the Heating Element

Turn your air fryer upside-down and use a damp cloth or nonabrasive sponge to wipe down the heating element.

Step 6: Clean the Exterior

Just like the interior, wipe down the exterior using a cloth or sponge with a bit of washing up liquid. Wipe away any remnants of the soap with a clean damp cloth, then polish the outside with a piece of kitchen paper.

Step 7: Reassemble Your Air Fryer

Check to make sure every nook and cranny of your air fryer is thoroughly dry. Assemble all of the removable parts into the main unit and voilà!

Possible Risks

Air frying does not guarantee a healthful diet

While air fryers are capable of providing healthier food options than deep fryers, limiting fried food intake altogether can significantly benefit a person's health.

Just replacing all deep-fried foods with air-fried foods in no way guarantees a healthier diet.

For optimal health, people should focus on a diet filled with vegetables, fruits, whole grains, and lean protein.

Air fried food is not guaranteed to be healthful

Air fryers are capable of making foods that are healthier than deep-fried food, but keep in mind that fried food is still fried food. When cooking excessively with oil, there will always be associated health effects.

Air Fryer Types: How to Find the Best One?

The Solo Air Fryer is the best option for the majority of individuals (and most budget-friendly)

The simplest basic air fryer resembles a little robot. They are usually just acylindrical base with a basket that pulls in and out to store the food. These are available in sizes ranging from two quarts to six or seven quarts. These variants are available with either digital or manual controls. There are also air fryers with dual chambers that allow you to cook two types of food at different temperatures at the same time. Ninja manufactures a decent one with two 4-quart cooking baskets (8 quarts overall).

Solo air fryers are also the lowest priced, with prices starting at £25. If you only want to test air frying but don't want to spend a lot of money or kitchen space, I'd recommend one of these.

Air frying toaster oven: bake, grill, roast, and toast

These versions have the appearance and functionality of a regular countertop toaster oven, but they also include an air fry capability. Because they can grill, roast, bake, toast, and do so much more, an advanced form is almost like adding a second main oven to your kitchen. Some even include a rotisserie feature. The extra oven space they give may feel like a lifesaver to someone who celebrates Christmas or large family gatherings. Furthermore, they air fry; but, because of their bigger size, these models often do not cook as rapidly or as strongly as smaller solitary air fryer ovens.

Breville, KitchenAid, and Cuisinart all manufacture great (and huge) models. Ninja's Foodi, which blasted chicken wings and chips to crispy golden perfection in a test of these types of air frying toaster ovens, was my favorite in a test of these types of air frying toaster ovens, I suspect this was due in part to the smaller cooking cavity, which helps the air fry function work properly. It also produced delicious grilled fish and toast. These air fryers begin about £125 and rise in price from there.

Air fryer and multicooker: An all-in-one air frying

These are the most modern and flexible air fryers, capable of doing far more than simply air fry. Consider an Instant Pot with an air fryer option. Ninja's Foodi multicooker and the Instant Pot Duo Crisp are the two most popular models, and if you want an air fryer, multicooker, or pressure cooker but don't have much room to spare in your kitchen, one of them is a wonderful alternative. I've used the 6-quart Duo Crisp a lot and it works great, producing some of the most delicious fried chicken I've ever had (with no frying at all.) These versions typically cost between £145 and £200.

An air fryer attachment for your Instant Pot is an excellent choice.

If you already have an Instant Pot, you can connect an Instant Pot air fryer cover (£75) or a Mealthy (£50), which clamps on top and air fries food down below. Although they don't have a great frying capacity, I found the air fryer lids to perform incredibly well.

Should you choose a digital air fryer over an analog air fryer?

No. This is a matter of personal choice, although the controls have nothing to do with performance or ultimate outcome. Digital air fryers offer settings for things like chicken wings, chips, and fish, but I find that even if the presets exist, it only takes a few runs for me to understand how long items need to cook and the proper temperatures, and I end up skipping them anyway. Digital air fryers are more expensive, and there is a possibility of the panel shorting out, but having a digital display of the temperature and cook time can be useful.

Breakfast

1. Scrambled Eggs & Bacon

Serving size: 2 servings	**Preparation time:** 4 minutes	**Cooking time:** 10 minutes	**Total time:** 14 minutes

Ingredients

- 2 eggs
- 2 tablespoons milk
- 1/3 tablespoons butter, unsalted
- 90 grams cheddar cheese
- 90 grams bacon, diced
- Salt
- Pepper

Instructions

- Place butter in an oven/air fryer-safe pan and place inside the air fryer.
- Cook at 220 degrees C until butter is melted, for about 2 minutes.
- Whisk together the eggs and milk, then add the bacon and the salt and pepper to taste.
- Place the eggs in pan and cook at 200 degrees C for 3 minutes, then push the eggs to the inside of the pan and stir them around.
- Cook for 2 more minutes then add cheddar cheese, stirring the eggs again.
- Cook for a further 2 minutes.
- Remove the pan from the air fryer and enjoy them immediately.

2. Eggs and Avocado

Serving size: 2 servings	**Preparation time:** 5 minutes	**Cooking time:** 10 minutes	**Total time:** 15 minutes

Ingredients

- 2 eggs
- 1 avocado
- Salt
- Pepper

Instructions

- Preheat the Air Fryer to 220 degrees C.
- Cut the avocado in half and remove the seed
- Scoop out a bit extra of the avocado and set aside
- Set avocado halves in the air fryer
- Crack 1 egg into each avocado half
- Sprinkle with salt and pepper.
- Air fry at 220 degrees C for 10 minutes.

3. Eggs with Yellow Potatoes

 Serving size:
4

 Preparation time:
5 minutes

Cooking time:
20 minutes

Total Time:
25 minutes

Ingredients

- Potatoes: 400 grams potatoes, diced
- Olive oil
- Salt
- Pepper
- Eggs: 4 eggs
- 400 grams baby spinach
- ½ tomato
- Salt
- Pepper
- 2 tablespoons salsa

Instructions

- Toss your diced potatoes in olive oil and season with salt and pepper. Place them in the air fryer at 220 degrees C for 10 minutes. If your air fryer has a basket, you'll want to stop cooking after 10 minutes and shake the potatoes. This keeps the potatoes at the bottom from becoming underdone. Place the basket back in the air fryer and cook for another 10 to 15 minutes. (Total air fryer cooking time is 20 to 25 minutes.) Potatoes should be crispy and fully cooked.
- When your potatoes are almost finished, it's time to add your cooking fat of choice to the pan. Heat pan to medium or medium low heat.
- In a bowl, whisk together your eggs with a splash of water. This helps make them fluffy!
- Pour your egg mixture into the hot pan. Season with salt and pepper. When your eggs are close to done add your spinach and tomatoes. Reduce heat to low. Stir and cover for 1 – 2 minutes. Spinach should be wilted.
- To eat, layer your potatoes on bottom. Top with the scrambled egg. Add a scoop of your favorite salsa.

4. Sweet Potatoes Hash

 Serving size:
4

 Preparation time:
10 minutes

 Cooking time:
25 minutes

 Total Time:
35 minutes

Ingredients

- 3 medium sweet potatoes, chopped into chunks about 1 inch thick.
- 2 white onions, diced
- 3 slices bacon
- 2 chopped green peppers
- 2 garlic cloves chopped
- 1 diced celery
- 1 tablespoon olive oil
- 1/2 teaspoon paprika
- 1/2 teaspoon dried chives
- Salt
- Pepper

Instructions

- Combine the sweet potato chunks, onions, celery, green peppers, and garlic in a large bowl.
- Drizzle with olive oil and then sprinkle pepper, salt and paprika. Stir and mix well to combine.
- Add the sweet potato mix to the air fryer basket. Do not overcrowd the basket. Cook in batches if needed.
- Air fry for 10 minutes at 220 degrees.
- Open the air fryer and shake the basket. Air fry for an additional 2-7 minutes until the sweet potatoes are crisp on the outside and tender to touch when pierced with a fork.
- Sprinkle the crumbled bacon and dried chives throughout.

5. Yellow Potatoes Hash

 Serving size:
5

 Preparation time:
10 minutes

Cooking time:
30 minutes

 Total Time:
40 minutes

Ingredients

- 2 medium russet potatoes, diced
- 1 onion, diced
- 1 teaspoon salt
- 1/2 teaspoon pepper
- 2 teaspoons garlic powder
- 1 teaspoon thyme
- 2 tablespoons olive oil
- olive oil spray, as needed

Instructions

- Dice up russet potatoes, and onions into the same sized small chunks (be sure the onion is not too small as it might burn)
- Toss potatoes and onion with 2 tablespoons of olive oil, salt, pepper, garlic powder, and thyme
- Transfer mixture to the air fryer basket
- Turn air fryer to 220 degrees and cook for 20 - 30 minutes. Check the mixture at least 3 times. Stir and spray the top with olive oil spray if needed (I found this helps it get perfectly crisp).
- Once done, hash should be crispy on the outside but not burnt

6. Eggs with Baby Spinach and Plum Tomatoes

Serving size: 2		**Preparation time:** 10 minutes	
Cooking time: 7 minutes		**Total Time:** 17 minutes	

Ingredients

- 2 large eggs
- 1 tablespoon grated Parmesan cheese
- 2 tablespoons milk
- 1 teaspoon salt
- 1/4 teaspoon black pepper
- 150 grams diced plum tomatoes
- 2 tablespoons cooked onions, diced
- 100 grams diced baby spinach (fresh)
- 90 grams grated cheddar cheese

Instructions

- Start by cracking the eggs, and pour the grated Parmesan cheese, milk, salt, and pepper into a medium-sized mixing bowl. Beat the eggs until they are frothy.
- Fold in the diced spinach, onions, and plum tomatoes.
- Pour into a small air fryer-safe pan that has been sprayed with olive oil. Set the timer for 7 minutes at 220 degrees C, air fryer setting.
- When there is a minute left, sprinkle the cheddar cheese on top. Remove when the cheese is melted.
- Garnish with fresh herbs to your taste.
- Plate, serve and enjoy!

7. Breakfast Casserole

Serving size: 6		**Preparation time:** 10 minutes	
Cooking time: 20 minutes		**Total Time:** 30 minutes	

Ingredients

- 200 grams fresh broccoli florets
- 100 grams cream cheese, room temperature
- 60 ml. sour cream
- 100 grams grated cheddar
- 1 teaspoon salt
- 1/2 teaspoon cracked pepper
- 100 grams crushed crackers
- 2 tablespoons melted butter

Instructions

- Spray a 17 cm round baking dish with non-stick spray. See notes.
- Add the broccoli to a large microwave safe bowl along with 60 ml. of water. Cover tightly with cling film and microwave for 5 minutes. Let stand, covered, for 3 minutes.
- Carefully remove the cling film and drain the liquid.
- Add the cream cheese, sour cream, and cheddar to the bowl with the broccoli and stir well to combine.
- Pour the broccoli mixture into the prepared baking dish. Cover with foil.
- Air fry at 220 degrees for 10 minutes.
- Stir together the cracker crumbs and melted butter.
- Remove the foil and top the casserole with the cracker crumbs.
- Return the pan to the air fryer and cook, uncovered, for 5 minutes. Serve immediately.

8. Eggs with English Sausages

Serving size: 3		**Preparation time:** 15 minutes	
Cooking time: 12 minutes		**Total Time:** 27 minutes	

Ingredients

- 0,5 kg sausage meat (no skins)
- 6 eggs
- 250ml. milk
- 90 grams grated cheese

Instructions

- On medium-high heat cook the sausage for 5 minutes.
- Then, mix the eggs, milk, salt, sausage, and cheddar cheese in a large mixing bowl.
- Spray your casserole dish with olive oil spray.
- Then pour the egg/sausage mixture into the casserole dish.
- Set the dish in the air fryer basket or tray.
- Set the temperature to 220 degrees C for 12 minutes.
- After 5 minutes, check and see if your eggs are done. The Omni has a preheating setting, which is an additional few minutes. Sprinkle the extra cheese on top (optional) and close the air fryer, and wait for it to melt, about a minute.
- Plate, serve and enjoy!

9. Ramekins Eggs Omelette and Bacon

 Serving size:
4

 Preparation time:
5 minutes

 Cooking time:
15 minutes

 Total Time:
20 minutes

Ingredients

- 4 eggs
- 2 tablespoons single cream or half cream
- Salt and pepper to taste
- 90 grams bacon

Instructions

- Crack one egg into each of the ramekins. Add in the single cream. Whisk together.
- Then add the bacon together with the salt and pepper.
- Add ramekins to air fryer basket and cook for 15 minutes at 175 degrees C. Check on the eggs 2-3 times and give each a stir with a fork or whisk.

10. Ramekins with Mushrooms, Baby Spinach and Eggs

 Serving size:
4

  Preparation time:
5 minutes

 Cooking time:
15 minutes

 Total Time:
20 minutes

Ingredients

- 4 eggs
- 2 tablespoons single ceam or half cream
- Salt and pepper to taste
- 90 grams baby spinach
- 90 grams mushrooms

Instructions

- Crack one egg into each of the ramekins. Add in the single cream. Whisk together.
- Then add the mushrooms together with the spinach and salt and pepper.
- Add ramekins to air fryer basket and cook for 15 minutes at 175 degrees C. Check on the eggs 2-3 times and give each a stir with a fork or whisk.

11. Grilled Tomato Toast

 Serving size:
1

 Preparation time:
5 minutes

 Cooking time:
13 minutes

 Total time:
18 minutes

Ingredients

- 1 piece of Toast
- 30 grams Feta Cheese
- 2 slices Tomatoes
- 1/2 tablespoon Olive Oil
- for seasoning Paprika
- for seasoning Black Pepper

Instructions

- Brush the toast with olive oil. Place the tomato slices and the feta cheese on top. Season with black pepper.
- Air fry for 10 minutes at 180 degrees C. Season with paprika.

12. British Blueberry Pancakes

 Serving size:
4

 **Preparation time:**
10 minutes

 Cooking time:
15 minutes

Total time:
25 minutes

Ingredients

- 130 grams pancake mix
- 1 large egg
- 120 ml. water
- ¼ teaspoon ground cinnamon
- 100 grams fresh blueberries

Instructions

- In a large mixing bowl, add the pancake mix, egg and water.
- Mix well.
- Fold in the blueberries and ground cinnamon.
- Spray with non-stick cooking spray or olive oil, your air fryer safe pan.
- Pour your mixture into the prepared pan.
- Set your temperature to 220 degrees C on your air fryer, for 10 to 12 minutes.
- Check and make sure it's cooked all the way through; if it needs a couple of additional minutes, just add another 3 minutes.
- Plate, serve, and enjoy!

13. Waffles with Orange Marmalade

 Serving size:
4

 Preparation time:
10 minutes

 Cooking time:
4/5 minutes

 Total time:
15 minutes

Ingredients

- 1 jar of orange marmalade
- 4 frozen waffles

Instructions

- Preheat the air fryer to 200 degrees C.
- Remove the frozen waffles from the freezer and place them on the air fryer tray once it is hot. If you can't fit four waffles in your air fryer due to its size, just use however many you can fit in one layer without overlap.
- Cook the waffles for 4-5 minutes total. Flip them over after 3 minutes. Depending on your preferred level of crispiness, you can cook them slightly longer.
- Remove the waffles from the air fryer and serve them with orange marmalade on top.

14. Chorizo and Potato Frittata

 Serving size:
4

 Preparation time:
7 minutes

 Cooking time:
18 to 20 minutes

 Total time:
25 minutes

Ingredients

- 200 grams potatoes
- 4 eggs, lightly beaten
- 150 grams chorizo
- 2 tablespoons red pepper, diced
- 1 onion, chopped
- 1 pinch cayenne pepper (optional)
- cooking spray

Instructions

- Combine sausage, eggs, potatoes, pepper, onion, and cayenne in a bowl and mix to combine.
- Preheat the air fryer to 180 degrees C. Spray a nonstick 6x2-inch cake tin with cooking spray.
- Place the egg mixture in the prepared cake pan.
- Cook in the air fryer until the frittatas are set, 18 to 20 minutes.

15. Egg and Ham Ramekins

 Serving size:
4

 Preparation time:
10 minutes

 Cooking time:
5 minutes

 Total time:
15 minutes

Ingredients

- 4 eggs
- 150 grams diced ham
- 150 grams grated cheddar cheese
- 4 tablespoon double cream
- salt and pepper to taste
- 4–5 tablespoons cheddar cheese (optional)

Instructions

- In a small mixing bowl, whisk together the eggs, ham, grated cheese, cream, salt, and pepper.
- Spray your ramekins with olive oil spray.
- Pour the egg mixture into the cups, evenly.
- Set the ramekins in the air fryer basket or tray.
- Set the temperature to 200 degrees C for 5 minutes.
- After 5 minutes, check and see if your eggs are done.
- Plate, serve, and enjoy!

16. Filled Hash Browns

 Serving size:
5

 Preparation time:
20 minutes

 Cooking time:
20 minutes

 Total time:
40 minutes

Ingredients

- 4 large russet potatoes
- 100 grams Greek yogurt
- 2 tablespoons breadcrumbs
- 2 teaspoons kosher salt, divided
- 1 teaspoon ground black pepper
- 1 teaspoon garlic powder
- 1 teaspoon onion powder
- 2 teaspoons vegetable oil

Instructions

- Peel and grate the potatoes.
- Place the grated potatoes in a bowl of cold water for 10 to 20 minutes to draw out the excess starch.
- Drain and rinse the potatoes. Wipe out the bowl and return the potatoes to the bowl.

- Microwave on a high heat for 4 to 5 minutes, stirring after each minute to parcook the potatoes.
- Lay them on kitchen paper-lined baking tray and pat them completely dry with more kitchen paper
- Return the potatoes to the bowl and add the breadcrumbs, 1 teaspoon of the salt, along with the pepper, garlic powder, and onion powder. Combine until the seasonings are evenly distributed among the potatoes.
- Line a baking tray with baking paper. Using a cookie scoop or spoon, to scoop up balls of the potato mixture and place them into an egg mould or round cookie cutter on the baking sheet. Press down to form patties within the ring. Remove the ring and repeat with the remaining potatoes.
- Fill them with Greek yogurt.
- Place the baking sheet into the fridge and chill for 20 minutes. Preheat the air fryer to 200 degrees C.
- Brush the basket of your air fryer with the oil and place the hash browns into the basket in one layer. You may have to fry them in batches.
- Air fry for 15 minutes, flipping halfway through until golden brown on both sides.
- Be careful not to spill the Greek yogurt.

17. Apple Fritters

	Serving size: 15		Preparation time: 10 minutes
	Cooking time: 10 minutes per batch		Total time:

Ingredients

- 90 grams all-purpose flour
- 40 grams sugar
- 2 teaspoons baking powder
- 5 teaspoons ground cinnamon
- Salt
- 50 ml. 2% milk (skimmed)
- 2 large eggs, room temperature
- 1 tablespoon lemon juice
- 3 teaspoons vanilla extract, divided
- 2 medium Honeycrisp apples, peeled and chopped
- Cooking spray
- 50 grams butter
- 30 grams icing sugar
- 1 tablespoon 2% milk (skimmed)

Instructions

- Preheat air fryer to 220°C. In a large bowl, combine flour, sugar, baking powder, cinnamon and salt. Add milk, eggs, lemon juice and 1 teaspoon of vanilla extract; stir just until moistened. Fold in apples.

- Line air-fryer basket with baking paper (cut to fit); spray with cooking spray. In batches, drop dough by 1/4 cupfuls, 2 in. a part onto the paper. Spray with cooking spray. Cook until golden brown, 5-6 minutes. Turn fritters; continue to air-fry until golden brown, 1-2 minutes.
- Melt butter in a small saucepan over a medium-high heat. Carefully cook until the butter starts to brown and foam, about 5 minutes. Remove from the heat; cool slightly. Add icing sugar, 1 tablespoon of milk and the remaining 1/2 teaspoon of vanilla extract to the browned butter; whisk until smooth. Drizzle over fritters before serving.

18. British French Toast

	Serving size: 1		Preparation time: 5 minutes
	Cooking time: 2-3 minutes		Total time: 7-8 minutes

Ingredients

- 2 eggs
- 2 tablespoons milk, cream, or single/half cream
- 1/2 teaspoon ground cinnamon
- 1/2 teaspoon vanilla extract
- 1 brioche bread, cut into 8 thick slices

Instructions

- In a medium bowl, add egg, milk, vanilla, and cinnamon; whisk to combine completely; set aside
- Make an assembly line: setup the whisked egg mixture and bread next to each other.
- Spray the air fryer basket with nonstick oil spray
- Dip the slices of bread into the egg mixture. being sure to flip and coat both sides. Lift out of the mixture and allow to drip for a few seconds, then place into the air fryer basket. Repeat for remaining slices
- Close the Air Fryer. Set to 200 degrees C and cook for 5 minutes. After 5 minutes, open the basket and carefully flip the french toast slices. Close the air fryer and cook for 3-4 more minutes at 200 degrees C.
- Remove the french toast when finished and then cook remaining french toast slices.
- Serve with warm maple syrup and icing sugar or your favorite toppings!

19. Air Fryer Granola with Sour Cream and Blueberries

 Serving size:
20

 Preparation time:
5 minutes

 Cooking time:
20 minutes

 Total time:
25 minutes

Ingredients

- 300 grams rolled oats
- 200 grams nuts and seeds (mixed)
- 150 grams blueberries
- 120 grams honey
- 1 teaspoon cinnamon
- 120 ml. sour cream

Instructions

- Preheat your air frier to 200 degrees C.
- Roughly chop any large nuts. Combine the ingredients in a mixing bowl. Stir to coat every piece evenly with the honey.
- Spread the granola over the air fryer's baking tray. You want the grains and nuts to stick together nicely.
- Bake the granola in the air fryer for 15-20 minutes, or until the grains are slightly golden on the edges.
- Remove the granola from the air fryer, and leave it to cool down completely while it's still in the baking tray. Then, break it up into bite sized clusters. Add blueberries and sour cream on top and serve.

20. French Toast Sticks with Strawberry Marmalade

 Serving size:
6

 Preparation time:
10 minutes

 Cooking time:
8 minutes

 Total time:
18 minutes

Ingredients

- 12 slices thick white bread
- 130 ml. milk
- 5 large eggs
- 4 tablespoons butter, melted
- 1 teaspoon vanilla extract
- 50 grams granulated sugar
- 1 tablespoon cinnamon
- Strawberry marmalade/jam

Instructions

- Slice each bread slice into thirds.
- In a bowl, add the milk, eggs, butter, and vanilla. Whisk until combined.
- In a separate bowl, add the cinnamon and sugar.
- Dip each bread stick quickly into the egg mixture.
- Sprinkle the sugar mixture onto both sides.
- Place into the air fryer basket and cook at 200°C for about 8 minutes or until just crispy.
- Remove from basket and allow to cool. Serve with strawberry marmalade.

21. Fluffy Omelette

 Serving size:
1

 Preparation time:
5 minutes

Cooking time:
10 minutes

 Total time:
15 minutes

Ingredients

- 2 eggs
- 2 cherry tomatoes
- 1 small onion
- 2 mushrooms
- 2 slices of turkey
- 1 spring onion
- Pinch salt
- Fresh ground black pepper
- Cheese (optional)
- Cooking spray

Instructions

- Dice the onion, pepper , spring onion, mushroom, and turkey.
- In a small bowl, mix the eggs, a pinch of salt, and fresh ground pepper.
- Add the vegetables and turkey to the egg and mix to combine.
- Preheat the air fryer to 200 degrees C and grease a cake tin with butter or oil.
- Put the tin into the air fryer basket and cook for 8-10 minutes.
- After 4 minutes sprinkle the egg with shredded cheese.
- Take a spatula and slide the omelette out of the tin onto a plate and serve immediately.

22. Tofu, and Plum Tomatoes Omelette

 Serving size:
2

 Preparation time:
5 minutes

 Cooking time:
10 0minutes

 Total time:
15 minutes

Ingredients

- Half a block of organic tofu
- 3 eggs

Instructions

- Dice the tofu and mix it with the eggs, together with pepper and salt.
- Preheat the air fryer to 200 degrees C and grease a cake tin with butter or oil.
- Put the tin into the air fryer basket and cook for 8-10 minutes.

23. Savoury French Toast

 Serving size:
1

 Preparation time:
5 minutes

 Cooking time:
10 minutes

 Total time:
15 minutes

Ingredients

- 4 slices of bread
- 2 slices of cheese or to taste (I used colby jack cheese)
- 2 slices of ham or to taste
- 1 avocado pitted and cut into thin slices.
- 2 tablespoon pickled jalapeno chopped (optional)
- 2 tablespoon mayonnaise
- 2 eggs

Instructions

- Crack two eggs into a shallow plate and whisk for about 10 seconds. Set aside.
- Line the fryer basket with a grill matt or a sheet of lightly greased aluminum foil.
- Spread some mayonnaise to one side of each slice of bread Then, assemble the sandwich by putting ham, cheese, jalapeno and avocado in between two slices of bread.
- Dip the both sides of the sandwich in egg mixture, each side for about 3 seconds. Put the sandwiches inside the fryer basket.
- Spray some oil onto the sandwiches and air fry at 190 degrees C for 8-10 minutes, turn over once in the middle of the cooking time, cook until the surface is golden brown.

24. Egg Muffins

 Serving size:
8

 Preparation time:
5 minutes

 Cooking time:
12 minutes

 Total time:
17 minutes

Ingredients

- 6 large eggs
- 90 grams double cream
- 100 grams cheddar
- 90 grams breakfast sausage
- Olive oil
- 1 teaspoon of garlic
- 250 grams spinach

Instructions

- Heat a nonstick pan on a medium-low heat.
- Add breakfast sausage meat (no skin) and cook for 12-16 minutes or until cooked through and browned. Crumble the sausage with a wooden spoon or cooking utensil of choice.
- Remove the breakfast sausage from the pan. Let the sausage cool.
- Add 1 teaspoon of olive oil and garlic to the pan. Cook until the garlic is fragrant and Add the spinach to the pan and cover; allow to cook 5 minutes. Take the spinach out of the pan let it cool like you did with the sausage.
- In a medium bowl add the eggs and milk and whisk until combined. Fold in the cheddar, breakfast sausage, and spinach.
- Place the silicone muffin cups into the air fryer basket and set the temperature to 200 degrees C. Fill the cups with the egg mixture (do not overfill).
- Set the air fryer time to 12 minutes at 200 degrees C.

25. Traditional English Breakfast

 Serving size:
2

 Preparation time:
3 minutes

 Cooking time:
15 minutes

 Total time:
18 minutes

Ingredients

- 6 English sausages
- 6 bacon rashers
- 2 large tomatoes
- 4 black pudding
- ½ can baked beans
- 2 large eggs
- 1 tablespoon whole milk
- 1 teaspoon butter
- salt & pepper

Instructions

- Crack your eggs into a ramekin and stir in butter, milk and salt and pepper. Place in the air fryer. Add to the air fryer bacon rashers, black pudding, and sausages. Slice tomatoes in half and season the top with salt and pepper.
- Close the air fryer basket, making sure first that there is room for each of the breakfast items to cook. Then cook for 10 minutes at 180 degrees C. Though at the 5 minute interval stir your eggs with a fork.
- When the air fryer beeps, check to make sure the eggs are scrambled and remove the scrambled eggs with an oven glove or kitchen tongs. Replace the ramekin space with a ramekin of cold baked beans. Cook for a further 5 minutes at the same temperature.

26. Beef Rolls

Serving size: 8	Preparation time: 15 minutes
Cooking time: 25 minutes	Total time: 40 minutes

Ingredients

- 500 grams minced beef
- 16 egg roll wrappers
- 1 onion, chopped
- 2 garlic cloves chopped
- 1 can diced tomatoes
- Half a can black beans
- 130 grams grated Mexican cheese
- Half a can sweetcorn
- cooking oil spray

Instructions

- Add the ground beef to a pan on a medium high heat along with the salt, pepper, and the taco seasoning. Cook until browned while breaking the beef into smaller chunks.
- Once the meat has started to brown add the chopped onions and garlic. Cook until the onions become fragrant.
- Add the diced tomatoes and chillis, Mexican cheese, beans and sweetcorn. Stir to ensure the mixture is combined.
- Lay the egg roll wrappers on a flat surface. Dip a cooking brush in water. Glaze each of the egg roll wrappers with the wet brush along the edges. This will soften the crust and make it easier to roll.
- Load 2 tablespoons of the mixture into each of the wrappers. Do not overstuff. Depending on the brand of egg roll wrappers you use, you may need to double wrap the egg rolls.
- Fold the wrappers diagonally to close. Press firmly on the area with the filling, cup it to secure it in place. Fold in the left

and right sides as triangles. Fold the final layer over the top to close. Use the cooking brush to wet the area and secure it in place.
- Spray the air fryer basket with cooking oil.
- Load the egg rolls into the basket of the Air Fryer. Spray each egg roll with cooking oil.
- Cook for 8 minutes on 200 degrees C. Flip the egg rolls. Cook for an additional 4 minutes or until browned and crisp.

27. Breakfast Chicken Pie

Serving size: 4	Preparation time: 10 minutes
Cooking time: 10 minutes	Total time: 20 minutes

Ingredients

- 100 grams frozen vegetables of choice
- 150 grams chicken, shredded
- 90 ml. chicken soup
- 1 package Pillsbury flaky grands

Instructions

- Spray the baking dish with nonstick cooking spray.
- Place 4 biscuits in the bottom of the dish and press down until you have an even layer.
- Place in the air fryer and cook for 3 minutes at 200°C. This will allow the bottom crust to be cooked through.
- In a small bowl mix together the diced chicken, soup, and vegetables. Mix well.
- Place your filing in the centre of the bottom crust.
- With the leftover 4 biscuits, place on top of the chicken mixture.
- Set into the air fryer and set the temperature to 220 degrees C, for 5-7 minutes, air fryer setting, remove once golden brown.

28. Oats with Cream Cheese

Serving size: 6	Preparation time: 10 minutes
Cooking time: 33 minutes	Total time: 43 minutes

Ingredients

- 200 grams rolled oatmeal, dry
- 150 grams fresh pineapple, chopped
- 90 ml. milk
- 100 grams mashed banana, very ripe (about 3 bananas)
- 1 teaspoon vanilla
- 100 grams pecans, chopped
- cooking oil spray

Instructions

- Spray a piece of foil with cooking oil spray. Cover the pan with the foil (oiled side facing the oatmeal), securing the foil around the edges of the pan.
- Preheat the air fryer to 170°C for 5 minutes. Carefully put the foil covered pan in the middle of the air fryer oven. Air fry the oatmeal for 30 minutes together with the milk, and pecans. Then remove the foil and air fry for an additional 3 minutes.
- Allow the oatmeal to cool and top it with the rest of ingredients.

29. Egg and French Beans Mixture

 Serving size:
8

 Preparation time:
15 minutes

 Cooking time:
8 minutes

 Total time:
23 minutes

Ingredients

- 250 grams green beans rinse and pat dry
- 90 grams all-purpose flour
- 2 eggs
- 130 grams seasoned panko bread crumbs
- 130 grams Parmesan cheese grated
- 1/2 teaspoon garlic powder
- 1/2 teaspoon onion powder
- 1/2 teaspoon paprika
- Dipping sauce for serving (optional)

Instructions

- Preheat air fryer to 200 degrees C.
- Set up a dredge station using three shallow bowls. To the first bowl add the flour. To the second bowl, add the eggs and beat them. To the third bowl, add the seasoned panko, Parmesan cheese, garlic powder, onion powder, and paprika.

- First, toss a few dried green beans in the flour. Then dip them into the egg, and then coat in the panko bread crumb mixture. Repeat with the remaining green beans.
- Place the coated green beans into the basket of the air fryer. (Don't overfill it!)
- Cook for 8 minutes until tender and the crust is golden.

30. Asparagus Frittata

 Serving size:
1

 Preparation time:
10 minutes

 Cooking time:
8 minutes

 Total time:
18 minutes

Ingredients

- 2 large eggs
- 1 tablespoon fresh grated Parmesan cheese
- 2 tablespoons milk
- 5 steamed asparagus tips
- pinch salt and pepper
- non-stick cooking spray

Instructions

- In a bowl, whisk together the eggs, cheese, milk, salt and pepper.
- Spray an oven safe dish with non-stick cooking spray and place in the air fryer basket.
- Pour the egg mix into the dish and place the asparagus into it. Cook at 200 degrees C for 8 mins. Check that it is set by inserting a toothpick in the centre. When it comes out clean, the eggs are done.

Poultry

31. Portuguese Whole Chicken

Serving size: 6 servings	**Preparation time:** 5 minutes	**Cooking time:** 1 hour	**Total time:** 1 hour and 5 minutes

Ingredients

- 1 whole chicken, medium sized, giblets removed
- 2 tablespoons avocado oil
- 1 tablespoon Kosher salt
- 1 teaspoon freshly ground black pepper
- 1 teaspoon garlic powder
- 1 teaspoon paprika
- ½ teaspoon dried basil
- ½ teaspoon dried oregano
- ½ teaspoon dried thyme

Instructions

- Combine all of the seasonings with the oil to make a paste and spread it all over the chicken.
- Spray the air fryer basket with cooking spray. Place the chicken in the basket breast side down and cook at 360F for 50 minutes. Flip the chicken to breast side up and cook for an additional 10 minutes.
- Check to make sure the breast meat has an internal temperature of 165F. Carve and serve.

32. Chicken Wings with Cayenne Spice and Potatoes

Serving size: 2 servings	**Preparation time:** 10 minutes	**Cooking time:** 30 minutes	**Total time:** 40 minutes

Ingredients

- 500 grams chicken wings flats and drumettes separated
- 500 grams
- 1 tablespoon avocado oil or olive oil
- 1/2 teaspoon coarse sea salt kosher salt, to taste
- 1/2 teaspoon garlic powder
- 1/4 teaspoon onion powder
- 1/4 teaspoon cayenne pepper or smoked paprika
- freshly cracked black pepper to taste
- fresh chopped parsley for garnish
- ranch dressing for serving
- chopped celery and carrots for serving

Instructions

- If your air fryer requires preheating, preheat to 220°C, as needed.
- Pat the wings dry on both sides with kitchen paper. Drizzle with oil then sprinkle evenly with salt, black pepper, garlic powder, onion powder and cayenne (or smoked paprika).
- Working in batches (depending on the size of your air fryer), place the wings in the air fryer basket in a single layer, making sure they are not crowding or overlapping.
- Cook at 220°F for 12 minutes, then remove the basket and use tongs to flip the wings. Cook again for 10-12 minutes, until golden brown or to desired crispiness.
- Transfer to a serving platter and sprinkle with coarse salt, chopped fresh parsley.
- Then make the potatoes. In a large bowl, toss potatoes with oil, pepper, and salt.
- Place potatoes in the basket of the air fryer and cook at 220° for 10 minutes. Shake basket and stir potatoes and cook until potatoes are golden and tender, 8 to 10 minutes more.
-

33. Salsa Verde Chicken Kebobs

 Serving size:
5

 Preparation time:
5 minutes

 Cooking time:
15 minutes

 Total time:
20 minutes

Ingredients

- 1 kg. skinless, boneless chicken breasts, cut into cubes
- 2 tablespoons soy sauce
- 1 tablespoon chicken seasoning
- 1 teaspoon smoked paprika
- Kosher salt, to taste
- Ground black pepper, to taste
- ½ green pepper, cut into chunks
- ½ red pepper, cut into chunks
- ½ yellow pepper, cut into chunks
- ½ courgete, sliced into thin rounds
- ¼ red onion, cut into chunks
- 8 grape tomatoes

Instructions

- Marinate the chicken by placing the chunks of chicken in a resealable plastic bag along with the soy sauce, chicken seasoning, paprika, salt and pepper. Remove the air from the bag and seal. Refrigerate for at least one hour, but perferably overnight.
- Remove the chicken from the marinade.
- Place the chicken and vegetables on the skewers and spray with olive oil cooking spray.
- Preheat your air fryer for 3 minutes at 170 degrees C.
- Place the skewers in the air fryer basket. Cook for 10 minutes on 350 degrees.
- Flip the skewers and cook for an additional 7-10 minutes or until the chicken reaches an internal temperature of 170 degrees C.
- Serve immediately.

34. Chicken Wings with Sesame Seeds

 Serving size:
6 servings

 Preparation time:
20 minutes

 Cooking time:
1 hour

 Total time:
1 hour and 20 minutes

Ingredients

- 1,5 kg. chicken wing drumettes and flats
- 3 teaspoons baking powder
- 2 teaspoons kosher salt
- 2 tablespoons gochujang
- 2 tablespoons soy sauce
- 1 tablespoon rice wine vinegar
- 2 teaspoons sesame oil
- 1 teaspoon sugar
- 3 tablespoons butter, melted and kept warm

Instructions

- Pat the wings dry, if needed. In a large bowl, add the wings and toss them with the baking powder and salt until evenly coated.
- Spread the wings around the bowl so they are in a single layer and refrigerate them, uncovered, for at least 6 hours and up to 24 hours.
- Heat the air fryer to 170°C. Open the drawer and fit as many wings as you can in it without crowding them. Close the drawer. Cook for 25 minutes, shaking the drawer every 5 minutes to shuffle the wings around.
- As the wings cook, make the sauce. In a medium bowl, whisk together the gochujang, soy sauce, rice wine vinegar, sesame oil, and sugar. Set aside.
- Once the wings have cooked for 25 minutes, increase the temperature of the air fryer to 220°C. Cook the wings for another 5 minutes. This gets them nice and brown and especially crispy.
- Mix the melted butter with the sauce (it might solidify a bit, but the heat of the wings will re-melt it). Add the wings to a large bowl, pour over half the sauce and toss the wings in the sauce.
- Transfer to a serving platter and sprinkle with spring onions and sesame seeds, if you like. Serve immediately, accompanied by the cucumbers, radishes, and sesame mayonnaise for dipping.

35. Chicken Schnitzel with Mozzarella

 Serving size:
2

 Preparation time:
5 minutes

 Cooking time:
10 minutes

 Total time:
15 minutes

Ingredients

- 750 grams chicken breasts, butterflied
- 100 grams plain flour
- 1 teaspoon onion powder

- 2 teaspoon garlic powder
- Salt
- Black pepper
- 1 egg
- 180 grams panko breadcrumbs
- 1 tablespoon cooking oil
- 1 package mozzarella cheese

Instructions

- Pound out each piece of chicken breast, so they are an even thickness.
- In a bowl, combine the flour, onion powder, garlic powder, salt, and pepper.
- Crack the egg into a separate bowl and beat slightly.
- Lastly, add the breadcrumbs into yet another bowl.
- One by one, coat the chicken in the following order. First, in the seasoning mixture. Next, coat in the egg. Lastly, coat in the breadcrumbs. Repeat until you have coated all the chicken.
- Preheat the air fryer to 200°C. It should take roughly 5 minutes.
- Cook the chicken in batches so there is only a single layer. Cook for 10 minutes, flipping halfway through and adding a slice of mozzarella cheese on top of it.

36. Drumsticks with Cheddar Cheese Sause

 Serving size:
2

 Preparation time:
5 minutes

 Cooking time:
20 minutes

 Total time:
25 minutes

Ingredients

- 8-12 chicken legs
- 4 teaspoons paprika
- 2 teaspoons Italian Seasoning
- 2 teaspoon brown sugar
- Salt
- Pepper
- 4 tablespoons olive oil

The Sauce:
- 100 ml. 1% low-fat milk, divided
- 4 teaspoons all-purpose flour
- ¼ teaspoon salt
- 100 grams cheddar cheese, grated
- ¼ teaspoon freshly ground black pepper

Instructions

- Pat the chicken legs with kitchen paper to dry. Add them to a medium sized bowl.

- In a small bowl combine paprika, Italian seasoning, brown sugar, and salt and pepper. Add the olive oil to the bowl of chicken and sprinkle with the seasonings and toss until fully coated.
- Place the chicken legs skin side down in the basket of the air fryer. Cook at 200 degrees C for 10 minutes. Flip after 10 minutes and continue to cook for 7-8 more minutes until no longer pink and the internal temperature is 170 degrees.
- The Sauce
- Combine 1/4 of the milk and flour in a saucepan; stir with a whisk.
- Stir in remaining 3/4 milk and salt; bring to a boil over medium heat, stirring frequently.
- Reduce the heat to low; simmer 2 minutes or until slightly thickened, stirring constantly.
- Remove from heat.
- Stir in cheese and pepper, and continue stirring until cheese melts. Add the cheese sauce over the meat.

37. Chicken Bites with English Mustard

Serving size:
6

Preparation time:
10 minutes

Cooking time:
12 minutes

Total time:
22 minutes

Ingredients

- 1 kg boneless chicken breast or thighs
- 1 tablespoon paprika
- ½ teaspoon garlic powder
- ¼ teaspoon onion powder
- 1 teaspoon thyme
- ½ teaspoon parsley
- ¼ teaspoon black pepper
- Salt to taste
- 1 tablespoon olive oil
- 90 grams English mustard

Instructions

- Pat the chicken dry with kitchen paper then cut it into bite-size that is about an inch.
- Add the cut chicken into a bowl then add the mustard and then the seasoning. Mix till well combined and chicken evenly coated in seasoning.
- If you have time, put the chicken in the fridge to marinate for a few hours.
- Set the air fryer to a temperature of 190 degrees C then air fry the chicken chunks for 10-12 minutes or till cooked.
- Bring out of the air fryer, then serve the chicken.

38. Chicken with Peas and Carrots

 Serving size: 2

 Preparation time: 10 minutes

 Cooking time: 35 minutes

 Total time: 45 minutes

Ingredients

- 2 boneless skinless chicken breasts
- ½ tablespoon olive oil
- 1 teaspoon chili powder
- 1/2 teaspoon paprika
- 1/2 teaspoon onion powder
- 1/2 teaspoon garlic powder
- 1/2 teaspoon salt
- 1/2 teaspoon pepper
- 1/4 teaspoon cumin
- 400 grams peas
- 400 grams carrots

Instructions

- Set air fryer to "air fry" and preheat to 220 degrees C.
- In a small bowl combine all the chicken spices (chili powder, onion powder, garlic powder, salt, pepper, cumin and paprika) to make a spice rub. Coat the chicken breasts with olive oil followed by the spice rub. Set aside.
- Peel carrots and wash the peas. Cut the potatoes into medium-sized pieces. Add salt, pepper, and oil.
- Place the vegetables into the preheated air fryer basket. Place the chicken breasts on top of the vegetables and close the air fryer. Cook for 35 minutes. Halfway through cooking, flip the chicken and give the veggies agood shake.

39. Chicken Honey

 Serving size: 6

 Preparation time: 15 minutes

 Cooking time: 30 minutes

 Total time: 45 minutes

Ingredients

- 6 boneless, skinless, chicken thighs
- 130 grams cornstarch (or potato starch)
- 1 pinch black pepper
- 1/4 teaspoon ground ginger
- 1/4 teaspoon ground nutmeg
- 1/8 teaspoon ground thyme
- 1/8 teaspoon ground sage
- 1/8 teaspoon paprika

Honey Garlic Sauce:

- 2 tablespoons olive oil
- 3 to 4 garlic cloves, minced
- 130 grams honey
- 30 ml. soy sauce
- 1 teaspoon ground black pepper

Instructions

- Cut the chicken into cubed chunks, then toss it in a bowl with cornstarch & seasonings. Use enough to coat the chicken evenly.
- Place in the Air Fryer and cook according to 220 degrees C.
- In a medium saucepan add 2 tablespoons olive oil and minced garlic. Cook over a medium heat to soften the garlic but do not let it brown.
- Add the honey, soy sauce, and black pepper.
- Simmer together for 5-10 minutes, remove from heat and allow to cool for a few minutes. Watch this carefully as it simmers because it can foam up over the pot very easily.
- Once the sauce is made and the chicken is finished cooking, combine in aserving dish and toss to coat the chicken completely.

40. Chicken Fingers with Parmesan Cheese

 Serving size: 4

 Preparation time: 10 minutes

 Cooking time: 15 minutes

Total time: 25 minutes

Ingredients

- 500 grams skinless, chicken tenderloins or breast sliced/ cut into strips
- 60 grams grated parmesan cheese (I used freshly grated).
- 40 grams breadcrumbs
- 1 egg
- 30 grams all-purpose flour
- 1 teaspoon Italian Seasoning
- Salt
- Pepper
- cooking oil spray I used olive oil

Instructions

- Place the breadcrumbs, eggs, and flour in separate bowls.
- Add the grated parmesan, Italian Seasoning, salt and pepper to taste to the bowl with the breadcrumbs. Stir.
- Coat the sliced chicken breasts in flour, then egg, and then the breadcrumbs.
- Spray both sides of the chicken tenders with cooking oil.
- Add the chicken tenders to the air fryer basket. Do not stack the tenders. Cook in batches if needed. Cook for 8 minutes on 200 degrees.

- Open the basket and flip the tenders. Cook for an additional 6 to 8 minutes or until the chicken tenders are crisp. Exact cook time will vary based on the air fryer brand that you use. Keep an eye on the tenders to make sure the appropriate cook time is achieved.
- Ensure the chicken reaches an internal temperature of at least 170 degrees C. Use ameat thermometer.

41. Tarragon Chicken

 Serving size:
4

 Preparation time:
5 minutes

 Cooking time:
22 minutes

 Total time:
27 minutes

Ingredients

- 500 grams boneless skinless chicken breasts (4 chicken breasts)
- 2 teaspoons unsalted butter
- 4 teaspoons dried tarragon leaf
- 1/4 teaspoon kosher salt
- 1/4 teaspoon black ground peppercorn

Instructions

- Top each chicken breast with butter. Season with salt, tarragon and peppercorn.
- Wrap foil around the chicken loosely, making a tent shape allowing an opening for air flow.
- Place the foil-wrapped chicken into the Philips Air fryer basket. Cook at 200 degrees C for 22 minutes.

42. Sweet Chicken Breasts

 Serving size:
4

 Preparation time:
10 minutes

 Cooking time:
17 minutes

 Total time:
27 minutes

Ingredients

- 2 teaspoons brown sugar
- 1 teaspoon paprika
- 1 teaspoon dried oregano
- ½ teaspoon garlic powder
- ¼ teaspoon onion powder
- ¼ teaspoon salt
- ⅛ teaspoon black pepper
- 2 boneless, skinless chicken breasts
- 1 teaspoon olive oil

Instructions

- In a small bowl, combine the brown sugar, paprika, dried oregano, garlic powder, onion powder, salt and pepper. Stir or whisk until well combined.
- Pat the chicken dry with kitchen paper. Place chicken breasts in a zip-top bag or between two layers of baking paper and use a meat mallet or rolling pin to pound them to an even thickness.
- Rub the olive oil over all sides of the chicken breasts. Then rub the spice mixture on both sides of the chicken.
- Place chicken in a single layer in the air fryer. Cook at 220°C for 8 minutes, then flip chicken over and continue cooking for 5-12 more minutes, or until the internal temperature of the chicken is 170°C at the thickest part of the breast.
- Let chicken rest for 5 minutes before slicing and serving.

43. Spicy Chicken Breasts

 Serving size:

 Preparation time:

 Cooking time:

 Total time:

Ingredients

- 220 ml. buttermilk
- 2 tablespoons Dijon mustard
- 2 teaspoons salt
- 2 teaspoons hot pepper sauce
- 1-1/2 teaspoons garlic powder
- 8 bone-in chicken breast halves, skin removed
- 200 grams soft bread crumbs
- 130 grams cornmeal (polenta or maize meal)
- 2 tablespoons canolaoil
- 1/2 teaspoon poultry seasoning
- 1/2 teaspoon ground mustard
- 1/2 teaspoon paprika
- 1/2 teaspoon cayenne pepper
- 1/4 teaspoon dried oregano
- 1/4 teaspoon dried parsley flakes

Instructions

- Preheat air fryer to 220°C. In a large bowl, combine the first 5 ingredients. Add chicken and turn to coat. Refrigerate, covered, for 1 hour or overnight.
- Drain chicken, discarding marinade. Combine remaining ingredients in a shallow dish and stir to combine. Add chicken, 1 piece at a time, and turn to coat. Place in a single layer on greased tray in air-fryer basket. Cook until a thermometer reads 170°C, about 20 minutes, turning halfway through

cooking. Return all chicken to air fryer and cook to heat through, 2-3 minutes longer.

44. Chicken Lemon

 Serving size:
6

 Preparation time:
8 minutes

 Cooking time:
12 minutes

 Total time:
20 minutes

Ingredients

- 900 grams chicken tenders film skin and tender muscle removed
- 3/4 teaspoon black pepper fresh ground, more or less
- 60 ml. lemon juice
- 1 teaspoon paprika
- 2 tablespoons olive oil
- 3/4 teaspoon oregano dry
- 3/4 teaspoon salt more if need
- 4 cloves garlic chopped

Instructions

- Preheat the air fryer to 220 degrees C.
- Clean and trim the chicken tenders. Place in abowl and marinate with the remainder of the ingredients.
- Line the tenders in the preheated air fryer without overlapping them. You will need to do them in 2-3 batches, depending on the size of your air fryer.
- Cook the tenders in the air fryer for 6-8 minutes. (cooking time depends on their size). Use an instant read thermometer for accurate cooking. Internal temperature should be 170 degrees.
- When cooked, wrap with aluminum foil and let it rest for 5 minutes before serving.
- Garnish with some fresh chopped parsley and serve.

45. British Chicken Nuggets

 Serving size:
4

 Preparation time:
5 minutes

 Cooking time:
15 minutes

  Total time:
20 minutes

Ingredients

- 500 grams chicken breast cubed
- 60 grams flour
- 1/2 teaspoon salt
- 1/4 teaspoon pepper
- Olive oil
- 3 cloves garlic chopped
- 130 grams Panko breadcrumbs
- 90 grams grated parmesan
- 1 teaspoon dried parsley
- 1/4 teaspoon paprika

Instructions

- In a small bowl whisk together the flour, salt and pepper. In a separate small bowl whisk the oil and chopped garlic. In another small bowl combine the Panko, parmesan, parsley, and paprika.
- Place the tenders in the flour mixture, then the oil, and lastly the Panko. Make sure to evenly coat each one.
- Spray the air fryer basket with oil and place the tenders inside.
- Cook the at 200 degrees C for 7 minutes, then flip and cook another 7-10 minutes until crispy.

46. Chicken Breasts filled with Garlic and Sage

 Serving size:
2

  Preparation time:
15 minutes

 Cooking time:
25 minutes

 Total time:
40 minutes

Ingredients

- 2 kg boneless skinless chicken breasts
- 250 grams frozen broccoli florets, thawed
- 160 grams shredded cheddar cheese (or pepper jack cheese)
- salt, to taste
- pepper, to taste
- garlic powder, to taste
- steak seasoning, to taste
- a flour, for coating the chicken breasts
- olive oil cooking spray
- ranch dressing for drizzling
- about 10 toothpicks for skewering the chicken closed

Instructions

- Using a very sharp knife, butterfly the chicken breasts by starting to cut at one side but don't cut the entire way through. Open the butterflied chicken (like a book).
- Sprinkle a little salt, pepper, garlic powder, and Montreal Steak seasoning on both sides of the butterflied chicken, but don't over do it.
- On the right half, put a layer of the grated cheese. On top of the cheese, put a layer of the broccoli florets, laying them tightly together, side by side. On top of the broccoli florets, put a light layer of the grated cheese.
- Carefully lift the left side of the butterflied chicken and cover the right side with the left side (as though you were closing abook.)

- Using 5 or 6 toothpicks, "skewer" the chicken breasts through the upper layer of chicken down through the lower layer of chicken, all around the edges, to close them nice and tight.
- Lightly season (to taste) the top of each chicken bundle with a little more salt, pepper, garlic powder, and steak seasoning.
- Roll each bundle of chicken, both top and bottom in a little flour, just enough to coat it. Then spray each side with olive oil cooking spray.
- Place the chicken bundles inside the air fryer basket. Set the temperature to 220 degrees C (or as close to that as yours allows) and set it for 25 minutes.
- At the halfway point, open the air fryer and turn the bundles over to the other side and resume cooking.

47. Chicken Schnitzel with Cheddar and Mushrooms

 Serving size:
2

 Preparation time:
10 minutes

 Cooking time:
20 minutes

Total time:
30 minutes

Ingredients

- 450 grams chicken breast
- 2 eggs
- 2 tablespoons Dijon mustard
- 1 teaspoon garlic powder
- 130 grams punko breadcrumbs
- 100 grams cheddar cheese
- 6 springs thyme
- 1 teaspoon ground paprika
- 1 teaspoon marjoram
- ¾ teaspoon salt
- ½ teaspoon black pepper
- 1 lemon
- Sauce

- 450 grams button mushrooms
- 1 tablespoon olive oil
- 2 tablespoon butter
- 4 cloves of garlic
- 2 finely diced shallots
- 130 ml. sour cream
- 50 ml. white wine
- 60 ml. broth/stock (chicken or vegetable)
- 90 grams cheddar cheese
- Salt
- Pepper
- Thyme

Instructions

- Trim off any visible tendons and check the chicken breasts for tenderloins. If present, cut off any hanging flaps of tenderloins and set these aside. You can keep them in the fridge for other recipes.
- Lay the chicken breast on a chopping board with the smooth side facing upwards.
- Firmly place your hand on top and slice horizontally along the rounded side. Do not slice through, rather, cut about three-quarters into the breast. The unfolded chicken breast should resemble a butterfly. Flip the chicken breast and place on the chopping board spread out then cut along the middle and divide into two pieces.
- Get a piece of baking paper or plastic wrap (cling film) about 3 feet in size and lay the chicken pieces on top, making sure to leave some space between each chicken piece. Cover the chicken breasts with an equally large in size baking paper or plastic wrap. Using the flat side of your kitchen mallet, gently pound until each piece is thin, about an inch in size.
- Place the pounded pieces in a bowl. In another bowl, combine panko, chopped herbs, seasoning, salt, and pepper. Next, use a third bowl to beat the eggs with the dijon mustard until properly combined.
- Dip each of the now thin chicken breasts first into the bowl with the egg mixture making sure to properly coat each piece.
- Proceed on to place the chicken breast in the bowl with the panko crumb and seasoning mixture, then combine, shaking off any excess breading.
- Next, open the air fryer and spray the basket with cooking oil, then lay the coated chicken breasts on top, taking care not to overcrowd. If you overcrowd, the air will not circulate as it should and as a result, your schnitzel will not cook evenly. You certainly do not want that. Depending on the type of air fryer you have, you should be able to fit about 2-4 pieces.
- Make sure the basket sits properly in the air fryer, then spray the tops of the chicken pieces with cooking oil and close the lid. Set the temperature at 180°C and the time at 7 minutes then press the start button and cook. Once the time is up, flip to the other side, spray with some cooking spray and cook at 180°C for a further 7 minutes.
- Repeat the steps from breading with panko to cooking, until all chicken pieces are cooked.
- Finally, transfer the air-fried chicken schnitzel to plates, squeeze some lemon juice on top and serve with the cheese mushroom sauce and your favorite side dishes.
- Sauce
- Heat olive oil and butter in a pan under a medium heat. Add the shallots and mushrooms and allow these to cook for 5 minutes, or until golden brown. Stir in the garlic and cook for 1 minute.
- Next, stir in the white wine and use it to deglaze the pan, making sure to scrape off all the delicious bits from the bottom of the pan. The alcohol should have evaporated after about 1 minute.

- Add the broth, sour cream or crème fraîche, and parmesan cheese, then allow this to simmer and thicken, for about 3 minutes.
- Finally, add the thyme leaves, season with salt and pepper to taste, and serve the gravy over the chicken schnitzel.

48. Sweet Chilli Chicken Fillets

 Serving size:
4

 Preparation time:
2 hours

Cooking time:
15 minutes

Total time:
2 hours and 15 minutes

Ingredients

- 500 grams boneless, skinless chicken tights, cut in half
- 130 ml. buttermilk
- 60 grams pretzels, blended into grumbs
- 20 ml. sweet chilli sauce

Instructions

- Place chicken in a medium mixing bowl, add buttermilk and turn chicken to coat. Cover and marinate for 2 hours in the refrigerator.
- One at a time, remove chicken pieces from marinade, coat in pretzel crumbs and place in air fryer basket. When all the chicken has been coated, cook on chicken setting 220 degrees C for 15 minutes.
- In a medium mixing bowl, toss fried chicken in the sweet chilli sauce.

49. Parmesan Chicken

 Serving Size:
4

 Preparation Time:
5 Minutes

 Cooking Time:
15 Minutes

 Total Time:
20 Minutes

Ingredients

- 2 Large Chicken breasts
- 130 grams Parmesan grated
- 130 grams panko bread crumbs
- 50 grams mayonnaise
- 1 tablespoon garlic powder

Instructions

- Split chicken breasts in half and pound each piece with a meat hammer, then sprinkle with salt.
- Spread Mayo on both sides of each piece of chicken. Mix together panko, parmesan, and garlic powder and coat each piece of chicken in the panko/parmesan mixture.
- Preheat air fryer to 200 degrees C.
- In a single layer place in the air fryer. Cook for 15 minutes turning once after 10 minutes.

50. Crispy Chicken with Pickles

 Serving size:
6

 Preparation time:
15 minutes

 Cooking time:
8 minutes

Total time:
23 minutes

Ingredients

- 4 chicken breasts, cut in half lengthwise
- 200 ml. dill pickle juice
- 100 grams seasoned breadcrumbs
- 1 teaspoon salt
- 1/2 teaspoon pepper
- 2 large eggs, beaten
- Pickle slices for garnish, optional

Instructions

- In a ziplock bag, marinate chicken breasts in dill pickle juice for at least 4 hours.
- Preheat air fryer at 200 degrees C for 5 minutes.
- To make breading, combine breadcrumbs, salt, and pepper. Place the chicken in beaten eggs and then cover in breading.
- Place breaded chicken in a greased air fryer basket. Spray the top of chicken with olive oil.
- Air fry at 200 degrees C for 8 minutes.
- Flip, spritz with olive oil and air fry for 6-8 minutes or until internal temperature reaches 165° Fahrenheit.
- Garnish with a couple pickle slices and serve.

51. Chicken Breast Filled with Brie and Prosciutto

 Serving size:
2

 Preparation time:
5 minutes

 Cooking time:
20 minutes

 Total time:
25 minutes

Ingredients

- 2 thawed chicken breasts split
- 1 brie cheese
- 1 package prosciutto
- 1 Egg
- 1 box bread crumbs

Instructions

- Preheat your air fryer to 170°C.
- Split your breast, and add brie cheese and prosciutto.
- In a small bowl, beat an egg and in another bowl, add in panko bread crumbs.
- Dip your chicken into the egg, then into panko bread crumbs. You may need to dip twice for maximum coverage.
- Air fry at 170°C for 10 minutes, flip over, and air fry the stuffed chicken breast for an additional 10 minutes.

52. Chicken Casserole

 Serving size:
8

 Preparation time:
10 minutes

 Cooking time:
15 minutes

 Total time:
25 minutes

Ingredients

- 900 grams chicken breasts
- 8 slices bacon
- 3 gloves garlic
- 180 ml. Ranch dressing
- 120 grams mozzarella cheese
- 120 grams cheddar cheese
- 350 grams broccoli

Instructions

- Preheat air fryer to 200 degrees C.
- Meanwhile place the broccoli into a pot of water and bring it to boil. Simmer for 2 minutes.
- Combine the chicken, bacon, drained spinach or broccoli, garlic, ranch dressing, and half of the shredded cheeses in a large bowl. Stir until well incorporated.
- Place it in the air fryer and cook it for 15 minutes.

53. Pineapple and Pepper Chicken

 Serving size:
2

 Preparation time:
5 minutes

 Cooking time:
10 minutes

Total time:
15 minutes

Ingredients

- 2 raw chicken breasts
- 1 tablespoon butter
- 1/4 teaspoon salt
- 1/8 teaspoon pepper
- Sauce
- 50 ml. pineapple juice
- 60 grams brown sugar
- 60 ml. low-sodium soy sauce
- 1 clove garlic, minced (1 teaspoon)
- 1/8 teaspoon ground ginger (or 1 teaspoon freshly grated ginger)
- 2 teaspoons cornstarch
- 2 teaspoons water

Instructions

- Preheat air fryer to 220 degrees C.
- Add melted butter, salt, and pepper to a bowl and mix. Coat the chicken breasts with butter on both sides and place in the air fryer, cooking for 10-15 minutes and flipp halfway. They are done when they reach 165 degrees internally. Let chicken rest for at least 5 minutes.
- Meanwhile, start putting together the pineapple sauce by mixing the pineapple juice, brown sugar, soy sauce, minced garlic, and ginger in a small saucepan on a medium heat and simmer for 5 minutes.
- Mix together the cornstarch and water in a separate bowl and mix into the sauce. Let simmer for 1 more minute while stirring then remove from heat.
- Slice rested grilled chicken breasts into long strips and either coat chicken entirely with sauce or pour the sauce over top of the chicken and serve.
- Add chunks of canned or fresh pineapple if desired.

54. Christmas Chicken

 Serving size:
8

 Preparation time:
10 minutes

 Cooking time:
55 minutes

 Total time:
1 hour and 5 minutes

Ingredients

- 1 whole chicken
- 1 tablespoon olive oil
- 2 tablespoons butter, melted
- 1 teaspoon garlic powder
- 1 teaspoon onion powder
- 1 teaspoon oregano
- ½ teaspoon rosemary
- 1 teaspoon basil (substitute with parsley)
- 1 teaspoon salt or more to taste
- ½ teaspoon white pepper or black pepper
- 1 teaspoon paprika
- 1 small onion quartered
- 2 Sprigs fresh Rosemary

- ½ orange or lemon

Instructions

- Pat Chicken dry, mix oil and butter, salt and spice blend to form marinade.
- Brush marinade all over chicken and inside the cavity of the chicken. Let chicken marinade for 30 mins to an hour.
- When it's time to cook, stuff the cavity of the chicken with onions, fresh Rosemary and orange or lemon wedges. Tie the legs with a string if you like.
- Place the whole chicken in the air fryer breast side down and air fry at 180°C for 40 mins then flip over and cook for another 15 mins or until internal temperature reads 74°C on an instant read meat thermometer.

55. Easter Chicken

 Serving size:
5

 Preparation time:
15 minutes

 Cooking time:
55 minutes

 Total time:
1 hour and 25 minutes

Ingredients

- 1 whole chicken
- 1/2 fresh lemon
- 1/4 whole onion
- 4 sprigs of fresh thyme
- 4 sprigs of fresh rosemary
- olive oil spray
- 1 teaspoon ground thyme
- 1 teaspoon onion powder
- 1 teaspoon garlic powder
- Kosher salt to taste

Instructions

- Put 1/2 a fresh cut lemon and 1/4 of a chopped onion inside the cavity of the chicken, along with the fresh rosemary and thyme.
- Make sure the chicken is completely dry on the outside. Pat dry with kitchen paper if necessary. A dry chicken will help it crisp in the air fryer with the olive oil.
- Spray olive oil onto both sides of the chicken using an oil sprayer.
- Sprinkle the seasonings throughout and onto both sides of the chicken. You may elect to only season the bottom side of the chicken at this step. Because you will need to flip the chicken during the air frying process, you will likely lose some of the seasonings at this stage. My preference is to season both sides initially, and then re-assess if more seasoning (usually salt is needed later).

- Line the air fryer with baking paper. This makes for an easy clean up. Load the chicken into the air fryer basket with the breast side down.
- Air fry the chicken for 30 minutes on 220 degrees C.
- Open the air fryer and flip the chicken. I gripped the chicken cavity with tongs to flip.
- If more seasoning is needed on the breasts, legs, and wings add additional as required.
- Air fry for an additional 20-25 minutes until the chicken reaches an internal temperature of 170 degrees C. Use a meat thermometer.
- This step is important. Place the meat thermometer in the thickest part of the chicken, which is typically the chicken thigh area. I like to test the breast too, just to ensure the entire chicken is fully cooked.
- Remove the chicken from the air fryer basket and place it on a plate to rest for at least 15 minutes before cutting into the chicken. This will allow the moisture to redistribute throughout the chicken before you cut into it.

56. Chicken Souvlaki

 Serving size:
8

 Preparation time:
10 minutes

 Cooking time:
15 minutes

 Total time:
25 minutes

Ingredients

- 900 grams Boneless skinless Chicken thighs or breasts
- 1 tablespoon Mediterranean style Oregano
- 2 tablespoon Oil
- 3 teaspoons Garlic powder or 4 cloves of garlic
- 1 ¼ teaspoon Salt
- 1 teaspoon Paprika
- ½ teaspoon White pepper
- ½ teaspoon Black pepper
- ¼ teaspoon Cayenne pepper
- 3 Tablespoons Lemon juice

Instructions

- Wash and pat chicken dry with clean kitchen paper.
- Cut chicken thighs into 2 inch bite sized pieces.
- Combine the chicken bites with the marinade till well coated. Set aside in the refrigerator to marinate for at least 30 minutes.
- While the chicken is marinating soak the bamboo skewers in water to keep them from burning during cooking.
- When ready to bake, thread the chicken pieces on the skewers till all the meat has been threaded.

- Place chicken skewers in a baking paper lined air fryer basket. Mine takes 4 at a time.
- Bake at 200°C for 15 mins flipping half way through the cooking time.
- Let it rest for 2 minutes then bake the next batch. Serve with your favourites accompanyments

57. Chicken with Black Beans

 Serving size:
4

 Preparation time:
5 minutes

Cooking time:
20 minutes

 Total time:
25 minutes

Ingredients

- 3 boneless chicken thighs
- 1 tablespoon black bean sauce
- 1 tablespoon oyster sauce
- 1 tablespoon mirin
- 1 tablespoon rice wine
- Thinly sliced green onion to garnish

Instructions

- Combine the black bean sauce, oyster sauce, mirin, and rice wine. Marinate the chicken with the sauce mixture and refrigerate at least 3 hours or overnight.
- Take the chicken out of the refrigerator 30 minute prior to air frying. Line the fryer basket with lightly greased aluminum foil.
- Place the chicken thighs in the fryer basket, skin side down and air fry at 190 degrees C for about 12 minutes. Turn over, then air fry again at 190 degrees C for 6-7 minutes.
- Thinly slice the chicken, garnish with onion and drizzle with some drippings to serve
- .

58. Hot Chicken Drumsticks

 Serving size:
3

 Preparation time:
5 minutes

Cooking time:
15 minutes

 Total time:
20 minutes

Ingredients

- 200 ml. Italian dressing
- 60 ml. Worcestershire sauce
- 60 ml. hot sauce
- 12 chicken drumsticks

Instructions

- Combine Italian dressing, Worcestershire sauce, and hot sauce.
- Place chicken in a ziplock bag. Pour marinade over the chicken. Seal bag and toss to coat. Refrigerate a few hours to overnight.
- Remove chicken from the marinade. Discard marinade.
- Place chicken in the basket of the air fryer. Cook at 200 degrees C for 20 minutes. Shake basket. Reduce heat to 170degrees C and cook an additional 15 minutes.

59. Curry Chicken

 Serving size:
4

 Preparation time:
35 minutes

Cooking time:
15 minutes

 Total time:
50

Ingredients

- 900 grams chicken drumsticks
- 3/4 teaspoon salt, divided
- 2 tablespoons olive oil
- 2 teaspoons curry powder
- 1/2 teaspoon onion salt
- 1/2 teaspoon garlic powder
- Chopped fresh coriander, optional

Instructions

- Place chicken in a large bowl; add 1/2 teaspoon salt and enough water to cover. Let stand 15 minutes at room temperature. Drain and pat dry.
- Preheat air fryer to 220°C. In another bowl, mix oil, curry powder, onion salt, garlic powder and remaining 1/4 teaspoon salt; add chicken and toss to coat. In batches, place chicken in a single layer on tray in air-fryer basket. Cook for 20 minutes, turning halfway through.

60. Chicken Tights with 5 Different Spices

 Serving size:
4

 Preparation time:
20 minutes

Cooking time:
40 minutes

 Total time:
1 hour

Ingredients

- 1 tablespoon soy sauce
- 1 teaspoon salt
- 1 teaspoon five spice powder
- 1 tablespoon red onion (chopped)
- 2 cloves garlic (chopped)
- 1 teaspoon oil
- 1 tablespoon shaoxing rice wine
- 1 teaspoon sesame oil
- 8 bone-in, skin-on chicken thighs

Instructions

- Combine the soy sauce, salt, five spice, red onion, garlic, oil, shaoxing wine (or sherry), and sesame oil in a mixing bowl and set aside.
- Pat the chicken dry and add it to the marinade, making sure to get the marinade under the skin of the chicken. Marinate overnight or at least 20 minutes.
- Preheat the air fryer to 190 degrees C, place the chicken and cook it for 30 minutes.

61. Buffalo Chicken

 Serving size: 4

 Preparation time: 5 minutes

 Cooking time: 16 minutes

 Total time: 21 minutes

Ingredients

- 2 chicken breasts
- 1/2 teaspoon garlic powder
- 1/2 teaspoon paprika
- 1/2 teaspoon chili powder, use ground cayenne to make it hotter
- 1/8 teaspoon black pepper
- 100 grams seasoned panko breadcrumbs, or gluten-free crumbs
- olive oil spray
- 3 tablespoons Frank's Hot Sauce (or other available hot sauce)

Instructions

- Cut the chicken into small bite sized chunks. Season with garlic powder, paprika, chili powder and black pepper.
- Place panko in a small bowl. Place the hot sauce in another small bowl.
- Dip the chicken into the hot sauce, a few at a time, then into the crumbs and place on the air fryer basket in a single layer, in batches if needed.
- Spray the top generously with olive oil and air fry 8 minutes at 200 degrees C, flipping halfway and spraying the other side when you flip.

62. Spicy Chicken Drumsticks

 Serving size: 8

 Preparation time: 10 minutes

 Cooking time: 17 minutes

 Total time: 27 minutes

Ingredients

- 1 kg Chicken drumsticks
- 1 tablespoon avocado oil
- 1/2 teaspoon seasalt
- 1/4 teaspoon pepper
- 1/4 teaspoon garlic powder
- 1/2 teaspoon onion powder
- 1/2 teaspoon paprika
- 1/2 teaspoon chilli flakes
- 1 teaspoon chipotle powder or chilli powder
- 1/4 teaspoon cayenne pepper, optional for hotter spice

Instructions

- If necessary preheat the air fryer to 220°C.
- While it's preheating put the drumsticks in a bowl and drizzle with avocado oil. Mix to coat evenly.
- In a separate bowl combine all remaining spice ingredients and mix.
- Evenly sprinkle spice mixture over all sides of the chicken.
- Once the grill has preheated. open the top and place the drumsticks inside. Leave room so the chicken isn't crowded to get an even cook and close the lid. Set the time for a total of 17 minutes.
- Cook for 9 minutes, then flip the chicken with utensils. Cook another 8 minutes.
- Remove from the grill and let cool before eating.

63. Onion Chicken

 Serving size: 4

 Preparation time: 20 minutes

 Cooking time: 12 minutes

 Total time: 32 minutes

Ingredients

- 500 grams boneless, skinless chicken breast
- 60 grams flour
- Salt
- Pepper
- 1 egg
- 2 tablespoons mayonnaise
- 130 grams crushed fried onions
- Olive oil

Instructions

- Start by trimming the fat off your chicken.
- In your first bowl, add the flour, salt, and pepper.
- In your second bowl, add the mayo and egg, mix well.
- In your third bowl, place the crushed-up dried onions.
- Coat your chicken with the flour, then in the egg/mayo mixture, and lastly in the crushed fried onions. As you coat them, place them in a greased air fryer basket or a greased air fryer tray (both sprayed with olive oil)
- Set the temperature to 220 degrees C for 6 minutes. After 6 minutes, turn the chicken and air fry for another 6 minutes.
- Plate, serve, and enjoy!

64. Chicken Tenders with Special Chicken Sauce

 Serving size:
4

 Preparation time:
5 minutes

 Cooking time:
8 minutes

Total time:
20 minutes

Ingredients

- 14 chicken tenders
- 2 teaspoons kosher salt divided
- 2 large eggs
- 30 grams panko breadcrumbs
- 30 grams whole wheat breadcrumbs

- 2 teaspoons paprika
- 1 teaspoon garlic powder
- 1/4 teaspoon ground black pepper
- Olive oil spray

Sauce

- 60 grams mayonnaise
- 1 tablespoon English mustard

- 1 tablespoon dijon mustard
- 2 1/2 tablespoons honey
- 2 tablespoons BBQ sauce

Instructions

- With kitchen paper, pat the chicken tenders dry. Sprinkle with 1/2 teaspoon kosher salt.
- In a shallow bowl (a pie dish works well) beat the eggs together. In a second shallow bowl, stir together the panko, breadcrumbs, paprika, garlic powder, pepper, and remaining 1 1/2 teaspoons of salt. Line a baking tray with baking paper and keep it nearby.
- Coat the chicken tenders: Working a few at a time, dip each piece of chicken into the egg, then into the breadcrumb mixture, patting it gently as needed to adhere. Shake off excess.

- Transfer the chicken to the prepared baking tray. Repeat with remaining pieces.
- Preheat the air fryer to 220 degrees C. If you'd like to keep the chicken warm between batches, turn a regular oven to 170 degrees C.
- Coat the air fryer basket with the olive oil spray, then add chicken tenders in a single layer so that they are not touching. Coat the top of the chicken tenders with oil spray.
- Cook the chicken for 7 to 8 minutes, pulling out the air fryer basket and turning the pieces over once halfway through.
- In a medium bowl whisk all the sauce ingredients together.
- Serve with air fried chicken tenders.

65. Lemon Chicken with Thyme and Broccoli

 Serving size:
3

 Preparation time:
15 minutes

Cooking time:
15 minutes

Total time:
30 minutes

Ingredients

- 2 tablespoons all-purpose flour
- Salt
- Pepper
- 4 chicken breasts

- Olive oil
- 500 grams broccoli
- Parsley
- Lemon juice

Instructions

- On a plate, combine flour, salt and pepper, then add the chicken. Stir well to combine.
- Transfer the chicken into a large bowl and add the broccoli flourets. Mix well.
- Preheat the air fryer to 170 degrees C, and add the chicken and broccoli mixture.
- Cook until the broccoli is crisp-and tender.

66. Pesto Chicken

 Serving size:
4

 Preparation time:
5 minutes

Cooking time:
15 minutes

Total time:
20 minutes

Ingredients

Pesto:
- 50 grams basil leaves
- 60 grams cashews
- 60 grams parmesan cheese
- 2 medium garlic cloves
- 1 teaspoon salt
- 3 tablespoon olive oil

Chicken:
- 500 grams chicken tenders or chicken breasts cut into medium pieces
- Salt & Pepper to taste
- Cooking Spray

Instructions

- Blend basil, cashews, parmesan, garlic, ½ teaspoon salt, and 2 tablespoon olive into a smooth paste and keep to one side.
- Add salt and pepper onto the chicken pieces and spread the prepared pesto on top of the chicken. Toss well.
- Transfer the pesto-covered chicken to the air fryer basket and set the temperature to 200 degrees C, md the air fryer setting for 5 minutes, Turn and air fry for another 3-5 minutes until fully cooked.

67. Mozzarella and Parmesan Chicken

Serving size: 4	Preparation time: 10 minutes
Cooking time: 40 minutes	Total time: 50 minutes

Ingredients

- 2 large boneless chicken breasts
- Kosher salt
- Freshly ground black pepper
- 40 grams all-purpose flour
- 2 large eggs
- 130 grams panko breadcrumbs
- 40 grams freshly grated Parmesan
- 40 grams mozzarella
- 1 teaspoon dried oregano
- 1/2 teaspoon garlic powder
- 1/2 teaspoon crushed red pepper flakes
- 130 ml. marinara sauce
- Freshly chopped parsley, for garnish

Instructions

- Carefully butterfly chicken by cutting in half widthwise to create 4 thin pieces of chicken. Season on both sides with salt and pepper.
- Prepare dredging station: Place flour in a shallow bowl and season with a large pinch of salt and pepper. Place eggs in a second bowl and beat. In a third bowl, combine breadcrumbs, Parmesan, oregano, garlic powder, and red pepper flakes.
- Working with one piece of chicken at a time, coat in flour, then dip in eggs, and finally press into panko mixture making sure both sides are coated well.
- Working in batches as necessary, place chicken in the basket of the air fryer and cook at 200°C for 5 minutes on each side. Top chicken with sauce and mozzarella and cook at 200° for 3 minutes more or until cheese is melty and golden. Garnish with parsley to serve.

68. Cajun Chicken

Serving size: 4	Preparation time: 5 minutes
Cooking time: 20 minutes	Total time: 25 minutes

Ingredients

- 640 g chicken mini fillets
- Cajun seasoning

Instructions

- Add your chicken to a bowl.
- Add your cajun seasoning and rub all over the chicken fillets.
- Lightly oil the air fryer basket (if desired, I use spray rapeseed oil)
- Add your chicken mini fillets to the air fryer.
- Cook on 200 degrees C for 20 minutes, turning after 10 minutes.
- If you overload the air fryer basket a little, like me, then you'll want to give these a shake a couple of times during the 20 minutes.
- Check the temperature before serving.

69. Southern Drumsticks

Serving size: 8	Preparation time: 10 minutes
Cooking time: 17 minutes	Total time: 27 minutes

Ingredients

- 1 kg chicken drumsticks
- 80 ml. hot sauce
- 250 ml. butter milk
- Vegetable oil

Instructions

- Preheat prep: Preheat the air fryer (if this setting is available on the model your using).
- Buttermilk Marinade: Add the buttermilk, egg and hot sauce to a large bowl. Whisk until combined then add the chicken drumsticks to the bowl, stir and set aside to use straight away or for the best results marinate overnight in the fridge.
- Using hands take one drumstick out of the buttermilk marinade, shake of the excess liquid, then add to the seasoned flour. Use your hands to cover the drumsticks with the flour, apply pressure to ensure the flour adheres fully. Shake off the excess and place into the air fryer basket.
- Spray the dredged chicken drumsticks generously with vegetable oil, then air fry for 10 minutes at 180 degrees C. After the initial 10 minutes of cooking stop the air fryer and turn the chicken drumsticks over to crisp up the other side of the chicken. Spray the chicken with oil to cover any flour patches. Then air fry for afurther 7-8 minutes.

70. Asian Chicken with Rice

 Serving size:
2

 Preparation time:
5 minutes

 Cooking time:
20 minutes

 Total time:
25 minutes

Ingredients

- 350 grams rice
- 130 grams chicken
- 5 tablespoons tamari soy sauce
- 200 grams frozen vegetables of your choice
- 2 onions
- 1 teaspoon sesame oil
- 1 teaspoon vegetable oil
- 1 tablespoon chilli sauce
- Salt

Instructions

- Preheat the air fryer to 180 degrees C.
- Mix all the ingredients together in a large bowl.
- Then transfer to a non-stick pan that fits inside the air fryer basket.
- Cook for 20 mins, stirring the rice mixture a couple of times during cooking.

71. Chicken Scallopini with Sage

 Serving size:
4

 Preparation time:
10 minutes

 Cooking time:
25 minutes

 Total time:
35 minutes

Ingredients

- 4 skinless, boneless chicken breast halves
- 1/4 teaspoon salt
- 1/4 teaspoon black pepper
- Cooking spray
- 60 grams all-purpose flour
- 3 tablespoons butter
- 2 sage sprigs
- 1 tablespoon chopped shallots
- 1 teaspoon chopped fresh thyme
- 2 tablespoons lemon juice
- Fresh sage leaves

Instructions

- Place each breast half between 2 sheets of cling film; pound to desired thickness. Season with salt and pepper. Heat a large skillet over a medium-high heat; coat with cooking spray. Place flour in a shallow dish; dredge chicken in flour.
- Preheat air fryer to 200 degrees C. Add chicken to air fryer and cook for 20 minutes.
- Open the air fryer, add butter and sage sprigs to it, and cook at 170 degrees C for 10 more minutes.
- Discard sage. Add shallots and thyme and cook it for 5 more minutes at 170 degrees C.
- Add lemon on top and serve.

72. Breaded Cutlets

 Serving size:
6

 Preparation time:
5 minutes

 Cooking time:
30 minutes

 Total time:
35 minutes

Ingredients

- 6 chicken breasts
- 40 grams egg whites
- 100 grams Italian seasoned breadcrumbs
- Olive oil spray

Instructions

- Create a breading station by pouring your egg whites into one shallow bowl, and the breadcrumbs into another shallow bowl.

- Lay a piece of wax paper or a plate to the side to put your breaded chicken on.
- Dip each piece of chicken into the egg white, and then into the breadcrumbs to coat thoroughly.
- Spray the bottom of your air fryer with olive oil spray, then add half of the chicken pieces (depending on the size of your air fryer).
- Spray the tops of the chicken with olive oil spray.
- Air fry at 200 degrees C for 15 minutes. At the 7 minute mark, turn the chicken and spray the tops with more olive oil spray.
- Remove the cooked chicken and set aside on a plate, and repeat the process for the remaining pieces.

73. Asiago Chicken Tights

Serving size: 4	**Preparation time:** 5 minutes
Cooking time: 30 minutes	**Total time:** 35 minutes

Ingredients

- 8 boneless, skinless chicken thighs, fat trimmed, 32 oz total
- 30 ml. low sodium soy sauce
- 2 1/2 tablespoons balsamic vinegar
- 1 tablespoon honey
- 3 cloves garlic, crushed
- 1 teaspoon Srirachahot sauce
- 1 teaspoon fresh grated ginger
- 1 spring onion, green only sliced for garnish

Instructions

- In a small bowl combine the balsamic, soy sauce, honey, garlic, srirachaand ginger and mix well.
- Pour half of the marinade into a large bowl with the chicken, covering all the meat and marinate at least 2 hours, or as long as overnight.
- Reserve the remaining sauce for later.
- Preheat the air fryer to 200 degrees C.
- Remove the chicken from the marinade and transfer to the air fryer basket.
- Cook in batches 14 minutes, turning halfway until cooked through in the center.
- Meanwhile, place the remaining sauce in asmall pot and cook over a medium-low heat until it reduces slightly and thickens, about 1 to 2 minutes.
- To serve, drizzle the sauce over the chicken and top with spring onion.

74. Spicy Wings

Serving size: 4	**Preparation time:** 5 minutes
Cooking time: 25 minutes	**Total time:** 30 minutes

Ingredients

- 500 grams chicken wings
- 1 ¼ teaspoons baking powder
- ¾ teaspoon kosher salt
- ¼ teaspoon ground black pepper
- 1 tablespoon melted unsalted butter
- 1 teaspoon finely grated lemon zest
- 1 teaspoon fresh lemon juice
- ½ teaspoon honey, preferably dark
- ½ teaspoon Tabasco sauce
- ¼ teaspoon Srirachaor or other Asian chilli sauce

Instructions

- In a large bowl, toss chicken with baking powder, salt and pepper until the pieces are thoroughly coated. Spread the pieces out on a rack placed on a rimmed baking tray and refrigerate, uncovered, for at least 1 hour and up to overnight.
- Heat the air fryer to 200 degrees C, if preheating is necessary.
- Arrange chicken on the air fryer rack so all of the pieces are standing up against the edges of the basket, with as much space around each one as possible. Fry until golden brown and crispy, about 20 minutes.
- Meanwhile, in a large bowl, whisk together butter, lemon zest and juice, honey, Tabasco and sriracha.
- Immediately transfer the fried chicken wings to the bowl with the honey.-chilli sauce and toss well. Serve at once.

75. Duck Breast with Tomato Sauce

Serving size: 2	**Preparation time:** 10 minutes
Cooking time: 15 minutes	**Total time:** 25 minutes

Ingredients

- 2 duck breasts, boneless
- ½ teaspoon kosher salt
- ¼ teaspoon pepper
- 1 can tomato sauce

Instructions

- Score the skin of the duck breast with a sharp knife. Ensure you do not cut through to the meat.
- Season the duck breasts with salt and pepper.
- Place the duck breast in the air fryer basket skin-side up, and air fry at 195°C for 5 minutes.
- When the time is up, turn the temperature down to up to 160°C, and air fry the duck breast for an additional 10-12 minutes.
- Once the duck breast is cooked, remove it from the air fryer and cover with aluminum foil to rest for 10 minutes.
- Meanwhile, in a pan, heat up the tomato sauce.
- Add the tomato sauce over the duck and serve.

76. Chinese Duck Breast

 Serving size:
1

 Preparation time:
5 minutes

 Cooking time:
25 minutes

 Total time:
30 minutes

Ingredients

- 1 duck breast
- ½ tablespoon of (Lee Kum Kee) oyster sauce
- 3 tablespoons of soy sauce
- 1 tablespoon of five spice powder
- 2 tablespoons of honey
- ½ tablespoon chopped garlic

Instructions

- Pat the duck breast dry, especially the skin.
- Mix 2.5 tablespoons of oyster sauce, 2 tablespoons of soy sauce, ½ tablespoon of five-spice powder, chopped garlic, and 1 tablespoons of honey.
- Place the duck breast in the sauce and ensure that the skin isn't touching the sauce. Let it rest in the fridge overnight (make sure it's not shut closed and there is some air left) – poke holes in the cling film to allow air to flow in.
- Add duck in the air fryer skin side facing up and pat dry the skin one last time. Set it to 170 degrees C for 15 minutes.
- In a bowl, mix 1 tablespoon of honey, 3 tablespoons of warm water, ½ tablespoons of five-spice powder.
- After 15 minutes, add honey mixture all over the duck breast and fry at 220 degrees C for 10 minutes or until crispy and golden brown.

77. Spicy Duck Leg

 Serving size:
4

 Preparation time:
15 minutes

 Cooking time:
35 minutes

 Total time:
45 minutes

Ingredients

- 2 duck legs
- 1 orange, juiced
- 1/2 teaspoon fresh ginger
- 1 teaspoon granulated garlic
- 4 tablespoon olive oil
- Chilli powder, as much as you like
- Salt and pepper

Instructions

- Combine all marinate ingredients.
- Coat duck leg everywhere with the marinate and leave in the fridge, in an air tight container for at least 2-4 hours to marinate.
- Set ninja health grill on air frying mode, 180 degrees C for 25 min.
- Turn duck leg every 7-10 min.
- Serve with salad and grilled potatoes.

78. Juicy Duck Breast

 serving size:
4

 preparation time:
10 minutes

 cooking time:
22 minutes

 total time:
32 minutes

Ingredients

- 2 duck breasts
- salt & pepper
- thyme
- star anis powder
- melted butter

Instructions

- Preheat the air fryer to 200 degrees C.
- Score the fat of the duck breast several times and rub with salt and pepper. Put in the basket and cook for 10 minutes.
- Remove basket and transfer meat to a baking pan. Baste with melted butter and sprinkle with thyme and star anis powder. Bake for another 12 minutes.

79. Whole Duck with Potatoes, Carrots and Celery

 Serving size:

 Preparation time:
10 minutes

 Cooking time:
45 minutes

Total time:
55 minutes

Ingredients

- 1 whole duck
- 2 tablespoons olive oil
- 1 tablespoon rosemary chopped
- 1 teaspoon thyme
- ½ teaspoon salt
- ½ teaspoon black pepper
- 1 teaspoon garlic. chopped

Instructions

- If starting with a frozen duck, let it defrost in the refrigerator for 24 to 48 hours. Once the duck is thawed, remove the neck and any giblets that may be inside the duck. Rinse, and pat dry with kitchen paper. Let the duck sit until the seasonings are ready.
- In a small mixing bowl, combine all of the seasonings together. Lightly brush the olive oil all over the duck and then coat with the seasonings.
- Transfer the duck, breast side up, to the air fryer basket and air fry for at 220 degrees C, 45-55 minutes.
- Do not tie the legs during the cooking process, as they need to move freely so the juices and fat can drain from the duck.

80. Crispy Duck Breast

 Serving size:
8

 Preparation time:
10 minutes

 Cooking time:
40 minutes

 Total time:
50 minutes

Ingredients

- 8 duck breasts
- 1 tablespoon hoisin sauce
- 1 tablespoon five spices powder
- 1 tablespoon pepper
- 2 tablespoons Shaoxing rice wine
- 1 tablespoon sugar
- 1 tablespoon Sichuan peppercorn
- 4 pieces Sichuan
- 2 pieces star anise
- 2 slices cinnamon
- 1 piece spring onion

Instructions

- Prepare the marinade by mixing the hoisin sauce, five spices powder, pepper, 1 tablespoon Shaoxing wine, sugar and salt. Rub all over the cavity of the duck, and secure with a skewer.
- Put the Sichuan peppercorns, star anise, cinnamon, remaining 1 tablespoon Shaoxing wine, spring onion and ginger in a large saucepan. Add water and bring to boil. Blanch the duck for 2 minutes until the skin is tightened.
- Drain the duck and wipe dry. Hang the duck up and leave to air-dry for 6-8 hours.
- Put the duck into the Air fryer and roast at 150°C for 35 minutes.
- When finished, turn the heat up to 180°C and roast for another 15 minutes. Brush the skin with the honey wash in three intervals. Then remove the skewer.

81. Turkey Breast

 Serving size:
4

 Preparation time:
5 minutes

 Cooking time:
40 minutes

 Total time:
45 minutes

Ingredients

- 1 bone in turkey breast
- 3 tablespoons butter, room temperature
- 1 clove garlic, chopped
- 1 teaspoon salt
- 1 teaspoon pepper

Instructions

- Pat the turkey breast with kitchen towels to remove any moisture. Sprinkle the salt and pepper over the butter. In a small bowl, mix together the butter and garlic. Rub the butter mixture all over the turkey.
- Place the turkey into the basket of your air fryer, so the skin side is facing down. Set it to 220°C for 20 minutes. Turn the turkey breast over and set the air fryer for an additional 20 minutes.
- Remove turkey from the air fryer and allow it to rest for 10 minutes before slicing.

82. Garlic Herb Turkey Breast

 Serving size:
6

 Preparation time:
10 minutes

 Cooking time:
50 minutes

 Total time:
1 hour

Ingredients

- 500 grams turkey breast
- Salt
- Pepper
- 4 tablespoons butter
- 3 cloves garlic
- 1 teaspoon chopped thyme
- 1 teaspoon chopped rosemary

Instructions

- Pat turkey breast dry and season on both sides with salt and pepper.
- In a small bowl, combine melted butter, garlic, thyme, and rosemary. Brush butter all over the turkey breast.
- Place in the basket of the air fryer, skin side up and cook at 220°C for 40 minutes or until internal temperature reaches 170°C, turning halfway through.
- Let rest for 5 minutes before slicing.

83. Lemon Turkey Breast

 Serving size:
6

 Preparation time:
5 minutes

 Cooking time:
55 minutes

 Total time:
1 hour

Ingredients

- 1 kg de-boned uncooked turkey breast
- 2 tablespoons oil
- 1 tablespoon Worcestershire sauce
- 1 teaspoon lemon pepper
- Salt

Instructions

- Pat the turkey dry.
- Combine oil, Worcestershire sauce, lemon pepper or herbs, and salt in a bowl or plastic bag. Add the turkey to the marinade, making sure the marinade completely coats the turkey breast. If possible, marinate for 1-2 hours.
- Lightly oil the air fryer basket. Remove the turkey from the marinade and place the turkey breast skin-side down in the air fryer basket.
- Air Fry at 220°C for 25 minutes. Turn the turkey breast to skin side up, and Air Fry for another 25-35 minutes.
- If you're cooking bone-in turkey breast, cook for additional 5-10 minutes if needed.

84. Rosemary Turkey Breast with Potatoes

 Serving size:
4

 Preparation time:
5 minutes

 Cooking time:
35 minutes

Total time:
40 minutes

Ingredients

- 1 kg boneless turkey breast
- 2 tablespoons unsalted butter
- ½ teaspoon thyme
- ½ teaspoon rosemary
- ½ teaspoon sage
- Salt
- Black Pepper

Potatoes:
- 500 grams new potatoes
- 2 teaspoons extra-virgin olive oil
- 2 teaspoons dry Italian-style salad dressing mix

Instructions

- Turkey: Use kitchen paper to pat the turkey dry.
- In a small bowl, combine the seasonings with the melted butter. Brush the butter and completely coat the turkey on both sides.
- Place the turkey in the air fryer basket, or on a baking tray and place in the air fryer.
- Air fry at 220 degrees C for 30 minutes on each side. Confirm doneness with a meat thermometer.
- Let turkey rest for about 5 minutes before carving.
- Potatoes : Preheat air fryer to 200 degrees C.
- Wash and dry potatoes. Trim edges to make flat surface on both ends.
- Combine extra-virgin olive oil and salad dressing mix in a large bowl. Add potatoes and toss until potatoes are well coated. Place in a single layer into the air fryer basket. Cook in batches if necessary.
- Air fry until potatoes are golden brown, 5 to 7 minutes. Flip potatoes and air fry for an additional 2 to 3 minutes.
- Season with salt and pepper. Add them right next to the meat.

85. Olive Bried Turkey Breast

 Serving size:
14

 Preparation time:
10 minutes

 Cooking time:
20 minutes

 Total time:
30 minutes

Ingredients

- 100 ml. brine from a can of olives
- 60 ml. buttermilk (alternatives – yogurt or milk)
- 1 kg boneless, skinless turkey breast
- 1 sprig fresh rosemary
- 2 sprigs fresh thyme

Instructions

- Whisk together olive brine and buttermilk. Put the turkey breast into a resealable plastic bag and pour brine-buttermilk mixture into the bag. Add rosemary and thyme sprigs. Seal bag and refrigerate for 8 hours.
- Take the bag out of the fridge and allow to rest until the breast reaches room temperature.
- Preheat Air Fryer to 175 degrees C.
- Cook the breast in the air fryer for 15 minutes. Turn over the breast and cook for 5 minutes until the turkey breast is no longer pink in the center and the juices run clear.

86. Candied Turkey Breast

 Serving size:
4

 Preparation time:
10 minutes

 Cooking time:
1 hour and 5 minutes

 Total time:
1 hour and 15 minutes

Ingredients

- Turkey Breast
- 2 kg. bone-in, skin-on turkey breast
- 60 grams butter melted
- 1 tablespoon garlic chopped
- 1 sprig fresh rosemary chopped
- 1 sprig fresh thyme chopped
- 2 leaves fresh sage chopped
- Brown Sugar Orange Glaze
- 60 ml. Dijon mustard
- 40 ml. apple cider vinegar
- 30 grams light brown sugar packet
- 2 tablespoons orange juice
- 1/2 teaspoon orange zest
- 1 tablespoon butter

Instructions

- If turkey breast is frozen, thaw overnight in the fridge and then set out on the counter for 30 minutes before cooking. If there is a turkey neck or gravy packet in the cavity, remove and discard.
- Place the turkey breast in a baking dish or on a platter and cover with butter, garlic, and chopped herbs.

- Place the turkey breast into the air fryer basket, top side up. Cook at 220 degrees C for 60 minutes, turning halfway through the cooking time.
- When there are about 10 minutes left on the air fryer, start the glaze. Add the mustard vinegar, brown sugar, orange juice, and orange zest to a medium saucepan. Whisk together.
- Place the saucepan over a medium heat and bring to a simmer. Cook for 5 minutes. Remove from the heat and whisk in the butter.
- Brush the glaze all over the turkey breast and air fryer for another 3 minutes at 200 degrees C to caramelise the glaze. Remove to a board and rest for 10 minutes before serving.

87. Coconut Turkey Fingers

 Serving size:
6 servings

 Preparation time:
20 minutes

 Cooking time:
10 minutes per batch

 Total time:

Ingredients

- 2 large egg whites
- 2 teaspoons sesame oil
- 60 grams sweetened shredded coconut, lightly toasted
- 60 grams dry bread crumbs
- 2 tablespoons sesame seeds, toasted
- 1/2 teaspoon salt
- 1 kg. turkey breast tenderloins
- Cooking spray

Instructions

- Preheat air fryer to 200°C. In a shallow bowl, whisk egg whites and oil. In another shallow bowl, mix coconut, bread crumbs, sesame seeds and salt. Dip turkey in egg mixture, then in coconut mixture, patting to help coating adhere.
- Working in batches, place turkey in a single layer on greased tray in air-fryer basket; spray with cooking spray. Cook until golden brown, 3-4 minutes. Turn; spray with cooking spray. Cook until golden brown and turkey is no longer pink, 3-4 minutes longer.
- Meanwhile, in a small saucepan, mix sauce ingredients. Bring to boil; cook and stir until thickened, 1-2 minutes. Serve turkey with sauce. If desired, top turkey strips with grated lime zest and serve with lime wedges.

88. Cheese Turkey Breast

 Serving size:
2

 Preparation time:
10 minutes

 Cooking time:
15 minutes

 Total time:
25 minutes

Ingredients

- 4 turkey breast cutlets, 4 oz each
- 2 large egg whites, beaten
- 90 grams seasoned breadcrumbs
- 2 tablespoons Parmesan cheese
- Salt
- Pepper
- 1 tablespoon butter
- 1 teaspoon olive oil
- lemon wedges for serving

Instructions

- Season cutlets with salt and pepper.
- Combine breadcrumbs and Parmesan cheese in a medium bowl.
- In another bowl beat egg whites.
- Dip turkey cutlets in egg whites, then breadcrumb mixture, shaking off excess.
- Preheat the air fryer to 200 degrees C. Add the butter and olive oil.
- When the butter melts, add the cutlets and cook about 6 minutes on each side, until golden brown and cooked through. Serve with lemon wedges.

89. Turkey Nuggets with Thyme

 Serving size:
6

 Preparation time:
20 minutes

 Cooking time:
28 minutes

 Total time:
48 minutes

Ingredients

- 500 grams turkey breast
- Dredging Mixture
- 60 grams all purpose flour
- 3/4 teaspoon paprika
- 1/2 teaspoon salt
- 1/4 teaspoon garlic powder
- 1/4 teaspoon black pepper
- 1/8 teaspoon onion powder
- 1 tablespoon thyme
- Egg Mixture
- 1 egg
- 60 ml. buttermilk (alternative yogurt or milk)
- Coating
- 60 grams seasoned breadcrumbs
- 40 grams all purpose flour
- 1/2 teaspoon salt
- 1/8 teaspoon black pepper

Instructions

- Preheat air fryer to 200 degrees C for 10 minutes.
- Meanwhile, cut turkey breast into "nuggets", roughly half inch thick and 1.5-2 inches long.
- Combine flour, paprika, salt, garlic powder, thyme, pepper and onion powder in a large zip top bag.
- Add raw turkey nuggets. Seal the bag and turn and toss until all are coated.
- Gather two medium but shallow dishes.
- In one dish, whisk together egg and milk.
- In the other dish, stir together bread crumbs, flour, salt and pepper.
- Working one by one, remove turkey nuggets from the bag and dip each in the egg mixture, then coat in the breadcrumb mixture. Place on a large plate until all are coated and ready to cook.
- Place 8-10 nuggets on the rack in the Air Fryer and spray with non-stick or oil spray. Set the timer for 8 minutes at 200 degrees C. Turn the nuggets at the 4 minute mark and spray the other side with non stick spray before continuing to cook.

90. Sweet Turkey Bake

 Serving size:
4

 Preparation time:
10 minutes

 Cooking time:
35 minutes

 Total time:
45 minutes

Ingredients

- 1 kg. bone-in turkey breast
- 2 tablespoons olive oil
- 1 tablespoon Italian Seasoning
- 1 teaspoon paprika
- 1 teaspoon garlic powder
- 1/2 teaspoon salt
- 1/4 teaspoon pepper
- 2 Tablespoons butter

Instructions

- Rub the turkey in olive oil. In a small bowl combine Italian seasoning, paprika, garlic powder, salt, and pepper. Rub on the outside of the turkey.
- Slice the butter and put it under the skin of the turkey.
- Lay the turkey skin side down in the air fryer basket. Cook at 220 degrees C for 20 minutes. Turn the turkey and cook for and an additional 10-15 minutes depending on the size of your turkey.
- Remove the turkey and let rest for 10 minutes. Slice and serve.

91. Maple Turkey Breast

 Serving size:
2

 Preparation time:
15 minutes

 Cooking time:
40 minutes

Total time:
55 minutes

Ingredients

- 1 kg turkey breast
- 1 ½ tablespoon sage
- 1 ½ tablespoon rosemary
- 1 teaspoon onion powder
- 90 ml. maple syrup
- Salt
- Pepper
- 2 tablespoons butter

Instructions

- Prepare the maple herb glaze: In a small bowl, add the maple syrup, onion powder, and chopped rosemary and sage.
- Preheat the air fryer for 5 minutes at 200 degrees C.
- Remove the turkey breast from the package and use kitchen paper to pat it dry.
- First, brush the breast with melted butter, then maple and herb glaze – make sure to flip the breast and brush the bottom too. Sprinkle evenly with salt & black pepper.
- Cook: transfer the turkey breast into the air fryer (skin side down) and cook at 220 degrees C for 15-20 minutes, and then turn the turkey breast and baste it with the drippings from the bottom of the air fryer.

Beef, Lamb and Pork

92. Beef with Broccoli and Carrot

 Serving size:
6 servings

 Preparation time:
10 minutes

 Cooking time:
30 minutes

 Total time:
40 minutes

Ingredients

- 400 grams steak
- 1 teaspoon oil
- ½ teaspoon dried onion powder
- 1 teaspoon Montreal Steak Seasoning
- 1/8 teaspoon cayenne pepper
- 300 grams broccoli florets
- 300 grams cauliflower florets
- 3 teaspoon garlic powder
- 2 tablespoons olive oil
- ¼ teaspoon sea salt
- ¼ teaspoon paprika
- Salt

Instructions

- Preheat the air fryer to 200 degrees C.
- Add cauliflower, olive oil, garlic powder, sea salt, paprika, and black pepper to the bowl with the broccoli. Mix well to combine. Pour mixture into the air fryer basket.
- Cook for 12 minutes, tossing vegetables halfway through cooking time for even browning.
- Meanwhile, trim the steak of any fat and cut it into cubes. Then, toss with the ingredients for the marinade (oil, salt, black pepper, Montreal seasoning, onion and garlic powder & the cayenne pepper) and massage the spices into the meat to coat evenly. Do this in a ziplock bag for easier cleanup.
- Spray the bottom of the air fryer basket with nonstick spray if you have any and spread the prepared meat along the bottom of it. Cook the beef steak tips for about 4-6 minutes and check for doneness.
- Once the steak bites are browned to your liking, toss them around and move to one side. Cook for another 3 minutes.

93. Greek Meatballs with Basil

 Serving size:
4 servings

 Preparation time:
5 minutes

 Cooking time:
12 minutes

 Total time:
17 minutes

Ingredients

- 500 grams minced lamb
- 1 teaspoon ground cumin
- 2 teaspoon granulated onion
- 2 Tablespoon fresh parsley
- ¼ teaspoon ground cinnamon
- Salt and pepper

Instructions

- In a large bowl, combine the lamb, cumin, onion, parsley, and cinnamon. Mix thoroughly until all the ingredients are evenly incorporated.
- Create small balls from the meat.
- Place lamb meatballs in the air fryer basket and cook at 200 degrees C for 12-15 minutes. Shake the meatballs halfway through.

94. Kofta Kabobs with Cheese Sauce

 Serving size:
4

 Preparation time:
5 minutes

 Cooking time:
12 minutes

 Total time:
17 minutes

Ingredients

- 1 package frozen tater tots/ potato crunchies
- 100 grams grated cheddar cheese
- 100 grams bacon diced and cooked

Instructions

- Place the tater tots into the air fryer basket, and set the temperature to 200 degrees C, air fryer setting, cook for about 8 to 10 minutes. Turning halfway during the cooking process.
- Remove the tater tots from the air fryer, and let cool for a couple of minutes. Then use a skewer (if using wood, let it soak for about 4 minutes in water before threading the tater tots through it.)
- Sprinkle the cheese on top, followed by the bacon, set the temperature to 300 degrees F, air fryer setting, and cook until the cheese starts to melt.
- Plate, serve, and enjoy!

95. Italian Meatballs

 Serving size:
40 meatballs

 Preparation time:
15 minutes

 Cooking time:
10 minutes

 Total time:
25 minutes

Ingredients

- 1kg minced beef
- 100 grams parmesan cheese
- 90 grams breadcrumbs
- 6 cloves garlic
- 1 small onion
- 90 grams leaf parsley
- Salt
- Pepper
- 1 jar marinara sauce
- 150 grams mozzarella cheese, shredded

Instructions

- Preheat the air fryer to 200 degrees C.
- Gently mix together all of the meatball ingredients.

- Use a scoop to make your meatballs. After you scoop them out you can roll them by hand to give them a nice round shape before cooking, but it's not necessary.
- Spray the air fryer basket with cooking spray. Then place your meatballs in the basket. If you have a shelf accessory for your air fryer you can use it to cook more meatballs at once.
- If you only have one layer of meatballs cook them 7-8 minutes. If you have two shelves of meatballs cook them for 10 minutes total.
- Next, heat your marinara sauce in a large heavy saucepan over a medium heat. Then drop the meatballs into sauce, and bring to a gentle simmer. Cook for 3 minutes.
- Sprinkle on cheese and enjoy!

96. Mediterranean Lamb Chops

 Serving size:
4

 Preparation time:
5 minutes

 Cooking time:
8 minutes

 Total time:
13 minutes

Ingredients

- 700 grams lamb chops
- 2 tablespoon olive oil
- 1 tablespoon red wine vinegar
- 1 teaspoon dried rosemary
- ½ teaspoon dried oregano
- ½ teaspoon kosher salt
- ½ teaspoon garlic powder
- ¼ teaspoon black pepper

Instructions

- Combine lamb chops, olive oil, red wine vinegar, rosemary, oregano, salt, garlic powder, and black pepper in a bowl. Rub the marinade into the meat and cover and chill for 1 hour.
- Preheat air fryer to 200 degrees C.
- Add lamb chops to the air fryer basket and cook for 7-9 minutes, turning halfway through the cooking time.

97. Pork Tenderloins with Honey Garlic Sauce

 Serving size:
4

 Preparation time:
10 minutes

 Cooking time:
26 minutes

 Total time:
36 minutes

Ingredients

- 600 grams pork tenderloin
- 2 tablespoons brown sugar
- 1 tablespoons smoked paprika
- 1 teaspoon salt
- 1 teaspoon ground mustard
- ½ teaspoon onion powder
- ½ teaspoon ground black pepper
- ¼ teaspoon garlic powder
- ¼ teaspoon cayenne powder (optional)
- ½ tablespoon olive oil

Instructions

- Mix all dry ingredients in a bowl.
- Trim the pork tenderloin of any excess fat/silver skin. Coat with a ½ tablespoon olive oil. Rub spice mixture on entire pork tenderloin.
- Preheat air fryer to 200° C for 5 minutes. After 5 minutes, carefully place pork tenderloin into air fryer and air fry at 200° C for 20-22 minutes.
- When air fryer cycle is complete, carefully remove pork tenderloin to a cutting board and let rest for 5 minutes before slicing. Save any juices to serve over sliced meat.

98. Crispy Pork Chops

 Serving size:
4

 Preparation time:
10 minutes

 Cooking time:
8 minutes

 Total time:
18 minutes

Ingredients

- 600 grams pork chops
- 1/2 teaspoon kosher salt
- 1/4 teaspoon black pepper
- 60 grams plain flour
- 1 teaspoon garlic powder , divided
- 1 teaspoon onion powder , divided
- 2 large eggs
- splash of water
- 60 grams seasoned Italian breadcrumbs
- 60 grams grated parmesan cheese , plus more for garnish
- fresh chopped parsley , for garnish

Instructions

- Season pork chops on both sides with the salt and pepper, set aside.
- Set up your breading station with 3 shallow bowls:
- Bowl 1: whisk together the flour, 1/2 teaspoon of garlic powder, and 1/2 teaspoon of the onion powder.

- Bowl 2: thoroughly whisk together the eggs, splash of water, 1/2 teaspoon of the garlic powder, and 1/2 teaspoon of the onion powder.
- Bowl 3: mix together the breadcrumbs and parmesan cheese.
- Place the pork chops one by one into the flour mixture and evenly coat. Shake off any excess flour and immediately place into the egg mixture, evenly coat. Let any excess egg drip off the pork chop and immediately place it into the breadcrumb mixture and evenly coat, shake off any excess. Repeat with the remaining pork chops.
- If your air fryer requires preheating, set it to 200°C for 5 minutes.
- Spray the air fryer basket with cooking spray; place two pork chops in the basket or as many as you can fit without them touching. Spray the tops of the pork chops with cooking spray.
- Air fry for 4 minutes, turn them over, spray the top with more cooking spray and air fry an additional 4 minutes.
- Serve with a garnish of parsley and more grated parmesan, if desired.

99. Pork Chops with Onions and Apples

 Serving size:
2

 Preparation time:
5 minutes

 Cooking time:
20 minutes

 Total time:
25 minutes

Ingredients

- 2 boneless pork chops
- 1/2 small red cabbage, sliced thick
- 1 apple, sliced thick
- 1 sweet onion, sliced thick
- 2 tablespoons oil
- 1/2 teaspoon cumin
- 1/2 teaspoon paprika
- salt/pepper - to taste

Instructions

- Spray air fryer basket with nonstick spray.
- Toss apples, cabbage and onions with 1 tablespoon oil, 1/4 teaspoon cumin, 1/4 teaspoon paprika, salt and pepper.
- Coat pork chops with oil, rub on the remaining seasonings, salt and pepper. Place chops in air fryer basket.
- Air fry at 200ºC for 15 minutes. Check temp, toss the apples and cabbage and air fry 5 more minutes or to desired doneness.

100. Pork Burger Patties

 Serving size:
4

 Preparation time:
10 minutes

 Cooking time:
10 minutes

 Total time:
20 minutes

Ingredients

- 500 grams pork mince
- 2 tablespoons Cajun seasoning
- 100 grams fine breadcrumbs
- 1 egg
- salt and pepper
- olive oil
- Bun and toppings
- 2 burger buns
- 1 tomato, sliced
- ½ avocado, sliced
- cos lettuce leaves
- 1 tablespoon mayo
- 1 tablespoon sweet onion relish or onion jam

Instructions

- Combine the pork mince, Cajun seasoning, breadcrumbs egg and a pinch of salt and pepper.
- Shape the ground pork mixture into 2 evenly sized patties.
- Preheat air fryer to 180°C.
- Spray air fryer basket with oil.
- Add patties to air fryer basket. Ensure they are not touching.
- Air fry patties at 180°C for 10 minutes, until cooked through.
- Slice the burger buns in half and place under a hot grill for 2 minutes, until just starting to brown.
- Slice tomato and avocado.
- Spread onion jam onto burger bun base. Add a patty, top with slices of tomato and avocado, and cos leaves. Spread mayo inside top of burger bun. Enjoy.

101. Pork Ribs with Honey

 Serving size:
6

 Preparation time:
3 hours

 Cooking time:
15minutes

 Total time:
3 hours and 15 minutes

Ingredients

- 2 kg pork ribs
- 40 grams honey
- 40 grams soy sauce
- 40 grams ketchup
- 40 grams brown sugar
- 2 tablespoons rice vinegar
- 2 tablespoons lemon juice
- 2 teaspoon sesame oil
- 2 tablespoons minced garlic
- 1 tablespoon sesame seeds for garnish or to taste
- 70 grams spring onions for garnish or to taste

Instructions

- In a medium-size bowl, prepare the marinade by mixing honey, soy sauce, ketchup, brown sugar, vinegar, and lemon juice.
- Take a ziploc bag, and place the ribs inside the bag. Pour about 2/3 of the marinade into the bag, mix with the ribs, and marinate in the refrigerator for at least 3 hours or best overnight. Save the rest of the marinade for later use.
- Take the pork ribs out from the fridge 30 minutes prior to air frying.
- Line the fryer basket with a grill mat or a sheet of lightly greased aluminum foil.
- Put the ribs inside the fryer basket without stacking. Air fry at 190 degrees C for about 10-12 minutes, turn over once in the middle until the edges are slightly caramelised.
- In the meantime, use a wok to saute garlic and sesame oil until fragrant, about one minute. Then, add in the rest of the marinade. Stir constantly until the sauce thickens.
- When the ribs are done, toss the ribs in the wok along with sesame seeds. Sprinkle some spring onions on top to serve.

102. Crispy Roast Pork

 Serving size:
4

 Preparation time:
30 minutes

 Cooking time:
1 hour

Total time:
1 hour and 30 minutes

Ingredients

- 1 kg pork belly
- 300 ml. water
- 1 teaspoon sea salt
- 1 teaspoon sugar
- Skin Rub
- 1/2 tablespoon vinegar
- 1 teaspoon sea salt
- Meat Rub
- 1/4 teaspoon Chinese 5 spice powder
- 1/4 teaspoon sea salt

Instructions

- If there is any hair on the pork skin, scrape it off with a knife. Then wash the pork belly under a tap.
- In a frying pan on a medium high, add the water, salt and sugar.
- Once boiling add the pork belly skin side down and cook for 8 minutes on each side.

- Once done, remove the pork belly and let it cool on a rack. Pat dry with some kitchen paper when it is cool enough to do so.
- Get a meat skewer or a metal fork and punch lots of holes into the skin of the pork belly – this usually takes me about 5 – 10 minutes. Do not punch holes so deep that it reaches the meat.
- Brush the pork skin with vinegar and then sprinkle half the salt. Let it rest for 10 minutes and repeat the process.
- Put the pork belly into the fridge uncovered and allow the skin to dry for a minimum of 12 to 48 hours. If you can, check on it every now and then to wipe off any moisture that comes to the surface.
- Take your pork belly out of the fridge and apply the meat rub on the sides and the bottom of the pork belly.
- Preheat your air fryer for 5 minutes then cook the pork belly for 40 minutes at 200 degrees C.
- Once done, let it rest for 15 minutes before carving.

103. Char Siew Pork Ribs

 Serving size:
5

 Preparation time:
5 minutes

 Cooking time:
20 minutes

 Total time:
25 minutes

Ingredients

- 1 kg ribs country-style
- 1 teaspoon smoked paprika
- 1 ½ teaspoon garlic powder
- 2 teaspoon ground black pepper
- 60 ml. barbecue sauce

Instructions

- Rinse the ribs and then pat them dry. Add the garlic powder, smoked paprika, and ground black seasoning to a small bowl and set aside.
- Preheat the air fryer to 220 degrees C. Prepare the basket of the air fryer with nonstick cooking spray.
- Rub the ribs with a small amount of the seasoning mixture.
- Place the ribs in a single layer in the basket of the air fryer. Cook at 220 degrees C for 20 minutes. Remove the basket and brush barbecue sauce onto the tops and sides of the ribs. Place back into the air fryer and cook for an additional 2 minutes.
- Serve with your favorite sides.

104. Breaded Pork Chops

 Serving size:
3

 Preparation time:
10 minutes

 Cooking time:
16 minutes

 Total time:
26 minutes

Ingredients

- 170 grams pork chops
- 60 grams breadcrumbs
- 1 large egg
- salt , to taste
- black pepper , to taste
- garlic powder , to taste
- smoked paprika , to taste

Instructions

- Season the pork chops with salt, pepper, garlic powder, and smoked paprika. Place the breadcrumbs in a medium bowl. In another bowl, beat the egg.
- Dip each pork chop in egg and then dredge it in the breadcrumbs, coating completely. Lightly spray both sides of coated pork chops with cooking spray right before cooking. Make sure to spray the pork chops well with oil. Don't leave any un-oiled areas because those bread crumbs will cook white and dry and won't go crispy.
- Preheat the Air Fryer at 220°C for 4 minutes.
- Place in the Air Fryer and cook at 194°C for 8-12 minutes. After 6 minutes of cooking, turn the pork chops over and then continue cooking for the remainder of time or until golden.

105. Stuffed Pork Loins with Bacon

 Serving size:
4

 Preparation time:
8 minutes

 Cooking time:
20 minutes

 Total time:
28 minutes

Ingredients

- 500 grams pork tenderloin
- 60 grams tub of chive and herb cream cheese spread
- 90 grams grated cheddar cheese
- 2-3 tablespoons Dijon mustard
- 90 grams panko breadcrumbs
- ½ teaspoon cayenne pepper
- ½ teaspoon salt
- ½ teaspoon black pepper

Instructions

- Butterfly the pork tenderloin by slicing against the long edge almost all the way through to the other side. Leave a little bit so that it opens like a hot dog bun.
- Open the pork tenderloin so that it is inside facing up. Spread a layer of cream cheese on the inside of the pork. Add a layer of grated cheddar cheese on top of the cream cheese.
- Carefully fold over the tenderloin and insert toothpicks to hold it closed. If your air fryer basket will not fit the entire tenderloin, slice it in half as I had to in the above photos. Brush Dijon mustard on the outside of the tenderloin.
- In a shallow dish, add breadcrumbs, cayenne pepper, salt, and black pepper. Roll the tenderloin in the breadcrumbs and press them in/down, so that they stick.
- Add the pork to the air fryer basket and lightly spray the breadcrumbs with cooking oil.
- Set the temperature to 200 degrees C and the timer to 10 minutes. Carefully turn them over and lightly spray with cooking oil. Cook an additional 8-10 minutes.

106. Bacon Wrapped Pork Chops

 Serving size:
4

 Preparation time:
10 minutes

 Cooking time:
20 minutes

 Total time:
40 minutes

Ingredients

- 500 grams pork tenderloin
- 5 slices bacon
- 1 teaspoon salt
- 1 teaspoon garlic powder
- 1/2 teaspoon onion powder
- 1/2 teaspoon smoked paprika
- 1/4 teaspoon pepper

Instructions

- Preheat air fryer to 350 degrees.
- In a small bowl, mix together salt, garlic powder, onion powder, paprika, and pepper. Season pork evenly on all sides with the seasoning mixture.
- Wrap slices of bacon around the pork tenderloin and add to the air fryer basket.
- Spray the top of the bacon wrapped pork tenderloin lightly with cooking spray.
- Cook 200 degrees C for 25-30 minutes.

107. Bacon-Wrapped Sausages

 Serving size:
4

 Preparation time:
20 minutes

 Cooking time:
15 minutes

 Total time:
35 minutes

Ingredients

- 200 grams sliced bacon
- 2 packages frozen fully cooked breakfast sausage links, thawed
- 60 grams plus 2 tablespoons packed brown sugar, divided

Instructions

- Cut bacon strips widthwise in half; cut sausage links in half. Wrap a piece of bacon around each piece of sausage. Place 1/2 cup brown sugar in a shallow bowl; roll sausages in sugar. Secure each with a toothpick. Place in a large bowl. Cover and refrigerate 4 hours or overnight.
- Preheat air fryer to 200°C. Sprinkle wrapped sausages with 1 tablespoon brown sugar. In batches, arrange sausages in a single layer in greased air fryer. Cook until bacon is crisp, 15-20 minutes, turning once. Sprinkle with remaining 1 tablespoon brown sugar.

108. Herbed Pork Chops

 Serving size:
2

 Preparation time:
3 minutes

 Cooking time:
12 minutes

 Total time:
15 minutes

Ingredients

- 500 grams pork loin chops
- 1 teaspoon olive oil
- 1 tablespoon herb and garlic seasoning

Instructions

- Add a spray or light coating of oil to both sides of chops and rub with seasoning.
- Add to air fryer basket and set to 220 degrees C for 12 minutes, flipping once.
- Allow to rest for 5 minutes before serving.

109. Tangy Pork Roast

Serving size: 6	Preparation time: 5 minutes
Cooking time: 40 minutes	Total time: 45 minutes

Ingredients

- 1 pork loin joint
- 2 teaspoon salt

Instructions

- Score the rind length ways. Rind can be quite hard to cut through, so you will have to carefully use a sharp knife. Make sure to only cut the rind, and not to cut through to the fat and meat underneath.
- Pat the rind dry with kitchen paper, and salt generously. Make sure to rub salt into the cuts you just made. Then, leave the pork roast to rest uncovered in a refrigerator skin side up for around 24 hours. Make sure to have a look at it once or twice while it rests, and wipe off any liquid that appears. This will ensure that the rind dries out completely.
- Preheat your air fryer to 200 degrees C.
- Transfer the pork roast to the air fryer, skin side up, and air fry for 40 minutes.
- Remove the cooked pork roast from the air fryer, and leave it for about 15 minutes before you carve and serve.

110. Pork Burgers

Serving size: 4	Preparation time: 10 minutes
Cooking time: 20 minutes	Total time: 30 minutes

Ingredients

- 1 tablespoon smoked paprika
- 1 teaspoon cumin
- 1 teaspoon sea salt
- 2 teaspoons dried coriander
- 1/2 teaspoon black pepper
- Burger
- 200 grams minced pork
- 200 grams minced beef
- 1 teaspoon Kosher salt
- 4 ciabatta rolls
- 60 grams butter, softened
- 130 grams blue cheese dressing
- 4 slices cheese
- 4 slices tomato
- 8 pickle slices

Instructions

- Combine the rub ingredients in a bowl.
- Combine the burger ingredients in a separate bowl.
- Shape the combined ingredients into four patties and coat each patty with the rub.
- Place the burgers on an Air Flow Rack. Place the rack on the middle shelf of the Air Fryer oven.
- Press the Power Button (220 degrees C) and increase the cooking time to 16 minutes. Turn the burgers over halfway through the cooking time (8 minutes).
- Cut the ciabatta rolls in half and butter them.
- Place two buns on a rack. Place the rack on the middle shelf of the Air Fryer.
- Press the Power Button (220 degrees C) and cook the buns until golden (about 3 minutes). Repeat until all the buns are toasted.
- Place the burgers on the buns and top with blue cheese dressing, cheese slices, tomato and pickle.

111. Pulled Pork with Bacon and Cheddar

Serving size: 4	Preparation time: 10 minutes
Cooking time: 4 minutes	Total time: 14 minutes

Ingredients

- 5 corn tortillas
- 4–5 tablespoons olive oil (enough to coat all of them)
- salt to taste
- 400 grams pulled pork, cooked and warmed
- 1 diced tomato
- 1 diced cucumber
- 100 grams grated cheddar cheese
- Guacamole
- 2 bacon slices, cooked and diced
- diced olives

Instructions

- Layout the tortillas in a stack, use a pizza cutter, make wedges, cut the tortilla in half, and then make your wedges.
- Place the wedges into a mixing bowl, and mix the olive oil and salt, being careful to coat each wedge.
- Then set the temperature to 200 degrees C, air fryer setting, for 4 minutes, turning them halfway through the cooking process.
- Spread the tortilla chips out on a large platter and scatter the toppings over the nachos
- Plate, serve, and enjoy!

112. Mustard Pork Chops

 Serving size:
4

 Preparation time:
10 minutes

 Cooking time:
20 minutes

 Total time:
30 minutes

Ingredients

- 4 pork chops
- 40 ml. avocado oil, can also use olive oil
- 70 grams Dijon mustard
- 1 teaspoon dried thyme or fresh thyme sprigs
- 1/2 teaspoon salt
- 1 teaspoon pepper
- nonstick cooking spray, for air fryer basket

Instructions

- Preheat your air fryer to 220 degrees C.
- Spray air fryer basket with nonstick spray.
- Cook pork chops for 8-10 minutes on 220 degrees C.
- Turn over and cook an additional 6-7 minutes.

113. Pork Rack with Macadamia Nuts

 Serving size:
4

 Preparation time:
10 minutes

 Cooking time:
2o minutes

 Total time:
3o minutes

Ingredients

- 1 garlic clove
- 1 tablespoon olive oil
- 800 grams rack of lamb
- pepper & salt
- 75 grams unsalted macadamia nuts
- 1 tablespoon breadcrumbs (preferably homemade)
- 1 tablespoon chopped fresh rosemary
- 1 egg

Instructions

- Finely chop the garlic. Mix the olive oil and garlic to make garlic oil. Brush the rack of lamb with the oil and season with pepper & salt.
- Preheat the Air fryer to 100°C.
- Finely chop the nuts and place them into a bowl. Stir in the breadcrumbs and rosemary. Whisk the egg in another bowl.

- To coat the lamb, dip the meat into the egg mixture, draining off any excess. Coat the lamb with the macadamia crust.
- Put the coated lamb rack in the Air fryer basket and slide the basket into the Air fryer. Set the timer for 25 minutes.
- After 25 minutes, increase the temperature to 200°C and set the timer for another 5 minutes. Remove the meat and leave to rest, covered with aluminium foil, for 10 minutes before serving.

114. Spicy Pork Kebabs

 Serving size:
3

 Preparation time:
10 minutes

 Cooking time:
20 minutes

Total time:
30 minutes

Ingredients

- 1 kg minced pork
- 40 grams shallot finely chopped (1 medium)
- 1 serrano chilli, finely chopped and de-seeded for mild heat
- 1 tablespoon ginger garlic paste (3 cloves of garlic + ½ inch ginger)
- 40 grams chopped coriander
- 1 carrot finely shredded (optional)
- 1 tablespoon garam masala
- 1 teaspoon Kashmiri red chilli powder or paprika for a milder flavour
- 1 teaspoon salt
- 2 teaspoon lime juice fresh
- 1 tablespoon olive oil + 2 tablespoons for forming kebabs
- 8 bamboo skewers, soaked in water for 10 minutes

Instructions

- In a small food processor, add peeled ginger, garlic cloves, shallot chunks (or onion), Serrano chilli and coriander. Pulse it until everything gets blended together.
- Add it to a large mixing bowl along with minced pork and grated carrots (if using). Add salt, garam masala, paprika, olive oil and lime juice. Mix well.
- Roughly divide the mixture evenly into 8 portions. Use food grade gloves for a mess-free process of making the kebabs.
- Pour 2 tablespoons of oil in a small bowl. Wet your palms with oil, take one portion of the pork mixture and roll it into an oblong or cylindrical shape by gently pressing it together.
- Thread a skewer through the spiced pork mix. Place the skewers on a plate and keep forming kebabs.

- Preheat air fryer at 200°C for 2 minutes. Place the skewers in the fryer basket, leaving ½-inch gap between them. Cook for 10-12 minutes.
- Rest for 5 minutes before serving. Serve with the coriander chutney as an appetizer or wrap it up in a paratha. For a low-carb meal, pair with a garden salad.

115. BBQ Ribs

	Serving size: 4		Preparation time: 2 minuts
	Cooking time: 28 minutes		Total time: 30 minutes

Ingredients

- 1 rack baby back pork ribs
- 3 teaspoons garlic powder
- 2 teaspoons paprika
- 1 teaspoon salt
- 1/2 teaspoon black pepper
- 1/2 teaspoon cumin
- 90 grams ketchup
- 2 tablespoons brown sugar
- 1 tablespoon apple cider vinegar
- 1 tablespoon olive oil
- 1/2 teaspoon ground cumin
- salt and pepper to taste

Instructions

- Remove the membrane: Peel off the silverskin from the back of the ribs.
- Cut the rack of pork ribs into 2-3 sections so that it can fit into your air fryer basket.
- Make the spice rub: In a small bowl, mix garlic powder, paprika, salt, pepper and cumin.
- Season the baby back ribs: Pat the ribs dry and rub the ribs on all sides with the spice rub.
- Cook the ribs in the air fryer: Preheat the air fryer to 190°C for a few minutes. Once hot, place the ribs into the basket with the meat side down and cook for 15 minutes.
- Turn the ribs using kitchen tongs, and cook for 10 more minutes at 190°C.
- Make the BBQ sauce: While the ribs are cooking, you can add BBQ sauce ingredients in a saucepan. Heat over a medium-low heat until the sugar and salt are completely dissolved.
- Brush with BBQ sauce: Remove the basket from the air fryer and brush generously with barbecue sauce on all sides.

- Place the basket back in the air fryer and cook for 3-5 more minutes at 200°C, or until the sauce has set and darkened slightly. (It may take more or less time based on the thickness or your ribs)
- Remove the ribs from the basket and let them rest for 5 minutes so that the juices can redistribute through the meat. Feel free to brush with more barbeque sauce if you like.

116. Sweet Beef and Vegetables

	Serving size: 4		Preparation time: 20 minutes
	Cooking time: 10 minutes		Total time: 30 minutes

Ingredients

- 500 grams beef sirloin
- 500 grams broccoli florets
- 2 red pepper cut into strips
- 2 green pepper cut into strips
- 2 yellow pepper cut into strips
- 2 onions diced
- 2 red onions diced

Marinade:
- 30 ml. hoisin sauce
- 2 teaspoons chopped garlic
- 1 teaspoon sesame oil
- 1 tablespoon soy sauce
- 1 teaspoon ground ginger
- 60 ml. water

Instructions

- Add all of the ingredients for the sauce (marinate) to a bowl, then add the meat.
- Then place in the refrigerator for about 20 minutes.
- Add one tablespoon of stir fryer oil, and mix it in with the vegetables.
- Place your vegetables in the air fryer basket, and cook them for about 5 minutes on 200 degrees C.
- Then open your air fryer, mix all of the vegetables, and make sure they are softened, not hard. If they aren't softened, add another 2 minutes.
- Remove the vegetables and place them in a bowl, then add your meat to the air fryer basket, and cook them for 4 minutes at 200 degrees C. Check and turn them, and do another 2 minutes if they aren't done.
- Plate, serve, and enjoy!

117. Beef Quesadillas

 Serving size:
2

 Preparation time:
2 minutes

 Cooking time:
8 minutes

 Total time:
10 minutes

Ingredients

- 2 medium flour tortillas (you should be able to fit one flat tortilla into the air fryer basket)
- 200 grams minced beef taco meat
- 100 grams Monterey jack cheese (grated)

Instructions

- Assemble the quesadillas by filling one half of each tortilla with half of the minced beef taco meat (or another filling of your choice) and top it with half of the grated Monterey jack cheese (or your favorite cheese). Fold the tortilla in half to close the quesadilla. *Add more of the filling and cheese if desired.
- Repeat with the second tortilla.
- Transfer the assembled quesadillas into your air fryer basket. Cook for 5 minutes at 175 degrees C then flip and cook an additional 3-5 minutes, or until golden and crispy.
- Remove the quesadillas from your air fryer and serve immediately.

118. Liver Muffins with Eggs

 Serving size:
2

 Preparation time:
10 minutes

 Cooking time:
11 minutes

 Total time:
21 minutes

Ingredients

- 500 grams baby calves liver
- 2 large onions sliced into rings
- 1 teaspoon salt
- 1/2 teaspoon black pepper
- 1 teaspoon smoked paprika
- 1 teaspoon garlic powder
- 1 teaspoon onion powder
- 1 teaspoon dry mustard
- 1 egg

Instructions

- Start by peeling the onions, and then slice them horizontally into rings.

- Place your onion rings into a large mixing bowl. Season them with salt, pepper, smoked paprika, dry mustard, garlic powder, and onion powder.
- Place the onions into an air fryer basket.
- Season your liver with salt, pepper, garlic powder, onion powder, dry mustard, and smoked paprika. Season on both sides.
- Place the liver on top of the onions in the basket, and add the egg (previously whisked). And set the temperature to 200 degrees C, for 7 minutes.
- Once the liver is fully cooked, remove it and place it on a plate.

119. Beef Schnitzel

 Serving size:
2

 Preparation time:
15 minutes

 Cooking time:
5 minutes

 Total time:
20 minutes

Ingredients

- 280 grams beef schnitzel
- 1 egg
- 2 tablespoons flour
- 130 grams panko breadcrumbs
- 2 tablespoons herbs

Instructions

- Pat beef dry, and cut any large pieces in half.
- Mix breadcrumbs and herbs de Provence in a shallow bowl.
- Add flour to another large bowl, place beef in flour and toss to coat.
- Add egg to the bowl with the beef, split the yolk, and toss to coat.
- Preheat air fryer to 180°C.
- Place each piece of beef into the breadcrumbs, and turn to coat thoroughly. Transfer to a plate, and press the panko crumbs onto the beef to help them stick.
- Place beef schnitzels in the air fryer basket. Ensure they are not touching. You may need to cook the schnitzels in batches depending on the size of your air fryer.
- Air fry beef schnitzels until golden brown and cooked through. This will take approximately 7-10 minutes. Carefully turn the beef halfway through the cooking time if required for your air fryer.

120. Meatballs with Tomato Sauce

 Serving size:
3

 Preparation time:
10 minutes

 Cooking time:
8 minutes

 Total time:
18 minutes

Ingredients

- 1 small onion
- 300 grams minced beef
- 1 tablespoon chopped fresh parsley
- ½ tablespoon chopped fresh thyme leaves
- 1 egg
- 3 tablespoons breadcrumbs
- pepper & salt to taste
- 200 ml tomato sauce

Instructions

- Finely chop the onion. Place all the ingredients into a bowl and mix well. Shape the mixture into 10 to 12 balls.
- Preheat the Air fryer to 200°C.
- Place the meatballs in the Air fryer basket and slide the basket in the Air fryer. Set the timer for 7 minutes.
- Transfer the meatballs to an oven dish, add the tomato sauce and place the dish into the basket of the Air fryer. Slide the basket into the Air fryer. Turn the temperature to 160°C and set the timer for 5 minutes to warm everything through.

121. Thai Roasted Beef

 Serving size:
4

 Preparation time:
20 minutes

 Cooking time:
20 minutes

 Total time:
40 minutes

Ingredients

- 500 grams flank steak
- 30 grams corn starch
- Cooking oil spray
- Sauce
- 2 teaspoons vegetable oil
- 1/2 teaspoon ginger
- 1 tablespoon chopped garlic
- 40 ml. soy sauce or gluten free soy sauce
- 40 ml. water
- 100 grams brown sugar
- Cooked rice

Instructions

- Thinly slice the steak in long pieces, then coat with the corn starch.
- Place in the Air Fryer, once in the air fryer coat it with a coat of grapeseed oil spray.
- Cook at 200 degrees C for 5 minutes on each side.
- While the steak cooks, warm up all sauce ingredients in a medium-sized saucepan on medium-high heat.
- Whisk the ingredients together until it gets to a low boil.
- Once both the steak and sauce are cooked, place the steak in a bowl with the sauce and let it soak in for about 5-10 minutes.
- When ready to serve, use tongs to remove the steak and let the excess sauce drip off.
- Place steak on cooked rice and green beans, top with additional sauce if you prefer.

122. Roast beef

 Serving size:
6

 Preparation time:
5 minutes

 Cooking time:
1 hour and 40 minutes

 Total time:
1 hour and 45 minutes

Ingredients

- 2 kg sirloin tip roast
- 2 tablespoons olive oil
- 6 tablespoons montreal steak spice

Instructions

- Preheat air fryer to 200°C. Trim excess fat off of roast.
- Brush roast with olive oil. Sprinkle with montreal steak spice on all sides, and press gently to coat.
- Place roast into preheated air fryer basket. Cook for 15 minutes. This is the sear.
- Reduce heat to 200°C. Cook for 1 hour 40 minutes, or 25 minutes per pound.
- Towards the end of cooking, check temperature with an instant read thermometer (cook to 135°F for medium rare).
- Place roast on a serving tray. Tent with foil, and rest for 10 minutes before slicing.

123. Peppercorn Meatloaf

 Serving size:
4

 Preparation time:
5 minutes

 Cooking time:
45 minutes

 Total time:
50 minutes

Ingredients

Meatloaf Ingredients:
- Instant pot no drain mashed potatoes
- 2 kg minced beef
- 1 small diced onion
- 1 teaspoon garlic puree
- 1 bread roll
- 2 large eggs
- 1 tablespoon Worcester sauce
- 2 teaspoon parsley
- 1 teaspoon paprika
- 2 teaspoon mixed herbs
- Salt & pepper

Meatloaf Glaze:
- 2 tablespoon Tomato Ketchup
- 1 teaspoon garlic puree
- 2 teaspoon Worcester sauce
- Salt & pepper
- Olive oil spray

Instructions

- Add into a bowl your meatloaf ingredients. Blend your bread roll into breadcrumbs in either a blender or a food processor.
- In your bowl give everything a good mix and make sure everything is well mixed in. You don't want an uneven spread of your seasoning.
- Make your meatloaf shape and wrap in tin foil, leaving a little space at the top. The tighter you wrap your tin foil around your meatloaf the easier it is for your meatloaf to keep its shape.
- Place your meatloaf in your air fryer basket and cook for 25 minutes at 160 degrees C.
- Remove the top layer of tin foil. You want the tin foil to still offer a good layer under the meatloaf but not over it. Cook for a further 15 minutes at 180 degrees C.
- While the meatloaf cooks make your glaze. Mix the glaze ingredients in a little bowl, until well mixed.
- When the air fryer beeps, spray the top of the meatloaf with extra virgin olive oil spray. Then using a spoon add your tomato ketchup glaze. Cook for a further 5 minutes at 200 degrees C.

124. Liver Souffle

 Serving size:
2

 Preparation time:
10 minutes

Cooking time:
10 minutes

 Total time:
20 minutes

Ingredients

- 500 grams beef or calf liver, fresh or frozen (thawed)
- 2 small onions, sliced then separated in rings
- 120 grams plain flour
- Cooking oil, as needed (I used vegetable oil)
- 1/2 tablespoon margarine or butter, optional
- Salt and black pepper, to taste

Instructions

- Preheat Air fryer to 200 degrees C.
- In a bowl add margarine, 1 teaspoon oil, onions, salt and pepper. Mix them well, and microwave them for 2 minutes.
- In another bowl put the flour together with salt and pepper and mix well to combine. Add the liver and once again mix well to combine.
- Combine both mixtures and air fry it for 10 minutes over 200 degrees C.

125. Beef Bulgogi

 Serving size:
6

 Preparation time:
10 minutes

 Cooking time:
12 minutes

 Total time:
22 minutes

Ingredients

- 900 grams sirloin steak
- 3 chopped spring onions, cut into 2-3 pieces each
- 2 grated carrots
- 3 tablespoons soy sauce
- 2 tablespoons brown sugar, or 2 teaspoons Splenda for low carb
- 2 tablespoons sesame oil
- 2 tablespoons sesame seeds
- 2 teaspoons chopped garlic
- 1/2 teaspoon ground black pepper

Instructions

- Place sliced beef, carrots, and spring onions into a plastic zip-top bag. Add soy sauce, brown sugar, sesame oil, sesame seeds, garlic, and ground pepper. Squish the bag well to get the meat and sauce to incorporate well.
- Allow the beef to marinate for 30 minutes or up to 24 hours in the fridge.
- Place the meat and veggies into the air fryer basket, leaving behind as much of the marinade as you can. Set air fryer to 200°C for 12 minutes, shaking halfway through.
- Serve with steamed rice, riced cauliflower, or over a mixed salad.

126. Beef with Hoisin Sauce with Vegetables

 Serving size:
2

 Preparation time:
3 minutes

 Cooking time:
8 minutes

Total time:
11 minutes

Ingredients

- 1 teaspoon oil
- 400 grams sirloin steak
- 1 onion
- Sauce
- 1 crushed garlic clove (or 1 teaspoon of garlic paste)
- 1 teaspoon honey
- 5 tablespoon hoisin sauce
- 2 tablespoon light soy sauce
- 120 ml. water
- 1 teaspoon sweet chilli sauce (optional)

Instructions

- Chop any ingredients you're planning on topping the dish with. If you're eating this with rice or noodles, start cooking them now too - the steak only takes 8 minutes.
- Chop the steak and onion into strips
- Add the onion and steak to the Air fryer with the 1 teaspoon of oil - cook for 3 minutes with the paddle in over 200 degrees C.
- Whilst the steak and onions are cooking, mix together the sauce ingredients.
- Once the onions and steak have cooked for 3 minutes, pour in the sauce.
- Cook for 5 minutes (or, until the steak is cooked to your liking, if you like it more med/rare cook for just 2 minutes here).

127. Traditional British Beef Recipe

 Serving size:
2

 Preparation time:
10 minutes

 Cooking time:
20 minutes

 Total time:
30 minutes

Ingredients

- 4 tablespoon. butter, softened
- 2 cloves garlic, crushed
- 2 teaspoons freshly chopped parsley
- 1 teaspoon freshly chopped chives
- 1 teaspoon freshly chopped thyme
- 1 teaspoon freshly chopped rosemary
- 900 grams bone-in ribeye
- Salt
- Freshly ground black pepper

Instructions

- In a small bowl, combine butter and herbs. Place in centre of a piece of cling film and roll into a log. Twist ends together to keep tight and refrigerate until hardened, 20 minutes.
- Season steak on both sides with salt and pepper.
- Place steak in the basket of the air fryer and cook at 200°C for 12 to 14 minutes, for medium, depending on thickness of steak, turning halfway through.
- Top steak with a slice of herb butter to serve.

128. Spicy Meatloaf with Tomato Basil Sauce

 Serving size:
8

 Preparation time:
15 minutes

 Cooking time:
15 minutes

 Total time:
30 minutes

Ingredients

- 1 can organic diced tomatoes with Italian herbs, drained
- 500 grams lean minced beef
- 500 grams lean minced pork
- 50 ml. marinara sauce
- 140 grams Italian style bread crumbs
- 1 egg, slightly beaten
- 1 teaspoon salt
- 1 teaspoon pepper

- 90 grams shredded mozzarella cheese (2 oz)
- 2 plum (Roma) tomatoes, chopped, if desired
- Chopped fresh basil leaves, if desired

Instructions

- Heat Air Fryer to 220 degrees C.
- Place diced tomatoes in a blender or food processor. Cover then blend on high speed for about 5 seconds or until the tomatoes are still slightly chunky. In large bowl, mix the beef and pork. Stir in tomatoes, marinara sauce, bread crumbs, egg, salt and pepper just until combined.
- Air fry the mixture for 20 minutes over 220 degrees C.
- Serve.

129. Ginger Beef Ribs

 Serving size: 6

 Preparation time: 20 minutes

 Cooking time: 30 minutes

 Total time: 50 minutes

Ingredients

- 1 kg. country-style pork ribs
- 2 tablespoons vegetable oil
- ¼ teaspoon salt
- ¼ teaspoon ground black pepper
- 2 teaspoons vegetable oil
- 1 shallot, finely chopped
- 30 ml. chilli sauce
- 40 grams apricot preserves
- 1 tablespoon reduced-sodium soy sauce
- 1 teaspoon grated fresh ginger
- ⅛ teaspoon ground dried chipotle pepper
- 2 tablespoons chopped fresh chives

Instructions

- Preheat an air fryer to 175 degrees C.
- Brush ribs with 2 tablespoons oil and season with salt and pepper. Arrange 1/2 of the ribs in a single layer in the air fryer basket.
- Cook in the preheated air fryer until ribs are fork-tender and fully cooked, 15 to 20 minutes.
- Meanwhile, heat 2 teaspoons oil in a small saucepan over medium heat. Add shallot; cook and stir until tender, about 3 minutes. Stir in chilli sauce, apricot preserves, soy sauce, ginger, and chipotle pepper. Heat and stir until bubbly, 3 to 5 minutes.
- Transfer ribs to a serving platter. Brush generously with glaze and garnish with chives.

130. Chipotle Steak

 Serving size: 4

 Preparation time: 30 minutes

 Cooking time: 30 minutes

 Total time: 1 hour

Ingredients

- 100 grams beef sirloin
- 180 grams Greek yogurt
- 15 grams coriander
- 1 chipotle chille in adobo sauce
- ½ teaspoon ground cumin
- ¼ teaspoon dried dill
- Kosher salt

Instructions

- Combine chipotle chilli, yogurt, coriander, cumin, and dill in a small bowl.
- Get a resealable bag and the chipotle sauce mixture. Add some salt to taste.
- Next, add the beef and massage making sure to coat all sides with marinade. Put in the fridge for at least 2 hours.
- Set your Air Fryer to 200 degrees C.
- Remove the marinated beef from the resealable bag into the Air Fryer basket.
- Cook the steaks in the Air Fryer for 15 minutes, turning half-way through cooking time.
- Transfer into a serving dish.

131. Avocado Lime Steak

 Serving size: 2

 Preparation time: 5 minutes

 Cooking time: 10 minutes

 Total time: 15 minutes

Ingredients

- 2 fillet steaks
- 1 tablespoon avocado oil
- 1 tablespoon montreal steak seasoning
- 1 tablespoon butter
- Pinch of coarse salt
- Ground black pepper
- Dried or fresh parsley

Instructions

- Prepare the steaks. Place the fillets onto a clean plate and pat them dry with clean kitchen paper.

- Season the steaks. Brush both sides of each piece of steak with some oil and generously season both sides of each fillet with the Montreal steak seasoning.
- Cook. Preheat the air fryer to 200 degrees C and place the steaks into the air fryer basket about 1 inch a part and cook for 4 minutes. Turn each piece of steak over and cook for 4 more minutes (see cooking chart below).
- Serve. Remove the steaks from the air fryer and place them onto a clean plate. Top each steak with a pat of butter, some parsley, a pinch of sea salt and some black pepper. Place a piece of foil loosely over the steak and let them rest for 5-10 minutes before slicing and serving. Serve warm with your favorite steakhouse sides.

132. Traditional British Beef Satay

 Serving size:
3

 Preparation time:
10 minutes

 Cooking time:
8 minutes

Total time:
18 minutes

Ingredients

- 500 grams beef flank steak
- 2 tablespoons oil
- 1 tablespoon fish sauce
- 1 tablespoon soya sauce
- 1 tablespoon chopped ginger
- 1 tablespoon chopped garlic
- 1 tablespoon sugar or other sweetener equivalent
- 1 teaspoon Sriracha sauce
- 1 teaspoon ground coriander
- 40 grams chopped coriander, divided
- 40 grams chopped roasted peanuts

Instructions

- Place beef strips into a large bowl or a ziplock bag.
- Add oil, fish sauce, soy sauce, ginger, garlic, sugar, Sriracha, coriander, and half of coriander to the beef and mix well. Marinate for 30 minutes or up to 24 hours in the fridge.
- Using a set of tongs, place the beef strips in the air fryer basket, laying them side by side and minimizing overlap.
- Leave behind as much of the marinade as you can and discard this marinade.
- Set your air fryer to 200 degrees C for 8 minutes, turning once halfway.
- Remove the meat to a serving tray, top with remaining chopped coriander and the chopped roasted peanuts.
- Serve with Easy Peanut Sauce.

133. Broccoli and Beef

 Serving size:
4

 Preparation time:
10 minutes

 Cooking time:
25 minutes

 Total time:
35 minutes

Ingredients

- 500 grams sirloin tip steak, thinly sliced
- 1 tablespoon soy sauce
- 1 teaspoon garlic powder
- 1 teaspoon onion powder
- 2 tablespoons cornstarch
- 500 grams broccoli florets, cut into bite-sized pieces

Sauce:
- 20 ml. soy sauce
- 3 tablespoons beef stock
- 2 tablespoons light brown sugar
- 1 tablespoon cornstarch (corn flour)
- 4 cloves garlic, chopped
- 1 1/2 teaspoon rice vinegar
- 1 teaspoon fresh ginger, chopped
- Cooking Spray
- Optional: Sliced spring onions for garnish

Instructions

- Place the steak in a medium-sized bowl and toss with the soy sauce, garlic powder, and onion powder. Add the cornstarch and mix it in, so the beef is coated. Set aside.
- Preheat the air fryer to 200 degrees C, air fryer setting. Add the broccoli to the basket and spray with cooking spray.
- Shake the basket to coat the broccoli and cook for 8 minutes, shaking the basket every 2 minutes until tender-crisp and starting to brown. Set aside.
- Spray the basket with cooking spray. Add the beef to the basket in a single layer, spray with cooking spray. Air Fry for 15 minutes, shaking the basket every 5 minutes, and coating with more cooking spray. Beef will be cooked through and lightly crispy.
- For the sauce, in a small bowl, whisk together the light soy sauce, beef stock, brown sugar, cornstarch, garlic, rice vinegar, and ginger. Set aside.
- In a large pan over a medium heat, add the cooked beef and broccoli to the pan. Add the sauce, and toss everything to coat. Cook until the sauce has thickened, about 2 minutes.
- Serve with scallion garnish. Plate, serve, and enjoy!

134. Beef Rice

Serving size: 2	**Preparation time:** 10 minutes
Cooking time: 20 minutes	**Total time:** 30 minutes

Ingredients

- 250 grams skirt steak sliced against the grain
- 500 grams cold cooked white rice
- 1 white onion diced
- 1 celery diced
- 2 carrots diced
- 4-6 tablespoons soy sauce or gluten free soy sauce
- Coconut oil cooking spray or olive oil cooking spray
- 2 hard-boiled eggs

Instructions

- Cut the steak and place it in the air fryer basket.
- Cook at 200 degrees C for 5 minutes.
- Turn and cook an additional 5 minutes.
- Line the air fryer basket with foil. Remember not to cover the entire basket to be sure air is still able to flow. I typically roll it up on the side.
- Spray the foil with the coconut oil or olive oil spray.
- Add all ingredients in order on top of the foil in the basket.
- Stir to mix together and add a nice coat of coconut oil spray to the top of the mixture.
- Cook in the air fryer on 170 degrees C for 5 minutes.
- Carefully open and stir up the rice and mixture again, adding an additional coat of spray or soy sauce if needed.
- Stir in the sliced or crumbled hard-boiled eggs.
- Continue cooking for an additional 3 minutes at 170 degrees C.
- Stir up and serve.

135. British Beef Roast

Serving size: 4	**Preparation time:** 5 minutes
Cooking time: 35 minutes	**Total time:** 40 minutes

Ingredients

- 900 grams beef
- 1 tablespoon olive oil
- 1 medium onion, (optional)
- 1 teaspoon salt
- 2 teaspoons rosemary and thyme, (fresh or dried)

Instructions

- Preheat air fryer to 200°C.
- Mix sea salt, rosemary and oil on a plate.
- Pat the beef roast dry with kitchen paper. Place beef roast on plate and turn so that the oil-herb mix coats the outside of the beef.
- If using, peel onion and cut it in half, place onion halves in the air fryer basket.
- Place beef roast in the air fryer basket.
- Set to air fry beef for 5 minutes.
- When the time is up, change the temperature to 180°C. Turn the beef roast over half way through the cooking time if required by your air fryer
- Set the beef to cook for an additional 30 minutes. This should give you a medium-rare beef. Though is best to monitor the temperature with a meat thermometer to ensure that it is cooked to your liking. Check it early, and cook for additional 5 minute intervals if you prefer it more well done.
- Remove roast beef from air fryer, cover with tin foil and leave to rest for at least ten minutes before serving. This allows the meat to finish cooking and the juices to reabsorb into the meat.
- Carve the roast beef thinly against the grain and serve with roasted or steamed vegetables, wholegrain mustard, and gravy.

136. Honey and Pork Dish

Serving size: 4	**Preparation time:** 10 minutes
Cooking time: 15 minutes	**Total time:** 25 minutes

Ingredients

- 4 pork chops
- salt and pepper to taste
- 40 grams honey
- 2 garlic cloves, chopped
- 2 tablespoons lemon juice
- 1 tablespoon sweet chilli sauce
- 1 tablespoon extra virgin olive oil

Instructions

- Preheat your air fryer to 200 degrees C.
- Season both sides of your pork chops with salt and pepper.
- Place your pork chops in a single layer in your air fryer. They can be touching, but make sure they lay flat on the bottom of the basket.

- Cook the pork chops for 10-15 minutes, turning halfway through until they reach 145 degrees F. The thicker your pork chops, the longer it will take to cook thoroughly.
- While cooking the pork chops, you can put your sauce together. Place olive oil in a small pan over a medium heat and sauté garlic until fragrant, usually 30 seconds to a minute.
- Add the lemon juice, sweet chilli sauce, and honey to the pan and mix until combined.
- Bring the sauce to a simmer and cook until thickened (3-4 minutes).The mixture will become a thicker consistency as it sits.
- Place pork chops in a serving dish and glaze sauce over top of them. Enjoy immediately!

137. Onion and Sausage Balls

 Serving size: 12

 Preparation time: 5 minutes

 **Cooking time:** 10 minutes

 Total time: 15 minutes

Ingredients

- 450 grams sausage meat
- 25 grams butter
- ½ small white onion
- ½ medium bread roll
- 2 tablespoons sage
- Salt & pepper
- Extra breadcrumbs for binding optional

Instructions

- Using a vegetable knife, chop your bread roll into small chunks. Also peel and thinly dice your onion. Get your butter and chop it into small chunks.
- Place all your ingredients into a mixing bowl and mix well.
- Make into small to medium sized sage and onion stuffing balls.
- Place in the fridge for an hour to chill and firm up.
- Cook for 10 minutes in the air fryer basket at 180 degrees C.

138. Juicy Pork Chops

 Serving size: 4

 Preparation time: 5 minutes

 Cooking time: 20 minutes

 Total time: 25 minutes

Ingredients

- 4 boneless pork chops
- 2 tablespoons extra-virgin olive oil
- 60 grams freshly grated Parmesan
- 1 teaspoon kosher salt
- 1 teaspoon paprika
- 1 teaspoon garlic powder
- 1 teaspoon onion powder
- 1/2 teaspoon freshly ground black pepper

Instructions

- Pat pork chops dry with kitchen paper, then coat both sides with oil.
- In a medium bowl, combine Parmesan and spices. Coat both sides of pork chops with Parmesan mixture.
- Place pork chops in basket of air fryer and cook at 220°C.

139. Sweet and Tender Pork Chops

 Serving size: 2

 Preparation time: 5 minutes

 Cooking time: 20 minutes

 Total time: 25 minutes

Ingredients

- 2 bone-in center cut pork chops, about 1 to 1-½ inch thick
- 2 tablespoons olive oil, or avocado oil
- 1 teaspoon light brown sugar
- 1 teaspoon chilli powder
- 1 teaspoon sweet paprika
- ½ teaspoon ground mustard
- ½ teaspoon salt
- ½ teaspoon fresh ground black pepper
- ¼ teaspoon garlic powder
- ¼ teaspoon onion powder

Instructions

- Preheat Air Fryer to 200°C.
- Grease the pork chops with olive oil.
- In a small mixing bowl combine brown sugar, chilli powder, sweet paprika, ground mustard, salt, pepper, garlic powder, and onion powder; mix until well incorporated.
- Season both sides of the pork chops with the prepared rub.
- Transfer pork chops to the air fryer basket.
- Cook for 5 minutes.
- Turn over and continue to cook for 4 to 6 more minutes.
- I don't recommend using thinner pork chops, but if you do, the cooking time will be less. For best and most accurate

results, use an instant read meat thermometer to check for doneness.

- Remove pork chops from the Air Fryer basket and transfer to a plate; let stand 5 minutes before cutting. Serve.

140. Butterbean Pork Ratatouille

 Serving size:
4

 Preparation time:
5 minutes

 Cooking time:
25 minutes

 Total time:
30 minutes

Ingredients

- ½ small aubergine, cut into cubes
- 1 courgette, cut into cubes
- 1 medium tomato, cut into cubes
- ½ large yellow pepper, cut into cubes
- ½ large red pepper, cut into cubes
- ½ onion, cut into cubes
- 1 fresh cayenne pepper, diced
- 5 sprigs fresh basil, stemmed and chopped
- 2 sprigs fresh oregano, stemmed and chopped
- 1 clove garlic, crushed
- salt and ground black pepper to taste
- 1 tablespoon olive oil
- 1 tablespoon white wine
- 1 teaspoon vinegar

Instructions

- Preheat Air Fryer to 200 degrees C.
- Place aubergine, courgette, tomato, peppers, and onion in a bowl. Add cayenne pepper, basil, oregano, garlic, salt, and pepper. Mix well to distribute everything evenly. Drizzle in oil, wine, and vinegar, mixing to coat all the vegetables.
- Pour vegetable mixture into a baking dish and put into the basket of the air fryer. Cook for 8 minutes. Stir; cook for another 8 minutes. Stir again and continue cooking until tender, stirring every 5 minutes, 10 to 15 minutes more. Turn off air fryer, leaving dish inside. Let rest for 5 minutes before serving.

141. Ham and Cheese Sandwich

 Serving size:
4

 Preparation time:
2 minutes

 Cooking time:
8 minutes

 Total time:
10 minutes

Ingredients

- 8 slices bread
- 8 slices cheese, cheddar
- 8 slices ham
- 4 tablespoon butter (softened, at room temperature)

Instructions

- Preheat your air fryer to 180 degrees C. For a convection style air fryer for 8 minutes.
- Butter the slices of bread. For a convection style oven, place half the buttered bread slices onto the air fryer racks facing down.
- Add sliced or grated cheese portions. Trim excess cheese from edges if desired.
- Add ham slices.
- Top the sandwich with the second buttered slice of bread facing upward. Add garlic salt, if desired.

142. Cashew Lamb Rack

 Serving size:
2

 Preparation time:
10 minutes

 Cooking time:
20 minutes

 Total time:
30 minutes

Ingredients

- 50 grams cashews
- 2 tablespoon peanut or vegetable oil
- 600 grams lamb eye of loin (backstraps), thinly sliced
- 15 grams fresh ginger, finely chopped
- 3 clove garlic, chopped
- 4 onions, cut into 5cm pieces
- 80ml. Chinese cooking wine (shaoxing) or dry sherry
- 2 teaspoon cornflour
- 2 tablespoon oyster sauce
- 1 tablespoon soy sauce
- 1 tablespoon rice vinegar
- 1 tablespoon white sugar
- Coriander leaves

Instructions

- In a wok, toss cashews over a high heat until they start to brown. Remove from the wok.
- Preheat your air fryer to 200 degrees C. Add the lamb and cook it for 20 minutes.
- In the previously used work, reduce heat to a medium-high, add the remaining oil, ginger and garlic.
- Stir-fry 1 minute or until fragrant; add onion. Stir in combined wine and cornflour. Remove the lamb from the air fryer and

return the lamb to wok with sauces, vinegar, sugar and cashews.

- Stir-fry for 1 minute or until heated through. Stir in the coriander.

143. Thyme Lamb Chops

 Serving size:
4

 Preparation time:
10 minutes

 Cooking time:
1 hour

 Total time:
1 hour and 10 minutes

Ingredients

- 1 teaspoon rosemary
- 1 teaspoon thyme
- 1 teaspoon oregano
- 1 teaspoon salt
- 1 teaspoon corinader
- 2 tablespoons olive oil
- 2 tablespoons lemon juice
- 1 grams lamb chops

Instructions

- Mix all of the ingredients, except for the lamb chops, in a ziploc bag. And shake to combine.
- Then place the lamb chops into the bag, and refrigerate for at least one hour. You will get a really nice flavor.
- Then place the lamb chops into the air fryer and set the temperature to 200 degrees C, and set the time for 3 minutes, then flip them, and do for another 4 minutes.
- I like to eat my lamb on a medium-rare. If you would like them done, increase the time.
- Plate, serve, and enjoy!

144. Lamb Steaks with Potatoes and Mushrooms

 Serving size:
4

 Preparation time:
5 minutes

 Cooking time:
1 hour and 10 minutes

 Total time:
1 hour and 15 minutes

Ingredients

- 1.2 kg lamb roast
- 300 grams potatoes
- 150 grams mushrooms
- 1 tablespoon extra virgin olive oil
- 2 tablespoon rosemary
- 1 teaspoon thyme
- 1 teaspoon bouquet garni
- Salt & pepper

Instructions

- Score the lamb and season well with salt, pepper, bouquet garni and thyme.
- Place in the air fryer basket and set the cook time to 30 minutes and the temperature to 160 degrees C.
- In a bowl add peeled and sliced roast potatoes. Add salt, pepper, rosemary, and extra virgin olive oil and mix with your hands. Add the mushrooms.
- When the air fryer beeps turn your lamb roast and place potatoes, and mushrooms in the gaps. Cook for a further 25 minutes at the same time and temp.
- When it beeps remove the potatoes, and mushrooms and allow the lamb to rest.

145. Rosemary and Garlic Lamb Chops

 Serving size:
4

 Preparation time:
10 minutes

 Cooking time:
14 minutes

 Total time:
24 minutes (marintion 1 hour)

Ingredients

- 567 grams rack of lamb
- 3 tablespoons olive oil
- 2 tablespoons chopped fresh rosemary
- 1 teaspoon garlic powder or 3 cloves garlic, chopped
- 1 teaspoon salt , or to taste
- 1/2 teaspoon black pepper , or to taste

Instructions

- Pat dry the lamb rack. Remove silver skin from underside of ribs if needed. Cut into individual chops.
- In a large bowl, combine olive oil, rosemary, garlic, salt, & pepper. Add the lamb and gently toss to coat in marinade. Cover and marinate for about 1 hour or up to overnight.
- Preheat the Air Fryer at 190°C for 4 minutes. Spray air fryer basket/tray with oil spray and place lamb chops in a single layer, making sure not to overlap the meat.
- Air Fry for 8 minutes.

146. Mediterranean Lamb Chops

 Serving size:
4

 Preparation time:
15 minutes

 Cooking time:
10 minutes

 Total time:
45 minutes (20 minutes marination)

Ingredients

- 8 lamb chops
- 1 tablespoon plain Greek yogurt
- 2 tablespoons olive oil or avocado oil
- 2 teaspoons chopped garlic or ½ teaspoon garlic powder
- 2 teaspoons paprika (regular) (reduce to 1 teaspoon if using smoked)
- 1 teaspoon cumin powder
- ⅛ teaspoon ground cinnamon
- ½ teaspoon red pepper flakes
- ¼ teaspoon cayenne pepper skip for mild taste
- 1 teaspoon lemon juice + zest
- ¾ teaspoon salt
- ½ teaspoon freshly ground black pepper

Instructions

- Lay the rack of lamb flat on a cutting surface. Remove excess fat. Take a sharp knife and using the bone as a guide, cut it into 8 chops of even thickness. Wipe dry chops to get rid of excess moisture.
- In a small bowl, combine all ingredients listed for marinade and mix well.
- Place all the chops on a large plate or bowl. Using a pastry brush, generously brush the marinade all over the lamb chops, coating all sides. Cover and keep aside for 20 minutes or up to 2 hours.
- Preheat the air fryer to 200°C for 2-3 minutes. Place the lamb chops in a single layer leaving a little space between them. You should be able to fit all lamb chops in one batch.
- Cook for 7-9 minutes, flipping halfway, for medium-rare, 10-12 minutes for medium-well. Keep in mind that the meat continues to cook while resting. Use a meat thermometer for accurate doneness.

Fish and Seafood

147. Fish Nuggets

 Serving size:
4 servings

 Preparation time:
10 minutes

 Cooking time:
10 minutes

 Total time:
20 minutes

Ingredients

- 60 grams white flour
- 2 large eggs
- 1 tablespoon finely chopped parsley
- 60 grams panko breadcrumb
- 500 grams cod, cut into 1-inch pieces
- 1 teaspoon lemon juice
- ½ teaspoon garlic powder
- Salt and black pepper to taste
- Cooking spray oil (avocado or olive oil)

Instructions

- Preheat air fryer to 200ºC for 10 minutes
- Mix flour and black pepper in a shallow dish and set aside.
- Lightly beat eggs and the chopped parsley in a second shallow dish and set aside.
- Mix panko and black pepper in a third shallow dish and set aside.
- Pat the fish dry with kitchen paper, season with lemon juice, garlic powder, salt, and black pepper to taste.
- Dredge the fish pieces one at a time in the flour mixture, shake off the excess. Dip in the egg mixture, letting the excess drip off. Then dredge in the panko breadcrumb, set it on a clean plate.
- Place the coated fish in the air fryer basket spray with cooking oil; cook at 200ºC for 5 minutes on each side or until the fish flakes easily.
- Serve with aside and tartar sauce or any dipping sauce you like.

148. Salmon with Thyme

 Serving size:
2 servings

 Preparation time:
5 minutes

 Cooking time:
10 minutes

 Total time:
15 minutes

Ingredients

- 2 salmon fillets
- Kosher salt
- Freshly ground black pepper
- 2 teaspoon extra-virgin olive oil
- 2 tablespoon whole grain mustard
- 1 tablespoon brown sugar
- 1 clove garlic, chopped
- 1/2 teaspoon thyme leaves

Instructions

- Season salmon all over with salt and pepper. In a small bowl, whisk together oil, mustard, sugar, garlic, and thyme. Spread on top of salmon.
- Arrange salmon in air fryer basket. Set air fryer to 200°C and cook for 10 minutes.

149. Crispy Salmon

 Serving size:
4

 Preparation time:
5 minutes

 Cooking time:
15 minutes

 Total time:
20 minutes

Ingredients

- 500 grams salmon fillet
- 1 tablespoon olive oil
- 40 grams punko breadcrumbs
- Salt
- Pepper

Instructions

- Remove the salmon from any packaging and pat it dry with kitchen paper.
- Drizzle on the olive oil, salt, and pepper. Rub them all over the salmon. Add breadcrumbs on top.
- Place the salmon in the air fryer tray skin side up and slide it in the air fryer.
- Turn the temperature to 170°C for 15-18 minutes.
- Check on the salmon half-way through the process to make sure it isn't burning.
- When it's golden brown around the edges remove and serve!

150. Traditional British Fish & Chips

 Serving size:
4

 Preparation time:
10 minutes

 Cooking time:
12 minutes

 Total time:
22 minutes

Ingredients

- 130 grams flour
- 2 tablespoons cornstarch/ corn flour
- ½ teaspoon baking soda
- 30 ml. beer
- 1 egg, beaten
- ½ teaspoon paprika
- Salt
- Pepper
- 1 teaspoon cayenne pepper
- 500 grams cod
- 500 grams potatoes

Instructions

- Combine half of the flour with cornstarch and baking soda in a large bowl. Add the beer and egg and stir until smooth.

Cover the bowl of batter with cling film and refrigerate for at least 20 minutes.
- Combine the flour, paprika, salt, black pepper and cayenne pepper in a shallow dredging pan.
- Make sure your pieces of fish are a certain thickness so they don't dry out in the air fryer. Pat the cod fish fillets dry with kitchen paper. Dip the fish into the batter, coating all sides. Let the excess batter drip off and then coat each fillet with the seasoned flour. Sprinkle any leftover flour on the fish fillets and pat gently to adhere the flour to the batter.
- Pre-heat the air fryer to 200°C.
- Generously spray both sides of the coated fish filets with vegetable oil and place them in the air fryer basket. Air-fry for 12 minutes at 200ºC. Spritz with more oil during the cooking process if there are any dry spots on the coating. Make the potatoes next. Place the Air fryer temperature to 180 degrees C and air fry them for 18 minutes.

151. British Prawn Recipe

 Serving size:
4

 Preparation time:
5 minutes

 Cooking time:
7 minutes

 Total time:
12 minutes

Ingredients

- 15 Fresh prawns (can substitute with frozen prawns or shrimps)
- 1 1/2 tablespoons olive oil
- 1 teaspoon chilli powder
- 1 teaspoon black pepper
- 1 tablespoon sweet chilli sauce
- 1 clove Garlic (chopped)
- 1/2 teaspoon salt

Instructions

- Wash and rinse the prawns.
- Preheat the air fryer at 200°C.
- Place the prawns into a mixing bowl. Add oil, chilli powder, black pepper, chili sauce, and garlic into the bowl.
- Stir and mix the ingredient until the prawns are evenly coated.
- Add salt to taste.
- Place the prawns into the air fryer and let them cook for 5 to 7 minutes.
- Check the prawns after 5 minutes and give them a toss.

152. Crispy Fish Fingers

 Serving size:
2

 Preparation time:
5 minutes

 Cooking time:
12 minutes

 Total time:
17 minutes

Ingredients

- 8 Frozen Breaded Fish Sticks

Instructions

- Place the frozen breaded fish sticks in the air fryer basket. Make sure they aren't overlapping. No oil spray is needed.
- Air Fry at 200°C for 8 minutes. Flip the fish sticks over and then continue to cook at 200°C for another 2-4 minutes or until cooked through and the coating is crispy.

153. Tuna Sandwich

 Serving size:
1

 Preparation time:
7 minutes

 Cooking time:
8 minutes

 Total time:
16 minutes

Ingredients

- 2 slices sandwich bread
- 1–2 tablespoons mayonnaise or room temperature butter
- 1 1/2–2 slices cheddar cheese
- 1 can tuna

Instructions

- Assemble the sandwich by placing every ingredient between the two slices of bread.
- Preheat the air fryer to 170 degrees C. The tuna melt is done when you see melty cheese and golden brown edges to your choice.

154. Hot Prawns

 Serving size:
4

 Preparation time:
5 minutes

 Cooking time:
8 minutes

 Total time:
11 minutes

Ingredients

- 500 grams large or jump shrimp
- Salt
- Pepper
- Olive oil
- 30 ml. red wine vinegar
- 3 garlic cloves, chopped
- 1 Tablespoon Italian seasoning
- 1 Tablespoon lemon juice
- 2 Tablespoons soy sauce
- 1 teaspoon dijon mustard
- 1 Tablespoon Worcestershire sauce

Instructions

- Salt and pepper the shrimp. In a medium sized bowl combine olive oil, red wine vinegar, garlic, Italian seasoning, lemon juice, soy sauce, Dijon mustard and Worcestershire sauce. Add the shrimp and let marinate for at least one hour or overnight.
- Remove the shrimp from the marinade and place in the air fryer basket. Cook at 200 degrees C for 8 minutes or until pink and cooked throughout.

155. Barramundi with Lemon Butter Garlic Sauce

 Serving size:
2

 Preparation time:
5 minutes

 Cooking time:
12 minutes

 Total time:
17 minutes

Ingredients

- 350 grams tilapia fillets
- ½ teaspoon garlic powder
- ½ teaspoon lemon pepper seasoning
- ½ teaspoon onion powder
- Salt
- Black pepper
- Lemon wedges
- Chopped parsley

Instructions

- Pre-heat Air Fryer to 220°C for 5 minutes.
- Rinse and pat dry the fish filets. Spray or coat with olive oil spray and season with garlic powder, lemon pepper, and/or onion powder, salt and pepper. Repeat for both sides.
- Lay perforated air fryer baking paper inside base of air fryer. Lightly spray the paper. (if not using a liner, spray enough olive oil spray at the base of the air fryer basket to make sure fish does not stick).
- Lay the fish on top of the paper. Add a few lemon wedges next to fish.

- Air Fry at 200°C for about 6-12 minutes, or until fish can be flaked with a fork. Timing will depend on how thickness of the filets, how cold the filets are and individual preference.
- Sprinkle with chopped parsley and serve warm with the toasted lemon wedges. Add additional seasonings or salt and pepper, if needed.

156. Crab Croquettes

 Serving size:
4

 Preparation time:
10 minutes

 Cooking time:
10 minutes

 Total time:
20 minutes

Ingredients

- 250 grams crab meat
- 200 grams red pepper
- 2 green onion chopped
- 2 tablespoon mayonnaise
- 2 tablespoon bread crumbs
- 1 tablespoon Dijon mustard
- 1 teaspoon old bay seasoning
- Oil for spraying
- Squeeze of lemon

Instructions

- Place crab, red pepper, onion, breadcrumbs, mayonnaise, Dijon mustard, and old bay in abowl and stir until combined.
- Gently form 4 patties with mixture.
- Place in Air Fryer basket and lightly spray tops with oil.
- Air fry on 220 degrees C 10 minutes. Open and squeeze a bit of lemon over the tops before serving.

157. White Fish Fillets with Chips

 Serving size:
4

 Preparation time:
10 minutes

 Cooking time:
15 minutes

 Total time:
25 minutes

Ingredients

- 4 large potatoes
- 2 White fillet fish
- 1 medium egg beaten
- 3 slices wholemeal bread made into breadcrumbs
- 25 grams bag tortilla chips
- 1 lemon rind and juice
- 1 tablespoon parsley
- Salt
- Pepper

Instructions

- Peel and slice your potatoes into chips. Load the potatoes into a bowl, cover with cold water and fridge for 15 minutes.
- Drain the potatoes, add seasoning and extra virgin olive oil and mix with your hands until nicely coated.
- Load the fries into the air fryer basket and cook for 15 minutes at 160 degrees C.
- Cut the fish fillets in half to make four nice sized pieces of fish ready for cooking. Season with lemon juice and then put to one side.
- Grind in a food processor the breadcrumbs, lemon rind, parsley, tortillas and salt and pepper. Place it into a large baking tray.
- Cover the fish in the beaten egg and then in the breadcrumbs mixture.
- Then cook for 15 minutes on 180 degrees C until nice and crispy.

158. Sesame Fish Fillets

 Serving size:
4

 Preparation time:
10 minutes

 Cooking time:
20 minutes

 Total time:
30 minutes

Ingredients

- 4 cod fillets
- Salt
- Pepper
- 3 tablespoons butter
- 2 tablespoons sesame seeds
- Vegetable oil
- 2 packets sugar snap peas
- 3 cloves garlic
- 1 orange

Instructions

- Brush the air fryer basket with vegetable oil and preheat to 200 degrees C.
- Thaw fish if frozen; blot dry with kitchen paper, and sprinkle lightly with salt and pepper.
- Stir together butter and sesame seeds in a small bowl. Set aside 2 tablespoons of the butter mixture for the fish. Toss peas and garlic with remaining butter mixture and place in the air fryer basket.
- Cook peas in the preheated air fryer in batches, if needed, until just tender, tossing once, about 10 minutes. Remove and keep warm while cooking the fish.
- Brush the fish with 1/2 of the remaining butter mixture. Place fillets in air fryer basket. Cook 4 minutes; turn the fish. Brush

with remaining butter mixture. Cook 5 to 6 minutes more or until fish begins to flake when tested with a fork. Serve with snap peas and orange wedges.

159. Calamari

 Serving size:
4

 Preparation time:
15 minutes

 Cooking time:
15 minutes

 Total time:
30 minutes

Ingredients

- 60 grams all-purpose flour
- 1 large egg
- 40 ml. milk
- 200 grams panko bread crumbs
- Salt
- Pepper
- 500 grams calamari rings
- Cooking spray

Instructions

- Preheat an air fryer to 200 degrees C.
- Place flour in a bowl. Whisk egg and milk in a separate bowl. Combine panko, salt, and pepper in a third bowl.
- Coat calamari rings first in flour, then in egg mixture, and finally in panko mixture.
- Place rings in the basket of the air fryer so that none are overlapping. Work in batches if needed. Spray the tops with nonstick cooking spray.
- Air fry for 4 minutes. Flip rings, spray with nonstick cooking spray, and cook for 3 minutes longer.

160. Breaded Scallops

 Serving size:
4

 Preparation time:
10 minutes

 Cooking time:
10 minutes

 Total time:
20 minutes

Ingredients

- 20 scallops
- Olive oil
- 60 grams breadcrumbs
- 2 teaspoons cajun seasoning
- Salt
- Avocado oil spray

Instructions

- Run your finger along the side of each scallop and remove the side muscle; discard it. Place scallops on a plate then pat them dry with kitchen paper. Drizzle the scallops with the olive oil.
- Next, combine the breadcrumbs, cajun seasoning and salt in abowl, then transfer the scallops to that bowl and stir so that the scallops are coated.
- Line your air fryer with foil, then place the scallops into it, making sure they're not overlapping. If they don't all fit, you'll have to cook them in batches. Spray the scallops with avocado oil spray.
- Air fry the scallops at 200°C for 8-10 minutes, shaking the basket half way through.

161. Air Fried Salmon with Broccoli

 Serving size:
2

 Preparation time:
5 minutes

 Cooking time:
10 minutes

 Total time:
15 minutes

Ingredients

- 600 grams salmon fillets
- 500 grams broccoli
- Oil
- Salt
- Pepper
- Lemon
- Crushed pepper flakes

Instructions

- Grease air fryer basket.
- Coat salmon fillet with oil, salt and pepper. Transfer to air fryer basket.
- Trim broccoli then toss with oil, salt and pepper. Arrange in an even layer around salmon fillet.
- Air fry at 200°C for 10 minutes or until salmon is flaky and cooked through. Toss the broccoli once during cook time.
- Serve with a squeeze of fresh lemon juice and sprinkle of crushed red pepper flakes.

162. Fish Tacos

 Serving size:
6

 Preparation time:
5 minutes

 Cooking time:
35 minutes

Total time:
40 minutes

Ingredients

- 2 tablespoons sour cream
- 1 tablespoon mayonnaise
- 1 clove garlic, finely chopped
- 1 teaspoon lime juice
- ¼ teaspoon salt
- 1 shredded green cabbage
- 1 thinly sliced red onion
- 2 tablespoons taco seasoning mix
- 1 egg
- 1 tablespoon water
- 90 grams punko crispy breadcrumbs
- 500 grams white fish fillets
- 12 mini flour tortilla taco bowls
- Sliced avocado, thinly sliced radishes, chopped fresh coriander leaves and lime wedges

Instructions

- In a medium bowl, mix sour cream, mayonnaise, garlic, lime juice and salt. Add cabbage and red onion and toss to coat. Cover and refrigerate cabbage mixture until ready to serve.
- Cut cooking baking paper. Place in bottom of air fryer basket.
- In a shallow dish, place the taco seasoning mix. In another shallow dish, beat an egg and water. In third shallow dish, place bread crumbs. Coat fish with taco seasoning mix; dip into egg mixture, then coat with breadcrumb mixture, pressing to adhere.
- Place fish on baking paper in the air fryer basket. Set to 220°C; cook 8 minutes. Turn fish; cook for 4 to 6 minutes. Cut it into chunks right after.
- Divide cabbage mixture among taco bowls. Top w

163. Tuna Tacos

Serving size: 4		**Preparation time:** 5 minutes	
Cooking time: 10 minutes		**Total time:** 15 minutes	

Ingredients

- 500 grams tuna
- 12 taco shells
- 1 teaspoon chilli powder
- ½ teaspoon oregano
- ½ teaspoon garlic powder
- ½ teaspoon paprika
- ¼ teaspoon cayenne (more or less for spiciness)
- ¼ teaspoon onion powder
- ¼ teaspoon cumin
- ½ teaspoon sea salt
- ½ teaspoon cracked pepper

Instructions

- Spray the air fryer basket with oil. In a small bowl, mix the spices, salt and pepper well to combine.

- Pat fish dry and then lay it in the air fryer basket. Brush with olive oil. Generously cover the fish with the spice rub and gently press it into the fish. Spray the top of the fish with oil to help it all hold to the fish and stay moist.
- Preheat air fryer to 200°C. Cook the fish for about 8-10 minutes.
- While the fish cooks, toss together the ingredients for the coriander lime slaw. Adjust the salt to taste or add more lime juice as desired.
- Take the taco shells and implement every ingredient inside.

164. Haddock with Pepper and Lemon

Serving size: 2		**Preparation time:** 5 minutes	
Cooking time: 12 minutes		**Total time:** 17 minutes	

Ingredients

- 500 grams haddock fish
- 90 grams flour
- 2 egg whites
- 50 grams panko breadcrumbs
- 2 teaspoons lemon pepper
- 2 slices of lemon
- Chopped parsley

Instructions

- Preheat air fryer to 200 degrees C. Spray air fryer pan with nonstick oil spray.
- In three bowls, place flour in one, eggs in another and breadcrumbs plus lemon pepper in another.
- Dredge haddock in first flour followed by egg, then lemon pepper bread crumbs.
- Place the haddock in the air fryer and cook for 12 minutes or until crispy.
- Top with some lemon juice and garnish with parsley.

165. Salmon Balls

Serving size: 4		**Preparation time:** 15 minutes	
Cooking time: 8 minutes		**Total time:** 21 minutes	

Ingredients

- 150 grams canned salmon
- 2 eggs
- 90 grams mayonnaise
- Salt
- 60 grams breadcrumbs
- 2 teaspoons dried dill

Instructions

- Mix ingredients together in alarge bowl, use a spatular to mix together the salmon (drained, mashed, and skin/bones removed if you'd like), eggs, mayo, salt, breadcrumbs, lemon zest and dill.
- Measure the patties according to your Air fryer dimensions and then form the patties.
- Heat air fryer to 200 degrees C. Spray the basket with oil, then add patties into the basket. Spray the tops of the salmon patties.
- Cook for a total of 8 minutes. Spray a second time 1-2 minutes before the patties are cooked through.

166. Coconut Shrimps

 Serving size:
4

 Preparation time:
10 minutes

 Cooking time:
12 minutes

 Total time:
22 minutes

Ingredients

- 500 grams shrimps
- 90 grams flour
- Salt
- Pepper
- 2 eggs
- 60 grams shredded coconut
- 90 grams Breadcrumbs
- Cooking spray
- Sweet chilli sauce

Instructions

- Preheat the air fryer to 200°C. When heated, spray the basket with cooking spray.
- Combine the flour, salt and pepper in one shallow bowl. Whisk the eggs in a second shallow bowl. Then combine the shredded coconut and panko breadcrumbs in a third shallow bowl.
- Dip the shrimp into the flour mixture, shaking off any excess. Then dredge the shrimp into the eggs, and finally into the coconut panko mixture, gently pressing to adhere.
- Place the coconut shrimp in the air fryer so they are not touching, and spray the top of the shrimp. Cook for 10-12 minutes, turning halfway through.

- Garnish with chopped parsley, and serve immediately with sweet chilli sauce, if desired.

167. Cod with Soy Sauce

 Serving size:
2

 Preparation time:
5 minutes

 Cooking time:
10 minutes

 Total time:
15 minutes

Ingredients

- 200 grams cod fillets
- 1 ½ tablespoon rice wine
- 1 Tablespoon butter melted
- 1 Tablespoon soy sauce
- 1 Tablespoon thinly sliced ginger
- 2 teaspoon honey
- 90 grams sliced green onion
- Coriander

Instructions

- Mix all the wet ingredients and set aside.
- Put the cod fillets in the middle of a large sheet of tin foil. Spread all of the ginger and half of the sliced onion over fish and pour the sauce mixture over the fish. Wrap the foil tightly and air fry at 180 degrees C for about 8 minutes.
- Garnish with the rest of the onion and some coriander to serve.

168. Cajun Shrimp

 Serving size:
6

 Preparation time:
10 minutes

 Cooking time:
20 minutes

 Total time:
30 minutes

Ingredients

- 1 tablespoon Cajun or Creole seasoning
- 25 cleaned and peeled extra jumbo shrimp
- 200 grams sausage
- 1 medium courgette, 8 ounces, sliced
- 1 medium yellow squash, sliced
- 1 large red pepper, seeded and cut into thin 1-inch pieces
- 1/4 teaspoon kosher salt
- 2 tablespoons olive oil

Instructions

- In a large bowl, combine the Cajun seasoning and shrimp, toss to coat.
- Add the sausage, courgettes, squash, peppers, and salt and toss with the oil.
- Preheat the air fryer 200 degrees C.
- In 2 batches (for smaller baskets), transfer the shrimp and vegetables to the air fryer basket and cook 8 minutes, shaking the basket 2 to 3 times.
- Set aside, repeat with remaining shrimp and veggies.
- Once both batches are cooked, return the first batch to the air fryer and cook 1 minute.

169. Shrimp Risotto

 Serving size:
2

 Preparation time:
5 minutes

 Cooking time:
30 minutes

 Total time:
40 minutes

Ingredients

- 300 grams risotto
- 300 ml. broth/stock
- 10 shrimps, cut
- 1 small onion
- 2 cloves garlic
- 2 tablespoons butter
- 1 tablespoon fresh parsley
- 2 tablespoon olive oil

Instructions

- Finely dice the onion and chop the garlic
- Preheat the Air Fryer to 200 degrees C for 3 minutes with a cake barrel inside.
- Add the olive oil into the cake barrel before adding the diced onion and garlic.
- Stir with a wooden spoon to coat the onion and garlic. Close the Air Fryer heat for 3 minutes.
- Stir again before adding the butter. Close the basket to let the butter melt.
- Cut the shrimps into small pieces. Now add the shrimps into the cake pan and coat the mushrooms with butter, onion-garlic mix.
- Close the Air Fryer and heat for 5 minutes.
- Add the risotto rice. Put it in the cake barrel and coat it with the mushroom mixture for about 1 minute.
- Then add ⅓ of the heated chicken or vegetable broth and close the Air Fryer for 5 minutes.
- Add the remaining ⅔ of the broth.
- Lower the Air Fryer temperature to 200 degrees C and cook for 20 minutes stirring halfway through the cooking time.

When the cooking time is done you leave the Air Fryer closed for 5 minutes then fluff the rice and serve.

170. Cod with Basil Vinaigrette

 Serving size:
4

 Preparation time:
10 minutes

 Cooking time:
15 minutes

Total time:
25 minutes

Ingredients

- 1 tablespoon olive oil
- 4 cod fillets
- A bunch of basil, torn
- Juice from 1 lemon, freshly squeezed
- Salt and pepper to taste

Instructions

- Preheat the air fryer for 5 minutes.
- Season the cod fillets with salt and pepper to taste.
- Place in the air fryer and cook for 15 minutes at 170 degrees C.
- Meanwhile, mix the rest of the ingredients in a bowl and toss to combine.
- Serve the air fried cod with the basil vinaigrette.

171. Almond Shrimps

 Serving size:
4

 Preparation time:
5 minutes

 Cooking time:
10 minutes

 Total time:
15 minutes

Ingredients

- 70 grams almond flour
- 1 tablespoon yellow mustard
- 500 grams raw shrimps, peeled and deveined
- 3 tablespoons olive oil
- Salt and pepper to taste

Instructions

- Place all ingredients in a Ziploc bag and give it a good shake.
- Place in the air fryer and cook for 10 minutes at 200 degrees C.

172. Apple Cod Fillet

 Serving size:
3

 Preparation time:
10 minutes

 Cooking time:
15 minutes

Total time:
25 minutes

Ingredients

- 50 grams mayonnaise
- 1 red onion, diced
- 500 grams frozen Alaskan cod
- 1 box whole wheat panko bread crumbs
- 1 granny smith apple, julienned
- 1 tablespoon vegetable oil
- 1 teaspoon paprika
- 1 cabbage, shredded
- Salt and pepper to taste

Instructions

- Preheat the air fryer to 200 degrees C.
- Place the grill pan accessory in the air fryer.
- Brush the fish with oil and dredge in the breadcrumbs.
- Place the fish on the grill pan and cook for 15 minutes. Make sure to turn the fish halfway through
- Meanwhile, prepare the slaw by mixing the remaining ingredients in a bowl.
- Serve the fish with the slaw.

173. Thai Cod

 Serving size:
4

 Preparation time:
5 minutes

 Cooking time:
20 minutes

 Total time:
25 minutes

Ingredients

- 50 ml. coconut milk, freshly squeezed
- 1 tablespoon lime juice, freshly squeezed
- 500 grams cod fillet, cut into bite-sized pieces
- Salt and pepper to taste

Instructions

- Preheat the air fryer for 5 minutes.
- Place all ingredients in a baking dish that will fit in the air fryer.
- Place in the air fryer.
- Cook for 20 minutes at 200 degrees C.

174. Garlic Scallops

 Serving size:
4

 Preparation time:
5 minutes

 Cooking time:
10 minutes

 Total time:
15 minutes

Ingredients

- 60 grams bread crumbs
- 1 tablespoon chopped parsley
- 16 sea scallops, rinsed and drained
- 2 shallots, chopped
- 3 pinches ground nutmeg
- 4 tablespoons olive oil
- 5 cloves garlic, chopped
- 5 tablespoons butter, melted
- salt and pepper to taste

Instructions

- Lightly grease the baking pan of air fryer with cooking spray.
- Mix in shallots, garlic, melted butter, and scallops. Season with pepper, salt, and nutmeg.
- In a small bowl, whisk olive oil and bread crumbs. Sprinkle over scallops.
- For 10 minutes, cook on 220 degrees C until tops are lightly browned.
- Serve and enjoy with a sprinkle of parsley.

175. Chilli Clams

 Serving size:
3

 Preparation time:
5 minutes

 Cooking time:
15 minutes

 Total time:
20 minutes

Ingredients

- 1 teaspoon basil leaves
- 2 tomatoes, chopped
- 1 tablespoon fresh lime juice
- 25 littleneck clams
- 4 cloves of garlic, chopped
- 6 tablespoons unsalted butter
- Salt and pepper to taste

Instructions

- Preheat the air fryer to 200 degrees C.
- Place the grill pan accessory in the air fryer.
- On a large foil, place all ingredients. Fold over the foil and close by crimping the edges.
- Place on the grill pan and cook for 15 minutes.
- Serve with bread.

176. Beer Cod Fillet

 Serving size:
2

 Preparation time:
10 minutes

 Cooking time:
15 minutes

 Total time:
25 minutes

Ingredients

- 100 grams plain flour
- ¾ teaspoon baking powder
- 200 ml. lager/beer
- 2 cod fillets
- 2 eggs, beaten
- Salt and pepper to taste

Instructions

- Preheat the air fryer to 200 degrees C.
- Pat the fish fillets dry then set aside.
- In a bowl, combine the rest of the ingredients to create a batter.
- Dip the fillets in the batter and place on the double layer rack.
- Cook for 15 minutes.

177. Wine Baked Cod

 Serving size:
2

 Preparation time:
10 minutes

 Cooking time:
12 minutes

 Total time:
22 minutes

Ingredients

- 1 tablespoon butter
- 2 tablespoons dry white wine
- 500 grams thick-cut cod loin
- 1-1/2 teaspoons chopped fresh parsley
- 1-1/2 teaspoons chopped onion
- 1/2 lemon, cut into wedges
- 1/4 sleeve buttery round crackers, crushed
- 1/4 lemon, juiced

Instructions

- In a small bowl, melt butter in microwave. Whisk in crackers.
- Lightly grease the baking pan of air fryer with the remaining butter. And melt for 2 minutes.
- In a small bowl whisk lemon juice, white wine, parsley, and onion.
- Coat cod fillets in melted butter.
- Pour dressing.
- Top with buttercracker mixture.

- Air fry it for 10 minutes at 200 degrees C.
- Serve and enjoy with a slice of lemon.

178. Garlic Sriracha Prawns

 Serving size:
2

 Preparation time:
5 minutes

 Cooking time:
15 minutes

 Total time:
20 minutes

Ingredients

- 1 tablespoon lime juice
- 1 tablespoon sriracha
- 500 grams large prawns, shells removed and cut lengthwise or butterflied
- 1 teaspoon fish sauce
- 2 tablespoons melted butter
- 2 tablespoons chopped garlic
- Salt and pepper to taste

Instructions

- Preheat the air fryer to 220 degrees C.
- Place the grill pan accessory in the air fryer.
- Season the prawns with the rest of the ingredients.
- Place on the grill pan and cook for 15 minutes. Make sure to turn the prawns halfway through.

179. Cajun Salmon

 Serving size:
1

 Preparation time:
5 minutes

 Cooking time:
15 minutes

 Total time:
20 minutes

Ingredients

- 1 salmon fillet
- 1 teaspoon juice from lemon, freshly squeezed
- 3 tablespoons extra virgin olive oil
- A dash of Cajun seasoning mix
- Salt and pepper to taste

Instructions

- Preheat the air fryer for 5 minutes.
- Place all ingredients in a bowl and toss to coat.
- Place the fish fillet in the air fryer basket.
- Bake for 15 minutes at 220 degrees C.
- Once cooked drizzle with olive oil.

180. Chipotle Crab Cakes

 Serving size:
4

 Preparation time:
5 minutes

 Cooking time:
10 minutes

 Total time:
15 minutes

Ingredients

Crab Cakes:

- 1 large egg
- 60 grams mayonnaise
- 1 small finely diced red pepper
- 2 tablespoons chopped fresh chives
- 2 tablespoons chopped fresh parsley
- 1 teaspoon grated lemon zest plus 2 tablespoons fresh lemon juice
- 2 teaspoons Dijon mustard
- 2 teaspoons seafood seasoning
- Kosher salt and freshly ground black pepper
- 500 grams crab meat
- 100 grams panko breadcrumbs
- Nonstick cooking spray, for the air-fryer basket and crab cakes
- Lemon wedges, for serving

Chipotle Sauce:

- 90 grams mayonnaise
- 60 grams sour cream
- 2 chipotle chillis in adobo sauce, finely chopped, plus 2 teaspoons adobo sauce
- 2 tablespoons chopped fresh chives
- 1 tablespoon chopped fresh parsley
- 1 teaspoon grated lemon zest plus 2 teaspoons fresh lemon juice
- Kosher salt and freshly ground black pepper

Instructions

- Whisk together the egg, mayonnaise, pepper, chives, parsley, lemon zest and juice, mustard, seafood seasoning, 1 teaspoon salt and several grinds of black pepper in a large bowl. With a rubber spatular or large spoon, very gently fold the crab and panko into the mixture. Try to avoid breaking up lumps of crab as much as possible.
- Cover the crab mixture with cling film and allow to rest in the refrigerator for at least 30 minutes and up to 1 day. This will allow the panko to absorb more liquid and help bind the crab cakes together better.
- For the chipotle sauce: While the crab mixture is resting, stir together the mayonnaise, sour cream, chipotles and adobo sauce, chives, parsley and lemon zest and juice in a small bowl until combined. Season with salt and black pepper and set aside.

- Just before cooking, divide the crab-cake mixture into 4 portions. Lightly compact each portion to form a patty with your hands to ensure they hold their shape while cooking and place onto a large plate.
- Preheat the air fryer to 200 degrees C and spray the basket with cooking spray. Place the crab cakes into the basket and spray the tops with cooking spray. Cook until deep golden brown and crisp, flipping halfway through and spraying again with cooking spray, about 16 minutes.
- Serve warm with chipotle sauce and lemon wedges.

181. Tuna Patties

 Serving size:
12

 Preparation time:
10 minutes

 Cooking time:
12 minutes

 Total time:
22 minutes

Ingredients

- 500 grams cans of tuna
- 2 eggs
- 100 grams seasoned breadcrumbs
- 4 tablespoons mayo
- 2 tablespoons lemon juice
- 1/2 diced white onion
- Salt
- Black Pepper

Instructions

- Drain the tuna and place into a large mixing bowl. Add the remaining ingredients and, using your hands, gently mix to combine. Note: you want the mixture to be reasonably firm. If it seems too squishy, add a little more breadcrumbs to the mixture.
- Spray your air fryer basket with cooking spray or olive oil.
- Form the mixture into patties and place about four, depending on the size of your air fryer basket, into the basket. Don't overcrowd them; you'll want room to be able to turn them easily.
- Cook at 200 degrees C. for 12 minutes, turning at the halfway mark. Remove and set aside, then continue this process until all of the patties have been cooked. Serve immediately.

182. Greek Fried Mussels

 Serving size:
4

 Preparation time:
25 minutes

 Cooking time:
10 minutes

 Total time:
35 minutes

Ingredients

- 500 grams mussels
- 1 tablespoon butter
- 150 ml. water
- 2 teaspoons chopped garlic
- 1 teaspoon chives
- 1 teaspoon basil
- 1 teaspoon parsley

Instructions

- Start by preheating your air fryer to 200 degrees C, air fryer setting.
- Then clean your mussels (soak for 30 minutes, as indicated in the instructions) and then use a brush and clean your mussels, and remove the "beard."
- Then in an air fryer safe pan, add the water, butter, garlic, chives, basil, parsley, and mussels.
- Place your pan into the air fryer.
- Set the time for 3 minutes, check, and see if the mussels are opened. If they are not opened, cook for another 2 minutes. Once all of the mussels are opened, they are ready for eating.
- Plate, serve and enjoy!

183. Chinese Shrimp Medley

 Serving size: 4

 Preparation time: 5 minutes

 Cooking time: 20 minutes

Total time: 25 minutes

Ingredients

- 1 bag of frozen mixed vegetables
- 500 grams small shrimps
- Olive oil
- Cooked rice

Instructions

- Add the shrimp and vegetables to your air fryer.
- Top it with the Cajun seasoning and spray with an even coating of spray.
- Cook on 200 degrees C for 10 minutes.
- Carefully open and mix up the shrimp and vegetables.
- Continue cooking for an additional 10 minutes on 200 degrees C.
- Serve over cooked rice.

184. British Seafood Bomb

 Serving size: 2

 Preparation time: 5 minutes

Cooking time: 15 minutes

 Total time: 20 minutes

Ingredients

- 500 grams frozen seafood medley
- Salt
- Pepper

Instructions

- Spray the air fryer basket with a non-stick cooking spray.
- Put frozen seafood medley in the air fryer basket. Cook at 200 degrees C for 15 minutes.
- Halfway through the cooking time, take out the air fryer basket. Season the seafood medley with salt, pepper and any other seasonings. Stir the seafood so it's coated with seasonings, then return to the air fryer and let it finish cooking.

185. Shrimp Bake

 Serving size: 4

 Preparation time: 5 minutes

 Cooking time: 20 minutes

 Total time: 25 minutes

Ingredients

- 1 bag of frozen mixed vegetables
- 1 tablespoons gluten free cajun seasoning
- Olive oil spray
- Season with salt and pepper
- 500 grams small shrimp peeled & deveined

Instructions

- Lightly grease the baking pan of the air fryer with cooking spray. Add all the ingredients and mix well then season well with pepper and salt.
- For 10 minutes, cook on 200 degrees C. Halfway through the cooking time, stir.
- Cook for 10 minutes at 200 degrees C.
- Serve and enjoy.

186. Celery and Garlic Turbot

 Serving size:
2

 Preparation time:
10 minutes

Cooking time:
20 minutes

Total time:
30 minutes

Ingredients

- 50 grams chopped celery leaves
- 1 clove of garlic, chopped
- 2 tablespoons olive oil
- 2 whole turbot, scaled and head removed
- Salt and pepper to taste

Instructions

- Preheat the air fryer to 220 degrees C.
- Place the grill pan accessory in the air fryer.
- Season the turbot with salt, pepper, garlic, and celery leaves.
- Brush with oil.
- Place on the grill pan and cook for 20 minutes until the fish becomes flaky.

187. Grilled Halibut

 Serving size:
6

 Preparation time:
5 minutes

 Cooking time:
20 minutes

 Total time:
25 minutes

Ingredients

- 1 tablespoon chilli powder
- 2 cloves of garlic, chopped
- 500 grams halibut fillet, skin removed
- 4 tablespoons dry white wine
- 4 tablespoons olive oil
- Salt and pepper to taste

Instructions

- Place all ingredients in a Ziploc bag.
- Allow to marinate in the fridge for at least 2 hours.
- Preheat the air fryer to 200 degrees C.
- Place the grill pan accessory in the air fryer.
- Grill the fish for 20 minutes making sure to turn over every 5 minutes.

188. Clams with Herbed Butter

 Serving size:
2

 Preparation time:
10 minutes

 Cooking time:
20 minutes

 Total time:
30 minutes

Ingredients

- 50 grams unsalted butter, diced
- 1 tablespoon dill, chopped
- 1 tablespoon fresh lemon juice
- 1 tablespoon parsley, chopped
- 24 littleneck clams, scrubbed clean
- Lemon wedges
- Salt and pepper to taste

Instructions

- Preheat the air fryer to 170 degrees C.
- Place the grill pan accessory in the air fryer.
- Then in a large piece of tin foil put the clams and the rest of the ingredients.
- Fold the foil and crimp the edges.
- Place on the grill pan and cook for 15 to 20 minutes or until all clams have opened.

189. Rainbow Prawns

 Serving size:
1

 Preparation time:
5 minutes

 Cooking time:
8 minutes

 Total time:
11 minutes

Ingredients

- ½ teaspoon black pepper
- ½ teaspoon sea salt
- 1 tablespoon ketchup
- 1 tablespoon white wine vinegar
- 1 teaspoon chilli flakes
- 1 teaspoon chilli powder
- 12 prawns, shelled and deveined

Instructions

- Preheat the air fryer to 170 degrees C.
- Place the shrimps in a bowl.
- Stir in the rest of the ingredients until the shrimps are coated with the sauce.
- Place the shrimps on the double layer rack and cook for 8 minutes.
- Serve with mayonnaise if desired.

190. Crisped Fillet with Crumb Tops

 Serving size:
4

 Preparation time:
5 minutes

 Cooking time:
15 minutes

 Total time:
20 minutes

Ingredients

- 130 grams dry bread crumbs
- 1 egg beaten
- 1 lemon, sliced
- 4 pieces of flounder fillets
- 5 tablespoons vegetable oil

Instructions

- Brush flounder fillets with vegetable oil before dredging in bread crumbs.
- Preheat the air fryer to 160 degrees C.
- Place the fillets on the double layer rack.
- Cook for 15 minutes.

191. Paprika Fish Nuggets

 Serving size:
6

 Preparation time:
5 minutes

 Cooking time:
25 minutes

 Total time:
30 minutes

Ingredients

- 500 grams fresh fish fillet, chopped finely
- 130 grams almond flour
- 1 tablespoon lemon juice
- 1 tablespoon olive oil
- 1 teaspoon chilli powder
- 1 teaspoon smoked paprika
- 2 cloves of garlic, chopped
- 2 eggs, beaten
- Salt and pepper to taste

Instructions

- Place all the ingredients in a bowl and mix until well-combined.
- Form small nuggets using your hands. Place in the fridge to set for 2 hours.
- Preheat the air fryer for 5 minutes.
- Carefully place the nuggets in the fryer basket.
- Cook for 25 minutes at 200 degrees C.

192. Lemon Fish Cakes

 Serving size:
3

 Preparation time:
5 minutes

 Cooking time:
20 minutes

 Total time:
25 minutes

Ingredients

- 130 grams dried coconut flakes
- 130 grams almond flour
- 500 grams cooked salmon, shredded
- 1 tablespoon chopped parsley
- 1 tablespoon lemon juice
- 2 eggs, beaten
- 3 tablespoons coconut oil
- Salt and pepper to taste

Instructions

- Mix the salmon, almond flour, eggs, salt, pepper, lemon juice and parsley in a bowl.
- Form small balls using your hands and dredge in coconut flakes.
- Brush the surface of the balls with coconut oil.
- Place in the air fryer basket and cook in a preheated air fryer for 20 minutes at 200 degrees C.
- Halfway through the cooking time, give the fryer basket a shake.

193. Cajun Shrimps

 Serving size:
3

 Preparation time:
5 minutes

 Cooking time:
8 minutes

 Total time:
11 minutes

Ingredients

- ¼ teaspoon cayenne pepper
- ¼ teaspoon smoked paprika
- ½ pound tiger shrimps,
- ½ teaspoon old bay seasoning
- 3 tablespoons olive oil
- A pinch of salt

Instructions

- Preheat the air fryer for 5 minutes.
- Toss all ingredients in a bowl that will fit the air fryer.
- Place the shrimps in the air fryer basket and cook for 8 minutes at 200 degrees C.

194. Parmesan Tilapia

 Serving size:
2

 Preparation time:
5 minutes

 Cooking time:
15 minutes

 Total time:
20 minutes

Ingredients

- 1 tablespoon lemon juice
- 1 teaspoon prepared horseradish
- 50 grams dry bread crumbs
- 2 tablespoons grated Parmesan cheese, divided
- 2 teaspoons butter, melted
- 2 teaspoons Dijon mustard
- 2 tilapia fillets
- 3 tablespoons reduced-fat mayonnaise

Instructions

- Lightly grease the baking pan of the air fryer with cooking spray. Place tilapia in a single layer.
- In a small bowl, whisk together well mayo, lemon juice, mustard, 1 tablespoon cheese and horseradish. Place on the fish,
- In another bowl, mix remaining cheese, melted butter, and bread crumbs. Sprinkle on top with Parmesan cheese .
- Cook on 170 degrees C for 15 minutes.
- Serve and enjoy.

195. Blackened Fish

 Serving size:
4

 Preparation time:
5 minutes

 Cooking time:
8 minutes

 Total time:
13 minutes

Ingredients

- 2 tablespoons paprika
- 2 teaspoons brown sugar
- 1 teaspoon dried oregano
- 1 teaspoon garlic powder
- 1/2 teaspoon cumin
- 1/4 teaspoon cayenne pepper
- 1 teaspoon salt
- 500 grams tailapia fillets
- olive oil spray

Instructions

- Start by making the rub, mix together the paprika, brown sugar, oregano, garlic powder, cumin, cayenne pepper and salt in a small bowl.
- Then rub the spices onto the fish.

- Spray this fish with olive oil spray, and then place into the air fryer basket. Set the temperature for 200 degrees C, for 4 minutes, after 4 minutes, turn (spray again) and add another 4 minutes.

196. Cod Fennel Platter

 Serving size:
4

 Preparation time:
10 minutes

 Cooking time:
17 minutes

 Total time:
27 minutes

Ingredients

- 350 grams cod fillet
- 250 grams green beans
- 3 tomatoes
- ½ fennel
- 250 ml coconut milk
- 3 garlic cloves
- 1 onion
- 2 tablespoon red curry paste
- 1 tablespoon cornstarch (cornflour) mixed with 2 tbsp water
- Fish sauce
- Rice

Instructions

- Start by preparing the cod fillets. removing any bones and skin. Cut the green beans in half and remove the ends. Cut the tomatoes into small cubes and remove the seeds. Slice the fennel in thin strips. Chop the onion and press the garlic.
- Put everything together in the oven proof dish and add some salt and pepper.
- Put a cooking pan with water and a saucepan on the stove. Mix the coconut milk with the curry paste and add a dash of fish sauce.
- In a small bowl, stir the cornstarch with two tablespoons of water and mix it with the curry sauce.
- Add rice to your boiling water and leave it for 10 minutes.
- Pour the sauce over the vegetables and place the dish in the Air Fryer for 10 minutes at 180 ºC.

197. Sockeye Fish

 Serving size:

 Preparation time:
10 minutes

 Cooking time:
17 minutes

 Total time:
27 minutes

Ingredients

- 350 grams cod fillet
- 250 grams green beans
- 3 tomatoes
- ½ fennel bulb
- 250 ml. coconut milk
- 3 garlic cloves
- 1 onion
- 2 tablespoons red curry paste
- 1 tablespoons cornstarch (corn flour) mixed with 2 tablespoon water
- Fish sauce
- Rice

Instructions

- Start by preparing the cod fillets, remove any bones and skin. Cut the green beans in half and remove the ends. Cut the tomatoes into small cubes and remove the seeds. Slice the fennel in thin strips. Chop the onion and press the garlic.
- Put everything together in the oven dish and add some salt and pepper.
- Put a cooking pan with water and a saucepan on the stove. Mix the coconut milk with the curry paste and add a dash of fish sauce.
- In a small bowl, stir the cornstarch with two tablespoons of water and mix it with the curry sauce.
- Add rice to your boiling water and leave it for 10 minutes.
- Pour the sauce over the vegetables and place the dish in the Air Fryer for 10 minutes at 180 [].

198. British Crab Legs

 **Serving size:**
1

 Preparation time:
5 minutes

 Cooking time:
5 minutes

 Total time:
10 minutes

Ingredients

- 500 grams crab legs
- Olive oil
- 1 teaspoon old bay seasoning
- 2 tablespoons butter

Instructions

- Lightly rinse the crab legs, being sure they don't have any leftover sand, dirt, or store packaging on them.
- Very lightly coat them with olive oil.
- Season the shells with Old Bay Seasoning, and then place the legs in the air fryer basket.
- Cook at 220 degrees C for 5-7 minutes, until the shells are hot to the touch.

199. Cod Nuggets

 Serving size:
4

 Preparation time:
5 minutes

 Cooking time:
12 minutes

 Total time:
17 minutes

Ingredients

- 500 grams cod
- 90 grams flour
- Salt
- Pepper
- 2 eggs
- 90 grams breadcrumbs
- 1 teaspoon garlic powder
- 90 grams Greek yogurt
- 2 tablespoons dill
- 1 lemon

Instructions

- Cut cod into small pieces.
- In a shallow dish, combine flour, salt, and pepper. In a second dish, whisk the 2 eggs. In a third dish, combine panko and garlic powder.
- Set the air fryer to 200° C.
- It takes 3 steps in order to properly bread the cod pieces. First, coat the cod pieces with the flour mixture. For the second coat, dip it in the eggs. Then the final coating, cover it with the panko mixture.
- Once all of your pieces are coated, cook in the air fryer for 10-12 minutes, turning halfway through.
- While cod is cooking, whisk together yogurt, dill, and lemon juice.
- Serve cod immediately with yogurt sauce.

200. Broiled Tilapia

 Serving size:
4

 Preparation time:
2 minutes

 Cooking time:
7 minutes

 Total time:
9 minutes

Ingredients

- 500 grams tilapia fillets
- 1 teaspoon old bay seasoning
- 1 teaspoon lemon pepper
- Salt
- Canola oil (rapeseed oil)

Instructions

- Thaw fillets, if frozen. Spray the basket of your air fryer with cooking spray.

- Place fillets in the basket (do not stack them) and season to taste with the spices. Spray lightly with oil.
- Set temperature at 200 degrees C and set timer for 7 minutes. When timer goes off, check for doneness. Fish should flake easily with a fork.

201. Garlic Lobster with Herbs

 Serving size:
2

 Preparation time:
10 minutes

 Cooking time:
20 minutes

 Total time:
30 minutes

Ingredients

- 2 lobster tails
- 4 tablespoons butter
- 1 teaspoon lemon zest
- 1 clove garlic, chopped

- salt and ground black pepper to taste
- 1 teaspoon chopped fresh parsley
- 2 wedges lemon

Instructions

- Butterfly lobster tails by cutting lengthwise through the centres of the hard top shells and meat with kitchen shears. Cut to, but not through, the bottoms of the shells. Spread the tail halves apart. Place tails in the air fryer basket with lobster meat facing up.
- Melt butter in a small saucepan over a medium heat. Add lemon zest and garlic; heat until garlic is tender, about 30 seconds. Transfer 2 tablespoons of butter mixture to a small bowl and brush onto lobster tails; discard any remaining brushed butter to avoid contamination from uncooked lobster. Season lobster with salt and pepper.
- Cook in an air fryer at 195 degrees C until lobster meat is opaque, 5 to 7 minutes. Spoon reserved butter from the saucepan over lobster meat. Top with parsley and serve with lemon wedges.

202. Trout Frittata

 Serving size:
4

 Preparation time:
5 minutes

 Cooking time:
16 minutes

 Total time:
21 minutes

Ingredients

- 4 eggs
- 2 trout fillets
- 3 tablespoons double cream
- 4 tablespoons grated cheddar cheese
- 4 mushrooms sliced

- 3 cherry tomatoes, halved
- 4 tablespoons chopped spinach
- 2 tablespoons fresh chopped herbs of choice
- 1 onion sliced
- salt to taste

Instructions

- Preheat the air fryer to 180 degrees C.
- Line a deep 7-inch baking dish/tin with baking paper, then oil the pan and set it aside.
- In a bowl, whisk together the eggs and cream.
- Add the rest of the ingredients to the bowl, and stir to combine.
- Pour the breakfast frittata mixture into the baking dish/tin and place inside the air fryer basket.
- Cook for 12-16 minutes, or until eggs are set. To check, insert a toothpick in the center of the air fryer frittata. The eggs are set if it comes out clean.

Vegetables, and Vegan

203. Vegetable Croquettes

Serving size: 4 servings	**Preparation time:** 10 minutes	**Cooking time:** 10 minutes	**Total time:** 20 minutes

Ingredients

- 2 medium-sized potatoes or use refrigerated mashed potatoes
- 2 tablespoons butter
- 1 tablespoon olive oil
- 130 grams bread crumbs
- 1 egg
- Salt and pepper

Instructions

- Start by making homemade mashed potatoes or purchasing mashed potatoes. The key is to make sure that the mashed potatoes are cold before starting. So, if you make them, place them into the refrigerator until cold.
- If you make homemade mashed potatoes, use a fork to mash them, add the butter, salt, and black pepper, mix well.
- Use your hands to shape the mashed potatoes into croquettes, then in one bowl, add the egg, and in the other bowl, add the bread crumbs and oil. Mix the bread crumb mixture well.
- Dip your potato croquettes into the egg mixture and then into the breadcrumb mixture. As you coat them, place them into a greased air fryer basket.
- When the basket or tray is full, Air Fry for 8-10 minutes at 200 degrees C, air fryer setting. Turn the potato croquettes halfway through the cooking process.
- Plate, serve, and enjoy!

204. Crispy Tofu

Serving size: 3 servings	**Preparation time:** 30 minutes	**Cooking time:** 10 minutes	**Total time:** 40 minutes

Ingredients

- 1 block of extra firm tofu, pressed for 30 minutes then cut into cubes
- 1 teaspoon garlic powder
- ½ teaspoon onion powder
- 1 teaspoon paprika
- ½ teaspoon sea salt
- 2 teaspoons cornstarch or corn flour
- ½ tablespoon light soy sauce or liquid aminos
- ½ teaspoon sesame oil or any oil
- ¼ teaspoon ground black pepper

Instructions

- In a medium size bowl place the pressed and cubed tofu. Add in liquid aminos and toss to coat. Add in all of the other seasoning ingredients including the oil and toss to thoroughly combine.
- Place in your air fryer in a single row, so that all the tofu has a little bit of space around each piece. Set your air fryer to 200°C. Cook for 10 minutes, shaking the basket after 5 minutes, then continue to cook.
- Remove after tofu is cooked. Allow to cool for a few minutes then serve.
- Enjoy!

205. Veggie Sushi

 Serving size:
3

 Preparation time:
1 hour and 10 minutes

 Cooking time:
10 minutes

 Total time:
1 hour and 20 minutes

Ingredients

- 1 batch Pressure Cooker Sushi Rice - cooled to room temperature
- 3 sheets of sushi nori
- ½ of a Haas avocado - sliced

Instructions

- Lay out a sheet of nori on a dry surface. With slightly damp fingertips, grab a handful of rice, and spread it onto the nori. The idea here is to get a thin layer of rice covering almost the entire sheet. Along one edge, you'll want to leave about ½ of the seaweed naked. Think of this as the flap that will seal your roll shut.
- On the end of the seaweed, opposite that naked part, lay out about 2-3 tablespoons of kale salad , and top with a couple of slices of avocado. Starting on the end with the filling, roll up your sushi, pressing gently to get a nice, tight roll. When you get to the end, use that naked bit of seaweed to seal the roll closed. If needed, get your fingertips wet, and moisten that bit of seaweed to make it stick.
- Repeat steps 2-3 to make 3 more sushi rolls.

206. Balsamic Vegetables

 Serving size:
4

 Preparation time:
10 minutes

 Cooking time:
8 minutes

 Total time:
18 minutes

Ingredients

- 4 tablespoons olive oil
- 4 tablespoons balsamic vinegar
- 2 tablespoons brown sugar
- 3 tablespoons soy sauce
- 1 tablespoon Dijon mustard
- 1/2 teaspoon pepper
- 6 ounces cherry tomatoes
- 1 yellow squash, sliced
- 1 courgette, sliced
- 150 grams mushrooms, halved
- 150 grams fresh asparagus

Instructions

- In a large mixing bowl, combine olive oil, balsamic vinegar, brown sugar, soy sauce, Dijon mustard, and pepper.
- Stir in vegetables, completely coating them.
- Refrigerate the vegetables and allow them to marinate for 30 minutes.
- Spray air fryer basket with olive oil and cook at 200° C for 8 minutes.
- Stir or shake and cook for another 5 minutes or until veggies are tender.

207. Cron Cakes

 Serving size:
10

 Preparation time:
10 minutes

 Cooking time:
20 minutes

 Total time:
30 minutes

Ingredients

- 1 can sweetcorn
- 2 eggs
- 1 or 2 teaspoons sugar (optional)
- 1 teaspoon salt
- ½ teaspoon pepper
- 90 grams plain flour
- 1 teaspoon baking powder
- 90 grams grated cheddar cheese
- 2 tablespoons butter
- 2 tablespoons olive or vegetable oil
- 50 grams cooked and crumbled bacon
- 1 diced jalapeno
- Chives as garnish
- Dipping sauce of your choice (I used sour cream and spicy ranch dressing)

Instructions

- Mix together the eggs, salt, pepper, sugar, and baking powder in a medium-sized bowl and combine.
- Add in the flour and whisk until incorporated.
- Add in the sweetcorn, grated cheese, bacon, and diced jalapeno. Shape into patties.
- Place in freezer for 30 minutes. Preheat Air Fryer to 200 degres C.
- Spray with cooking oil. Air Fryer for 10 minutes and flip over for an additional 5 minutes.
- Serve with favorite condiments and enjoy!

208. Halloumi with Vegetables

 Serving size:
2

 Preparation time:
1 minute

 Cooking time:
9 minutes

Total time:
10 minutes

Ingredients

- 1 block halloumi cheese
- 1 bag of mixed vegetables

Instructions

- Preheat the air fryer to 200 degrees C.
- Slice the halloumi cheese into cubes.
- Place the halloumi in a single layer in the air fryer basket, and add the vegetables on top.
- Cook for 7 minutes, then with a spatula mix the ingredients.
- Continue to cook for 2-3 minutes until browned and crispy.

209. Buttered Onion Rings

 Serving size:
3

 Preparation time:
5 minutes

 Cooking time:
15 minutes

 Total time:
20 minutes

Ingredients

- 60 grams almond flour
- 50 ml. coconut milk
- 1 big white onion, sliced into rings
- 1 egg, beaten
- 1 tablespoon baking powder
- 1 tablespoon smoked paprika
- Salt and pepper to taste

Instructions

- Preheat the air fryer for 5 minutes.
- In a mixing bowl, mix the almond flour, baking powder, smoked paprika, salt and pepper.
- In another bowl, combine the eggs and coconut milk.
- Soak the onion slices into the egg mixture.
- Dredge the onion slices in the almond flour mixture.
- Place in the air fryer basket.
- Close and cook for 15 minutes at 200 degrees C.
- Halfway through the cooking time, shake the fryer basket.

210. Corn in Turmeric

 Serving size:
5

 Preparation time:
10 minutes

 Cooking time:
8 minutes

 Total time:
18 minutes

Ingredients

- 30 ml. water
- ¼ teaspoon baking soda
- ¼ teaspoon salt
- ¼ teaspoon turmeric powder
- ½ teaspoon curry powder
- ½ teaspoon red chilli powder
- 130 grams chickpea flour or besan
- 10 pieces baby corn, blanched

Instructions

- Preheat the air fryer to 200 degrees C.
- Line the air fryer basket with aluminum foil and brush with oil.
- In a mixing bowl, mix all ingredients except for the corn.
- Whisk until well combined.
- Dip the corn in the batter and place inside the air fryer. Cook for 8 minutes until golden.

211. Marinara Aubergine

 Serving size:
3

 Preparation time:
5 minutes

 Cooking time:
45 minutes

 Total time:
50 minutes

Ingredients

- 1 clove garlic, sliced
- 1 large aubergine
- 1 tablespoon olive oil
- 1/2 pinch salt, or as needed
- 50 grams dry bread crumbs
- 50 grams ricotta cheese
- 50 grams grated Parmesan cheese
- 50 grams water, plus more as needed
- 1/4 teaspoon red pepper flakes
- 130 ml. prepared marinara sauce
- 1-1/2 teaspoons olive oil
- 2 tablespoons shredded pepper jack cheese
- salt and freshly ground black pepper to taste

Instructions

- Cut aubergine crosswise in 5 pieces. Peel and chop two pieces into cubes.

- Lightly grease the baking pan of the air fryer with 1 tbsp olive oil. For 5 minutes, heat oil at 200 degrees C. Then add the XXXXXX strips and cook for 2 minutes per side. Transfer to a plate.
- Add 1 ½ tsp olive oil and add garlic. Cook for a minute. Add chopped aubergines. Season and salt. Cook for 4 minutes. Lower heat to 200 degrees C and continue cooking aubergines until soft, XX minutes more.
- Stir in water and marinara sauce. Cook for 7 minutes until heated through. Stirring every Transfer to a bowl.
- In a bowl, whisk well pepper, salt, pepper jack cheese, Parmesan cheese, and ricotta. Evenly pour over the aubergine strips and then fold in half.
- Lay folded aubergine in baking pan. Pour marinara sauce on top.
- In a small bowl whisk the olive oil, and bread crumbs well. Sprinkle all over the sauce.
- Cook for 15 minutes at 200 degrees C until tops are lightly browned.
- Serve and enjoy.

212. Chilli Cheese Polenta

 Serving size: 3

 Preparation time: 5 minutes

 Cooking time: 10 minutes

 Total time: 15 minutes

Ingredients

- 1 polenta roll, sliced
- 130 grams cheddar cheese sauce
- 1 tablespoon chilli powder

Instructions

- Place the baking dish accessory in the air fryer.
- Arrange the polenta slices in the baking dish.
- Add the chilli powder and cheddar cheese sauce.
- Close the air fryer and cook for 10 minutes at 170 degrees C.

213. Baked Potatoes with Olives and Cream Cheese

 Serving size: 1

 Preparation time: 10 minutes

 Cooking time: 40 minutes

 Total time: 50 minutes

Ingredients

- ¼ teaspoon onion powder
- 1 medium russet potato, scrubbed and peeled
- 1 tablespoon chives, chopped
- 1 tablespoon Kalamata olives
- 1 teaspoon olive oil
- 1/8 teaspoon salt
- 50 grams vegan butter
- 50 grams vegan cream cheese

Instructions

- Preheat the air fryer to 200 degrees C.
- Place inside the potatoes in the air fryer basket and cook for 40 minutes. Be sure to turn over the potatoes at least once.
- Place the potatoes in a mixing bowl and pour in olive oil, onion powder, salt, and vegan
- Serve the potatoes with vegan cream cheese, Kalamata olives, chives, and other vegan toppings want.

214. Pepper with Tofu, and Spices

 Serving size: 8

 Preparation time: 5 minutes

Cooking time: 10 minutes

 Total time: 15 minutes

Ingredients

- ½ teaspoon red chilli powder
- ½ teaspoon turmeric powder
- 1 onion, finely chopped
- 1 packet firm tofu, crumbled
- 1 teaspoon coriander powder
- 3 tablespoons coconut oil
- 8 banana peppers, top end sliced and seeded
- Salt to taste

Instructions

- Preheat the air fryer for 5 minutes.
- In a mixing bowl, combine the tofu, onion, coconut oil, turmeric powder, red chi;li powder, and salt. Mix until well-combined.
- Scoop the tofu mixture into the hollows of the banana peppers.
- Place the stuffed peppers in the air fryer.
- Close and cook for 10 minutes at 170 degees C.

215. Pepper Tortilla

 Serving size: 4

 Preparation time: 5 minutes

 Cooking time: 15 minutes

 Total time: 20 minutes

Ingredients

- 1 small red pepper, chopped
- 1 small onion, diced
- 1 tablespoon water
- 2 cobs grilled, remove corn kernels
- 4 large tortillas
- 4 pieces store-bought vegan nuggets, chopped
- mixed greens for garnish

Instructions

- Preheat the air fryer to 200 degrees C.
- In a pan heated over medium heat, water sauté the vegan nuggets together with the onions, and corn kernels. Set aside.
- Place filling inside the corn tortillas.
- Fold the tortillas and place inside the air fryer and cook for 15 minutes until the tortilla gets golden.
- Serve with mix greens on top.

216. Balsamic Brussels Sprouts

 Serving size: 4

 Preparation time: 5 minutes

 Cooking time: 15 minutes

 Total time: 20 minutes

Ingredients

- ¼ teaspoon salt
- 1 tablespoon balsamic vinegar
- 400 grams Brussels sprouts, halved
- 2 tablespoons olive oil

Instructions

- Preheat the air fryer for 5 minutes.
- Mix all ingredients in a bowl until the brussels are well coated.
- Place in the air fryer basket.
- Close and cook for 15 minutes for 170 degrees C.

217. Mayo Carrot Courgette Dish

 Serving size: 4

 Preparation time: 10 minutes

 Cooking time: 25 minutes

 Total time: 35 minutes

Ingredients

- 1 tablespoon grated onion
- 2 tablespoons butter, melted
- 200 grams carrots, sliced
- 1-1/2 courgettes, sliced
- 50 ml. water
- 30 grams mayonnaise
- 1/4 teaspoon prepared horseradish
- 1/4 teaspoon salt
- 1/4 teaspoon ground black pepper
- 30 grams Italian bread crumbs

Instructions

- Lightly grease the baking pan of the air fryer with cooking spray. Add carrots. For 8 minutes, cook carrots. Then add the courgettes and continue cooking for another 5 minutes at 170 degrees C.
- Meanwhile, in a bowl whisk well pepper, salt, horseradish, onion, mayonnaise, and water. veggies. Toss well to coat.
- In a small bowl mix melted butter and bread crumbs. Sprinkle over veggies.
- Cook for 10 minutes at 200 degrees C until tops are lightly browned.
- Serve and enjoy.

218. Cauliflower Steak with Sauce

 Serving size: 2

 Preparation time: 5 minutes

 Cooking time: 15 minutes

 Total time: 20 minutes

Ingredients

- 40 ml. almond milk
- ¼ teaspoon vegetable stock powder
- 1 cauliflower, sliced into two
- 1 tablespoon olive oil
- 2 tablespoons onion, chopped
- salt and pepper to taste

Instructions

- Soak the cauliflower in salted water or brine for at least 2 hours.
- Preheat the air fryer to 200 degrees C.
- Rinse the cauliflower and place inside the air fryer and cook for 15 minutes.
- Meanwhile, heat oil in a pan over a medium flame. Sauté the onions and stir until they become translucent. Then add the vegetable stock powder and milk.
- Bring to boil and adjust the heat to low.
- Allow the sauce to reduce and season with salt and pepper.
- Place cauliflower steak on a plate and pour over the sauce.

219. Cauliflower Bites

 Serving size:
4

 Preparation time:
5 minutes

 Cooking time:
20 minutes

 Total time:
25 minutes

Ingredients

- salt and pepper to taste
- 1 flax egg (1 tablespoon flaxseed meal + 3 tablespoon water)
- 1 small cauliflower, cut into florets
- 1 teaspoon mixed spice
- ½ teaspoon mustard powder
- 2 tablespoons maple syrup
- 1 clove of garlic, chopped
- 2 tablespoons soy sauce
- 30 grams oats flour
- 30 grams plain flour
- 30 grams desiccated coconut

Instructions

- Preheat the air fryer to 170 degrees C.
- In a mixing bowl, mix together oats, flour, and desiccated coconut. Season with salt and set aside.
- In another bowl, place the flax egg and add a pinch of salt to taste. Set aside.
- Season the cauliflower with mixed spice and mustard powder.
- Dredge the florets in the flax egg first then in the flour mixture.
- Place inside the air fryer and cook for 15 minutes.
- Meanwhile, place the maple syrup, garlic, and soy sauce in a sauce pan and heat over a medium high heat until it boils and adjust the heat to low until the sauce thickens.
- After 15 minutes, take out the florets from the air fryer and place them in the saucepan.
- Mix well to combine with the sauce and serve.

220. Boccoli Bake

 Serving size:
2

 Preparation time:
10 minutes

 Cooking time:
30 minutes

Total time:
40 minutes

Ingredients

- 220 grams broccoli
- 2 tablespoons plain flour
- Salt
- 1 tablespoon dry bread crumbs
- ½ large onion, chopped
- ½ can evaporated milk
- 90 grams cheddar cheese
- 1 teaspoon butter
- 40 ml. water

Instructions

- Lightly grease the baking pan of the air fryer with cooking spray. Mix in half of the milk and flour, cook on 200 degrees C for 5 minutes. Halfway through the cooking time, mix well. Add broccoli and remaining milk. Mix well and cook for another 5 minutes.
- Stir in cheese and mix well until melted.
- In a small bowl mix the butter and bread crumbs well. Sprinkle on top of the broccoli.
- Cook for 20 minutes at 200 degrees C. until the tops are lightly browned.
- Serve and enjoy.

221. Creole Vegetables

 Serving size:
5

 Preparation time:
10 minutes

 Cooking time:
15 minutes

 Total time:
25 minutes

Ingredients

- 40 grams honey
- 30 grams English mustard
- 1 large red pepper, sliced
- 1 teaspoon black pepper
- 1 teaspoon salt
- 2 large yellow squash, cut into thick slices
- 2 medium courgettes, cut into thick slices
- 2 teaspoons creole seasoning
- 2 teaspoons smoked paprika
- 3 tablespoons olive oil

Instructions

- Preheat the air fryer to 200 degrees C.
- Place the grill pan accessory in the air fryer.
- In a Ziploc bag, put the courgette, squash, red pepper, olive oil, salt and pepper. Give vegetables a good shake.
- Place in the grill pan and cook for 15 minutes.
- Meanwhile, prepare the sauce by combining the mustard, honey, paprika, and creole seasoning.
- Serve the vegetables with the sauce.

222. Paprika Tofu

	Serving size: 4		**Preparation time:** 5 minutes
	Cooking time: 12 minutes		**Total time:** 17 minutes

Ingredients

- 50 grams cornstarch (cornflour)
- 1 block extra firm tofu, pressed to remove excess water and cut into cubes
- 1 tablespoon smoked paprika
- salt and pepper to taste

Instructions

- Line the air fryer basket with aluminum foil and brush with oil.
- Preheat the air fryer to 170 degrees C.
- Mix all ingredients in a bowl. Toss to combine.
- Place in the air fryer basket and cook for 12 minutes.

223. Olives with Sweet Potatoes

	Serving size: 4		**Preparation time:** 5 minutes
	Cooking time: 25 minutes		**Total time:** 30 minutes

Ingredients

- 500 grams sweet potatoes, peeled and cut into wedges
- 150 grams kalamata olives, pitted and halved
- 1 tablespoon olive oil
- 2 tablespoons balsamic vinegar
- A bunch of coriander, chopped
- Salt and black pepper to the taste
- 1 tablespoon basil, chopped

Instructions

- Combine the potatoes with the olives and the other ingredients and toss in a pan that fits the air fryer.
- Place the pan in the air fryer. Cook at 200 degrees C for 25 minutes.
- Divide between plates and serve.

224. Lemony Tomatoes

	Serving size: 4		**Preparation time:** 5 minutes
	Cooking time: 20 minutes		**Total time:** 25 minutes

Ingredients

- 200 grams cherry tomatoes, halved
- 1 teaspoon sweet paprika
- 1 teaspoon coriander, ground
- 2 teaspoons lemon zest, grated
- 2 tablespoons olive oil
- 2 tablespoons lemon juice
- A handful parsley, chopped

Instructions

- Mix the tomatoes with the paprika and the other ingredients in the air fryer's pan, toss and cook at 200 degrees C for 20 minutes.
- Divide between plates and serve.

225. Carrots with Garlic

	Serving size: 4		**Preparation time:** 5 minutes
	Cooking time: 20 minutes		**Total time:** 25 minutes

Ingredients

- 1 tablespoon avocado oil
- 250 grams baby carrots, peeled
- Juice of 1 lime
- ½ teaspoon sweet paprika
- 6 garlic cloves, minced
- 1 tablespoon balsamic vinegar
- Salt and black pepper to the taste

Instructions

- Combine the carrots with the oil and the other ingredients in a pan that fits the air fryer. Toss gently, put the pan in the air fryer and cook at 170 degrees C for 20 minutes.
- Divide between plates and serve.

226. Walnuts and Green Beans

 Serving size:
4

 Preparation time:
5 minutes

 Cooking time:
20 minutes

Total time:
25 minutes

Ingredients

- 250 grams green beans, trimmed and halved
- 100 grams walnuts, chopped
- 150 grams cherry tomatoes, halved
- 2 tablespoons olive oil
- A pinch of salt and black pepper
- 1 tablespoon chives, chopped

Instructions

- Mix the green beans with the walnuts and the other ingredients in a pan that fits the air fryer. Toss, put the pan in the air fryer and cook at 200 degrees C for 20 minutes.
- Divide between plates and serve.

227. Fried Portobello Mushrooms

 Serving size:
2

 Preparation time:
5 minutes

 Cooking time:
10 minutes

 Total time:
15 minutes

Ingredients

- 1 tablespoon cooking oil
- 150 grams Portobello mushroom, sliced
- salt and pepper to taste

Instructions

- Place the grill pan accessory in the air fryer.
- In a bowl, place all the ingredients: and toss to coat. Then season the mushrooms.
- Place in the grill pan.
- Close the air fryer and cook for 10 minutes at 200 degrees C.

228. Indian Broccoli

 Serving size:
6

 Preparation time:
5 minutes

 Cooking time:
15 minutes

 Total time:
20 minutes

Ingredients

- ¼ teaspoon turmeric powder
- 250 grams broccoli, cut into florets
- 1 tablespoon almond flour
- 1 teaspoon garam masala
- 2 tablespoons coconut milk
- salt and pepper to taste

Instructions

- Preheat the air fryer for 5 minutes.
- In a bowl, combine all ingredients until the broccoli florets are coated with the other ingredients.
- Place in a fryer basket and cook for 15 minutes until crispy.

229. Chickpa-Fig with Arugula

 Serving size:
4

 Preparation time:
10 minutes

 Cooking time:
20 minutes

 Total time:
30 minutes

Ingredients

- 150 grams chickpeas, cooked
- 1 teaspoon cumin seeds, roasted then crushed
- 2 tablespoons extra-virgin olive oil
- 300 grams rocket, washed and dried
- 4 tablespoons balsamic vinegar
- 8 fresh figs, halved
- salt and pepper to taste

Instructions

- Preheat the air fryer to 170 degrees C.
- Line the air fryer basket with aluminum foil and brush with oil.
- Place the figs inside the air fryer and cook for 10 minutes.
- In a mixing bowl, mix the chickpeas and cumin seeds.
- Once the figs are cooked, take them out and place the chickpeas in the air fryer. Cook the chickpeas.
- Meanwhile, mix the dressing by combining the balsamic vinegar, olive oil, salt and pepper.

- Place the rocket in a salad bowl and place the cooled figs and chickpeas on top.
- Pour over the sauce and toss to coat.
- Serve immediately.

230. Apple Chips

 Serving size:
1

 Preparation time:
5 minutes

 Cooking time:
6 minutes

 Total time:
11 minutes

Ingredients

- ½ teaspoon ground cumin
- 1 apple, cored and sliced thinly
- 1 tablespoon sugar
- A pinch of salt

Instructions

- Place all the ingredients in a bowl and toss to coat everything.
- Put the grill pan accessory in the air fryer and place the sliced apples on the grill pan.
- Close the air fryer and cook for 6 minutes at 200 degrees C.

231. Almonds, Cheese and Tomatoes

Serving size:
3

Preparation time:
5 minutes

Cooking time:
20 minutes

Total time:
25 minutes

Ingredients

- 100 grams toasted almonds
- 1 yellow pepper, chopped
- 3 large tomatoes
- Monterey Jack cheese
- Salt and pepper to taste

Instructions

- Preheat the air fryer to 200 degrees C.
- Place the grill pan accessory in the air fryer.
- Slice the tops off the tomatoes and remove the seeds to create hollow "cups."
- In a mixing bowl, combine the cheese, pepper, and almonds. Season with salt and pepper.
- Stuff the tomatoes with the cheese filling.

- Place the stuffed tomatoes on the grill pan and cook for 15 to 20 minutes.

232. Mushrooms with Pesto

 Serving size:
3

 Preparation time:
10 minutes

 Cooking time:
15 minutes

Total time:
20 minutes

Ingredients

- 1 tablespoon olive oil
- 50 grams cream cheese
- 100 grams pine nuts
- 1 tablespoon basil leaves
- 1 tablespoon lemon juice, freshly squeezed
- 250 grams cremini mushrooms, stalks removed
- Salt to taste

Instructions

- Place all ingredients. except the mushrooms. in a food processor.
- Pulse until fine.
- Scoop the mixture and place on the side where the stalks were removed.
- Place the mushrooms in the fryer basket.
- Close and cook for 15 minutes in a 200 degrees C preheated air fryer.

233. Pepper Pineapple with Sugar Glaze

 Serving size:
2

Preparation time:
5 minutes

 Cooking time:
10 minutes

 Total time:
15 minutes

Ingredients

- 1 medium-sized pineapple, peeled and sliced
- 1 red pepper, seeded and julienned
- 1 teaspoon brown sugar
- 2 teaspoons melted butter
- Salt to taste

Instructions

- Preheat the air fryer to 200 degrees C.

- Place the grill pan accessory in the air fryer.
- Mix all the ingredients in a Ziploc bag and give it a good shake.
- Place it into the grill pan and cook for 10 minutes making sure that you flip the pineapples half way trough.

234. Vegetable Tacos

 Serving size:
6

 Preparation time:
5 minutes

 Cooking time:
5 minutes

 Total time:
10 minutes

Ingredients

- 1 tablespoon olive oil
- 1 tablespoon lime juice
- 1 teaspoon chilli powder
- 1 teaspoon ground cumin
- 1 teaspoon sea salt
- ¼ teaspoon garlic powder
- 1 can chickpeas, drained
- 1 small head cauliflower, cut into bite-sized pieces
- 100 grams sour cream
- 1 handful chopped coriander
- 20 ml. lemon juice
- 1 tablespoon sriracha
- Salt
- 6 corn tortillas

Instructions

- Preheat an air fryer to 190 degrees C.
- Whisk together olive oil, lime juice, chilli powder, cumin, salt, and garlic powder in a large bowl. Add chickpeas and cauliflower and stir until evenly coated.
- Stir together sour cream, coriander, lime juice, and Sriracha in a bowl until evenly combined. Season with salt to taste.
- Place cauliflower mixture in the basket of the air fryer. Cook for 10 minutes, stir, and cook for another 10 minutes. Stir once more and cook until desired crispness, about 5 more minutes.
- Spoon cauliflower mixture into corn tortillas and top with sauce.

235. Tempura Vegetables with Sesame Sauce

 Serving size:
4

 Preparation time:

 Cooking time:

 Total time:

Ingredients

- 75 grams plain flour
- 65 grams Asian white rice
- 1 egg yolk
- 80 ml. iced water
- 50 ml. dressing sesame soy
- 2 medium courgettes
- 150 grams frozen corn kennels
- ½ red onion, thinly sliced
- 1 medium carrot
- 2 tablespoons sesame soy dressing
- 3 tablespoons roasted sesame dressing
- 2 tablespoons mayonaiise
- Toasted sesame seeds

Instructions

- Whisk the flour and rice in a bowl until combined. Whisk egg yolk, water and sesame soy dressing in a jug. Pour into dry mixture and whisk until combined. Stir in the courgettes, corn, carrot and onion. Season.
- Spray the basket of an XXL air fryer with oil spray. Place 9 tablespoons of mixture into the basket. Spray with oil and air fry at 200C for 10 minutes or until crisp and golden. Repeat with remaining mixture.
- To make the dipping sauce, combine sesame soy dressing, roasted sesame dressing and mayonnaise in a bowl.
- Serve tempura fritters with dipping sauce and a sprinkle of toasted sesame seeds.

236. Air-Fried Cauliflower

 Serving size:
4

 Preparation time:
5 minutes

 Cooking time:
15 minutes

 Total time:
20 minutes

Ingredients

- 1 small cauliflower head cut into florets
- 1 tablespoon olive oil
- ¼ teaspoon ground turmeric
- ½ teaspoon smoked paprika
- ½ teaspoon salt
- ¼ teaspoon ground black pepper

Instructions

- Drizzle the cauliflower florets with olive oil, then toss with turmeric, smoked paprika, salt, and pepper so that they're well coated in the seasoning.
- Roast in the Air Fryer at 200°C for around 15 minutes, turning every 3 minutes.

- When the air frying process is done, remove from the air fryer basket and serve on a plate. It can be enjoyed either warm or cold.

237. Polenta Fries

 Serving size:
4

 Preparation time:
5 minutes

 Cooking time:
30 minutes

 Total time:
35 minutes

Ingredients

- 1 package polenta, previously prepared according to instructions
- Nonstick olive oil cooking spray
- Salt
- Pepper

Instructions

- Preheat an air fryer to 175 degrees C.
- Slice polenta into long, thin slices resembling french fries.
- Spray the bottom of the basket with cooking spray. Place 1/2 of the polenta fries in the basket and lightly mist the tops with cooking spray. Season with salt and pepper.
- Cook in the preheated air fryer for 10 minutes. Flip the fries with a spatula and cook until crispy, about 5 minutes longer. Transfer fries to a kitchen towel-lined plate. Repeat with remaining half of fries.

238. Air-Fried Falafel

 Serving size:
25 balls

 Preparation time:
30 minutes

 Cooking time:
15 minutes

 Total time:
45 minutes

Ingredients

- 400 grams dried chickpeas (not canned or cooked chickpeas)
- 5 garlic cloves chopped
- 1 small onion chopped
- 130 grams parsley leaves chopped
- 60 grams coriander leaves chopped
- 2 teaspoon ground coriander
- 2 teaspoon ground cumin
- 1 1/2 teaspoon sea salt

- 1 teaspoon black pepper
- Red pepper flakes or cayenne pepper to taste
- 1 teaspoon baking powder
- Cooking spray

Instructions

- The day before you start making the falafel, place the dried chickpeas in a large bowl. Fill it with plenty of water (the chickpeas should be covered by at least 7 cm but add more water if needed) and soak for 18-24 hours. Drain the chickpeas completely and use kitchen paper to lightly pat them dry (if they are too wet).
- Transfer the chickpeas along with all other ingredients to a large food processor. If you have a small food processor, you will need to work in batches. Process everything for about 20 seconds, then scrape down the sides of the food processor and blend again. Do this a few times until the mixture is well combined, but not mushy.
- Put the falafel mixture in the fridge (in the food processor bowl) for about 45-60 minutes (or longer).
- Use an ice cream scooper to scoop the falafel mixture and shape it with your hands to form a ball (or make a patty/disk if you wish). Do this with the remaining falafel mixture.
- Use the cooking spray to lightly spray the falafel balls. Also, spray the basket of your air fryer to avoid sticking. Heat the air fryer to 190 degrees C and set the timer to 15 minutes. Cook the falafel balls in the air fryer, flip them after 10 minutes. They should be crispy and slightly brown on the outside. You might need to fry them in batches if necessary.
- Serve hot on its own or assemble the falafels in pitta bread with tahini, lettuce, tomato, and cucumbers. Enjoy!

239. Teriyaki Cauliflower

 Serving size:
8

 Preparation time:
20 minutes

 Cooking time:
30 minutes

 Total time:
50 minutes

Ingredients

- 1 medium cauliflower head, chopped into florets
- ½ teaspoon garlic powder
- 130 grams plain flour
- 90 ml. unsweetened non-dairy milk
- 200 grams breadcrumbs (use gluten-free if needed)
- Cooking spray
- For the teriyaki sauce
- 40 ml. low-sodium soy sauce (or tamari if gluten-free)

- 130 ml. water
- 2 tablespoons brown sugar
- 2 tablespoons rice vinegar
- 1 tablespoon toasted sesame oil
- 3 garlic cloves, chopped
- 2 teaspoons chopped ginger
- 2 tablespoon corn starch (or sub with arrowroot starch)
- ⅛ teaspoon freshly cracked black pepper
- A pinch of chilli flakes (optional, for heat)

Instructions

- Preheat air fryer to 180 degrees C.
- To a medium mixing bowl, mix flour and garlic powder together. Then slowly pour the milk, stirring constantly to prevent clumps. The mixture should be smooth and creamy.
- In another bowl, add the breadcrumbs. Start coating the cauliflower florets by dipping each one in the wet mixture first, letting any excess batter drip off. Then roll it in the breadcrumbs. Repeat until all florets are coated.
- Spray the air fryer basket with oil or cooking spray. Add florets to the basket in a single layer, then spray them with oil. Cook for 12-15 minutes, or until golden and crispy. Make sure to stop and shake the basket halfway through.
- In the meantime, make the teriyaki sauce. Add all of the ingredients to a saucepan- soy sauce, water, sesame oil, rice vinegar, sugar, garlic, ginger, cornstarch, black pepper, and chilli flakes (optional). Heat over a medium-high heat, stirring occasionally. When the sauce starts to boil, turn the heat to medium-low and start whisking constantly, simmering the sauce for 2-3 minutes until it thickens. Remove from the heat.
- Add wings to a bowl and pour in ⅔ of the sauce. Mix gently. Use the rest of the sauce to drizzle on spots that didn't get coated well. Top with toasted sesame seeds (optional) and serve right away!

240. Brussel Sprouts with Garlic

 Serving size:
2

 Preparation time:
15 minutes

 Cooking time:
15 minutes

 Total time:
30 minutes

Ingredients

- 10 fresh cauliflower florets, from one small head of cauliflower, about 250g
- 60 grams plain flour
- 2 grams all-purpose seasoning
- 120 ml plant-based milk

- 150 grams teriyaki sauce
- 1 teaspoon cayenne pepper
- 15 ml oil, or cooking spray

Instructions

- Preheat the air fryer to 200°C.
- In a bowl, combine the flour, all-purpose seasoning and chilli pepper . Gradually stir in enough plant-based milk to make a thick and smooth batter.
- Rinse and drain cauliflower then dip each piece into the batter, coating completely. Shake off the excess batter then place on an air fryer tray or basket coated with oil or cooking spray. Place them in one layer, without touching.
- Place the tray in the air fryer and cook for 10 to 15 minutes until golden brown. Remove the pieces, set aside and repeat with the remaining batch.
- Dip each piece of cauliflower in teriyaki sauce. Place back on the tray and into the air fryer for another 3 to 5 minutes or until the sauce becomes stickier.
- Repeat with the remaining pieces and serve warm.

241. Peppers Filled with Cheese

 Serving size:
20

 Preparation time:
30 minutes

 Cooking time:
35 minutes

 Total time:
1 hour and 5 minutes

Ingredients

- 250 grams Italian sausage
- 1 package miniature multi-coloured sweet peppers
- 2 tablespoons olive oil, divided
- 1 package cream cheese, softened
- 100 grams grated Cheddar cheese
- 2 tablespoons crumbled blue cheese (Optional)
- 1 tablespoon finely chopped fresh chives
- 1 clove garlic, chopped
- ¼ teaspoon ground black pepper
- 2 tablespoons panko breadcrumbs

Instructions

- Heat a large nonstick pan over a medium-high heat. Cook and stir the sausage in the hot pan until browned and crumbly, 5 to 7 minutes. Drain and discard grease; set aside.
- Preheat an air fryer to 175 degrees C.
- Cut a slit in one side of each sweet pepper lengthwise from stem to tip. Brush peppers with 1 tablespoon olive oil and place in the air fryer basket.

- Cook in the preheated air fryer for 3 minutes. Shake the basket and cook until peppers start to brown and soften, about 3 minutes more. Remove peppers and let stand until cool enough to handle; leave air fryer on.
- While peppers are cooling, stir together sausage, cream cheese, cheddar cheese, blue cheese, chives, garlic, and black pepper in a medium bowl until well combined. Mix breadcrumbs with remaining 1 tablespoon olive oil in a small bowl.
- Spoon cheese mixture into each pepper and sprinkle with the breadcrumb mixture. Place stuffed peppers in the air fryer basket, working in batches if necessary, and cook until filling is heated through and breadcrumbs are toasted, 4 to 5 minutes. Cool slightly; serve warm.

242. Cauliflower and Mushroom Balls

 Serving size:
6

 Preparation time:
15 minutes

 Cooking time:
11 minutes

 Total time:
26 minutes

Ingredients

- ½ head cauliflower, stems trimmed short and cut into bite sized pieces
- 60 grams flour
- 2 eggs, beaten
- 90 grams Panko breadcrumbs
- 90 grams parmesan cheese, grated
- 1 teaspoon Italian seasoning
- ½ teaspoon salt
- ½ teaspoon garlic powder
- ¼ teaspoon black pepper
- 100 grams mushrooms

Instructions

- You'll need three shallow bowls or resealable containers. Put the flour in the first one. In the second one, beat the eggs. In the third bowl, stir the Panko breadcrumbs, parmesan cheese, Italian seasoning, mushrooms, salt, garlic powder and black pepper.
- Take the cauliflower and place it in the first bowl. Toss to coat, or put the lid on and shake. Working in batches tap the excess flour off the cauliflower and dip it in the egg. Then place in the Panko crumbs. Toss to coat or again put the lid on and shake. Remove to a plate and repeat with remaining cauliflower.

- Preheat air fryer to 200 degrees C. Set for 11 minutes cook time. Once preheated, place in a single layer in the air fryer basket. You may need to work in batches to avoid overcrowding. Cook for 11 minutes or until golden brown. Serve hot.

243. Cauliflower Florets with Curry

 Serving size:
4

 Preparation time:
10 minutes

 Cooking time:
25 minutes

Total time:
35 minutes

Ingredients

- 1 large (or 2 small) head(s) cauliflower, cored, broken into large-ish florets, florets sliced into 1/2-inch slices
- 1/2 onion, peeled, thickly sliced, root to tip
- 4 cloves garlic, sliced
- 2 tablespoons lemon juice
- 80ml extra virgin olive oil
- 1 1/2 teaspoons yellow curry powder
- 1/4 teaspoon ground cinnamon
- 1/2 teaspoon salt
- 1/4 teaspoon ground black pepper

Instructions

- Preheat air fryer, line baking pan with foil:
- Pre-heat air fryer to 220°C with a rack on the top third of the oven. Line a large rimmed baking tray with foil.
- Put the garlic, lemon juice, olive oil, curry powder, cinnamon, salt, and pepper in a large bowl. Whisk vigorously until well combined:
- Add the cauliflower and onion slices to the bowl with the curry and toss to coat. Spread the cauliflower and onion slices on the baking sheet in a single layer.
- Roast in air fryer at 220°C for 25 to 30 minutes until well browned. Check halfway through the cooking, and rotate the pan for more even cooking.

244. Roasted Rosemary Squash

 Serving size:
4

 Preparation time:
15 minutes

 Cooking time:
20 minutes

 Total time:
25 minutes

Ingredients

- 500 grams cubed butternut squash
- 1 teaspoon cinnamon
- Olive oil cooking spray

Instructions

- Spray the air fryer basket with olive oil cooking spray or line it with foil and spray.
- Place the butternut squash in the basket.
- Sprinkle with cinnamon and coat with olive oil spray.
- Cook at 200 degrees for 20 minutes. It's best to check on it after 10 minutes, stir, coat and continue cooking. At this point, you can also add more cinnamon if you prefer.
- Serve.

245. Aubergine Gratin

	Serving size: 4		**Preparation time:** 10 minutes
	Cooking time: 20 minutes		**Total time:** 30 minutes

Ingredients

- 90 grams Italian breadcrumbs
- 90 grams freshly grated parmesan cheese
- 1 teaspoon Italian seasoning
- 1 teaspoon salt
- ½ teaspoon dried basil
- ½ teaspoon garlic powder
- ½ teaspoon onion powder
- ½ teaspoon freshly ground black pepper
- 60 grams flour
- 2 large eggs, beaten
- 1 medium aubergine, sliced into 1/2-inch rounds
- 1 can marinara sauce, or more to taste
- 8 slices mozzarella cheese, or as needed

Instructions

- Combine breadcrumbs, parmesan cheese, Italian seasoning, salt, basil, garlic powder, onion powder, and black pepper in a shallow bowl. Place flour in a separate shallow bowl and beaten eggs in a third shallow bowl.
- Dip sliced aubergine first in flour, then in beaten eggs, and finally coat with bread crumb mixture. Place coated aubergine on a plate and let rest for 5 minutes.
- Preheat an air fryer to 185 degrees C.
- Place breaded aubergine rounds in the air fryer basket, making sure they are not touching; work in batches if necessary. Cook for 8 to 10 minutes, turn each round, and cook

until desired crispiness is achieved, 4 to 6 minutes more. Top each aubergine round with marinara sauce and 1 slice of mozzarella cheese. Place basket back in the air fryer and cook until cheese has started to melt, 1 to 2 minutes. Repeat with remaining aubergine, if necessary.

246. Winter Vegetable Delight

	Serving size: 4		**Preparation time:** 10 minutes
	Cooking time: 10 minutes		**Total time:** 20 minutes

Ingredients

- 1 red pepper chopped
- 200 grams mushrooms halved
- 1 small courgette cut into ½" moons
- 2 cloves garlic chopped
- 1 tablespoon olive oil
- ½ teaspoon Italian seasoning
- salt & pepper to taste
- 1 tablespoon parmesan cheese grated

Instructions

- Preheat air fryer to 200°C.
- Mix all the ingredients together, except the parmesan cheese.
- Place in a single layer in the air fryer.
- Cook 6 minutes, toss and sprinkle with parmesan cheese.
- Cook for an additional 3-5 minutes or until tender crisp.

247. Courgette Chips

	Serving size: 4		**Preparation time:** 10 minutes
	Cooking time: 10 minutes		**Total time:** 20 minutes

Ingredients

- 500 grams of courgette, sliced thin*
- nonstick oil spray
- 1 tablespoon apple cider vinegar
- 2 teaspoon seasoned salt
- 1 teaspoon garlic powder

Instructions

- Using a mandoline slicer or chef knife, slice the courgettes into thin slices.

- Place courgettes in a mixing bowl. Add vinegar and mix to combine.
- Spray air fryer basket with non-stick cooking spray.
- Add courgette chips in a single layer in air fryer basket.
- Air fry at 200 degrees for 4-5 minutes. Turn the chips over and fry for an additional 4-5 minutes, until they reach desired crispness. Check the chips frequently and remove early if they start to burn.
- Once done frying, sprinkle with seasoned salt and garlic powder.
- Enjoy!

248. Potato Chips

Serving size: 6	**Preparation time:** 15 minutes
Cooking time: 20 minutes	**Total time:** 35 minutes

Ingredients

- 2 large potatoes
- Olive oil-flavored cooking spray
- 1/2 teaspoon sea salt
- Chopped fresh parsley, optional

Instructions

- Preheat air fryer to 200°C. Using a mandoline or vegetable peeler, cut potatoes into very thin slices. Transfer to a large bowl; add enough ice water to cover. Soak for 15 minutes; drain. Add more ice water and soak another 15 minutes.
- Drain potatoes; place on kitchen towels and pat dry. Spray the potatoes with cooking spray and sprinkle with salt. In batches, place potato slices in a single layer on a greased tray in the air-fryer basket. Cook until crisp and golden brown, 15-17 minutes, stirring and turning every 5-7 minutes. Feel free to sprinkle with parsley if you would like to.

249. Aubergine Chips

Serving size: 4	**Preparation time:** 10 minutes
Cooking time: 25 minutes	**Total time:** 35 minutes

Ingredients

- 1 large aubergine sliced into ¼-inch rounds
- ½ teaspoon garlic powder
- ½ teaspoon chilli powder
- ½ teaspoon dried oregano
- ½ teaspoon salt
- 1 tablespoon olive oil

Instructions

- Mix together the garlic powder, chilli powder, oregano, and salt.
- In a large bowl, add the aubergine slices, olive oil and the prepared spice mix. Toss well to coat each aubergine slice with the spice mix.
- Lightly spray the air fryer basket with olive oil spray. Arrange the aubergine slices in a single layer in the air fryer basket.
- Air fry at 200° C for 20 to 25 minutes, turning the aubergine slices once, till they are slightly crispy.
- Place the aubergine slices on a wire rack to cool down. They will continue to crisp up as they cool down.
- Repeat process with the remaining slices.

250. Filled Mushrooms with Cheddar and Bacon

Serving size: 4	**Preparation time:** 5 minutes
Cooking time: 7 minutes	**Total time:** 12 minutes

Ingredients

- 250 grams mushrooms stems removed
- 150 grams cream cheese softened
- 4 strips turkey bacon or pork bacon, crumbled
- 150 grams cheddar cheese grated
- ½ teaspoon salt
- ½ teaspoon garlic powder
- ¼ teaspoon pepper

Instructions

- To make this recipe, clean the mushrooms using cold water. Then, remove the tops of mushrooms from the stems and set aside.
- In a medium bowl, mix the softened cream cheese with the crumbled bacon, grated cheese, salt, pepper, and garlic. Stir together until the mixture is well combined and creamy.
- Scoop the cream cheese mixture into mushroom caps, filling the mushroom cavity. Once all mushrooms are filled, lightly spray or brush the basket with oil, and then gently place the

stuffed mushrooms into the air fryer basket without stacking or overlapping.

- Air fry 200 degrees C 5-7 minutes, until the tops of the mushrooms are golden brown.

251. Feta and Pesto Tomato Sandwiches

 Serving size:
2

 Preparation time:
5 minutes

 Cooking time:
8 minutes

 Total time:
13 minutes

Ingredients

- 4 pieces of sour dough bread
- 4 tablespoons room temperature butter
- 1 tomato, sliced thinly
- 60 grams fresh basil
- 2 slices feta cheese

Instructions

- Spread butter on one side of the bread, and then place it butter side down into the air fryer basket. Then add the tomato slices and feta.
- Add the basil on top, and then cover with a piece of bread buttered, placing the butter side up.
- Set the temperature for 170 degrees C, air fryer setting, for 8 minutes. Turning halfway.
- Plate, serve, and enjoy!

252. Parmesan Courgette

 Serving size:
4

 Preparation time:
2 minutes

 Cooking time:
8 minutes

 Total time:
10 minutes

Ingredients

- 2 large courgettes
- 1 tablespoon olive oil
- 1 teaspoon garlic powder
- salt (to taste)
- pepper (to taste)
- 130 grams Parmesan cheese

Instructions

- Slice the courgettes into ¼ inch rounds
- Transfer to a large mixing bowl and drizzle with olive oil, garlic powder, salt, and pepper. Gently toss to combine.
- Transfer to the air fryer and top with grated parmesan.
- Set your air fryer to 200°C for 5 minutes. After 5 minutes open air fryer and turn over the courgettes, then sprinkle parmesan on the other side. Close the air fryer and cook for another 4-5 minutes.
- The courgette rounds are ready once the parmesan cheese is golden brown and the edges of the courgettes are crisp. Enjoy with your favorite dip or condiment.

253. Three Cheese Vegetable Frittata

 Serving size:
4

 Preparation time:
10 minutes

 Cooking time:
15 minutes

 Total time:
25 minutes

Ingredients

- 6 large eggs
- 30 ml. milk of choice (see notes for substitutions)
- 2 red/white onions chopped
- 1 pepper chopped any colour
- 150 grams crimini mushrooms chopped or white button mushrooms
- 150 grams baby spinach chopped or baby kale
- 20 grams coriander or parsley chopped
- ½ teaspoon salt adjust to taste
- ½ teaspoon crushed black pepper
- 300 grams of cheddar, mozzarella and feta (100 grams of each, mixed together)

Instructions

- Saute veggies in olive oil in an oven-safe pan/dish for 2-3 minutes over a medium-high heat, then let them cool.
- Meanwhile, combine eggs, milk, salt and pepper in a large bowl and whisk until blended. Stir in half the cheese mixture. Keep to one side.
- Spread the sautéed veggies evenly in the pan (or a shallow baking dish). Now pour the egg mixture over that. Spread chopped herbs on top. Top that with the remaining grated cheese.

- Assemble the frittata in a shallow baking dish. Place it in the fryer basket and cook on 200°C for 15-18 minutes, or until an inserted toothpick comes out clean.
- Let the frittata rest for 5-10 minutes before serving. Using a serrated knife, slice it into as many slices as you prefer.

254. Feta Triangles

 Serving size:
3

 Preparation time:
20 minutes

 Cooking time:
9 minutes

 Total time:
29 minutes

Ingredients

- 1 egg yolk
- 100 grams feta
- 2 tablespoons flat-leafed parsley, finely chopped
- 1 onion, finely sliced into rings
- Freshly ground black pepper
- 5 sheets of frozen filo pastry, defrosted

Instructions

- Beat the egg yolk in a bowl and mix the feta, parsley and onion; season with pepper to taste.
- Cut each sheet of filo pastry into three strips.
- Scoop a full teaspoon of the feta mixture on the underside of a strip of pastry. Fold the tip of the pastry over the filling to form a triangle, folding the strip zigzag until the filling is wrapped up in a triangle of pastry. Fill the other strips of pastry with feta in the same manner.
- Preheat the Air Fryer to 200°C.
- Brush the triangles with a little oil and place five triangles in the basket. Slide the basket into the Air Fryer and set the timer to 3 minutes. Bake the feta triangles until they are golden brown. Bake the other feta triangles in the same manner.
- Serve the triangles in a platter.

255. Aubergine Caviar

 Serving size:
6

Preparation time:
20 minutes

 Cooking time:
15 minutes

Total time:
25 minutes

Ingredients

- 1 medium aubergine, halved lengthwise

- ½ teaspoon kosher salt
- 5 ½ tablespoons olive oil, divided
- 1 bulb garlic
- 90 grams tahini (sesame seed paste)
- 2 tablespoons lemon juice, or more to taste
- ¼ teaspoon ground cumin
- ⅛ teaspoon smoked paprika
- 2 tablespoons crumbled feta cheese
- 1 tablespoon chopped fresh parsley
- ½ teaspoon lemon zest

Instructions

- Sprinkle cut sides of aubergine with salt. Let stand for 20 to 30 minutes. Blot dry with paper towels.
- Preheat an air fryer to 200 degrees C.
- Brush cut sides of aubergine with 1 tablespoon olive oil. Cut off the top 1/4 inch from the garlic bulb, exposing the cloves. Brush cloves with 1/2 tablespoon olive oil and wrap bulb in aluminum foil. Place aubergine and garlic in the air fryer basket.
- Cook in the preheated air fryer until aubergine and garlic are tender and aubergine is a deep golden brown, 15 to 20 minutes. Remove and allow to cool, about 10 minutes.
- Scoop flesh from aubergine and place into the bowl of a food processor. Add tahini, lemon juice, 4 cloves of roasted garlic (reserve remaining roasted garlic for another use), remaining 4 tablespoons olive oil, cumin, and paprika; pulse to a moderately smooth consistency. Top with feta cheese, parsley, and lemon zest.

256. Ratatouille

 Serving size:
2

 Preparation time:
15 minutes

 Cooking time:
35 minutes

Total time:
45 minutes

Ingredients

- 220 grams aubergine, peeled and diced to 3/4 inch cubes
- 2 sweet peppers, diced
- 10 cherry tomatoes, left whole
- 6-8 garlic cloves, sliced in half lengthwise
- 3 tablespoons oil
- 1 teaspoon dried oregano
- 1 teaspoon Kosher salt
- 1/2 teaspoon ground black pepper
- 1/2 teaspoon dried thyme

Instructions

- In a medium bowl, mix together the aubergine, pepper, tomatoes, garlic, oil, oregano, salt, pepper, and thyme.
- Place the vegetables in the air fryer basket. Set the air fryer to 200°C for 20 minutes or until the vegetables are tender and roasted.
- The vegetables shrink down considerably when this is cooked, and you will get about 200 grams of cooked veggies from this recipe, making it a great side dish.

257. Tofu Enchiladas with Cheese

 Serving size:
6

 Preparation time:
15 minutes

 Cooking time:
1o minutes

 Total time:
25 minutes

Ingredients

- 1 block firm tofu
- 1 tablespoon oil
- 1 diced onion
- 1 teaspoon cumin
- 1 teaspoon chilli powder
- 100 grams black beans cooked
- 100 grams rice cooked
- 1 can fire roasted tomatoes
- 1 lime juiced, optional
- 12 tortillas
- 100 grams shredded Mexican cheese
- 150 grams enchilada sauce
- 1 lime quartered, for garnish

Instructions

- Start by pressing the tofu for about 10 to 12 minutes, tightening every 3 to 4 minutes.
- In a pan over a medium heat, add oil and sauté onions.
- When the onions have softened, add tofu to pan. Mash tofu with a fork and sauté the tofu and onion mixture for about 6 to 8 minutes.
- Add the spices to the pan mixture and stir to combine.
- Add the cooked black beans, cooked rice, and fire roasted tomatoes to the tofu mixture. Heat for about 2 minutes.
- If using lime juice, add to the mixture here and remove from heat.
- Roll mixture into tortillas.
- Line air fryer basket with foil before adding rolled tortillas with the seams facing down. This will need to be cooked in a few batches, depending on your air fryer size.
- Top enchiladas with sauce and then cheese.
- Cook for about 4 minutes at 200°C or until cheese melts. Repeat until all enchiladas are cooked.

258. Cabbage Steaks

 Serving size:
6

 Preparation time:
15 minutes

 Cooking time:
10 minutes

 Total time:
25 minutes

Ingredients

- 1 head cabbage
- 2 tablespoons melted butter (or olive oil)

Seasoning:
- 1 tablespoon Old Bay seasoning
- 1/2 teaspoon onion powder (for each cabbage steak piece)
- 1 teaspoon garlic powder
- 1 teaspoon smoked paprika
- 2 tablespoons shredded parmesan (very finely)
- 1 teaspoon dried parsley

Instructions

- Pour half of water underneath your air fryer basket.
- Preheat the air fryer to 200 degrees C for 5 minutes.
- Slice the cabbage in thick steaks.
- Mix all the seasoning ingredients in a bowl.
- Place cabbage steak pieces on a cutting board and using a kitchen brush grease them with butter. Then sprinkle seasoning on top.
- Place the cabbage steak piece into the preheated air fryer basket, close basket, and set the timer to 8 minutes, for crispier edges add 2 more minutes and check again.
- Repeat with the rest of the steaks.
- Serve with lemon wedges and chopped parsley.

259. Cauliflower Rice with Tofu

 Serving size:
3

 Preparation time:
10 minuts

 Cooking time:
20 minutes

 Total time:
30 minutes

Ingredients

- ½ block firm or extra firm tofu
- 2 tablespoons reduced sodium soy sauce
- 1 diced onion
- 1 diced carrot - about 1 ½ to 2 carrots
- 1 teaspoon turmeric
- 250 grams riced cauliflower

- 2 tablespoons soy sauce
- 1 ½ tablespoons toasted sesame oil
- 1 tablespoon rice vinegar
- 1 tablespoon chopped ginger
- 90 grams chopped broccoli

Instructions

- In a large bowl, crumble the tofu (you're going for scrambled egg-size pieces, not ricotta here), then toss with the rest of the Round 1 ingredients. Air fry at 200 degrees C for 10 minutes, shaking once.
- Meanwhile, mix together all of the Round 2 ingredients in a large bowl*.
- When the first 10 minutes of cooking are done, add all of the Round 2 ingredients to your air fryer, shake gently. Fry at 200 for 10 more minutes, shaking after 5 minutes.
- Riced cauliflower can vary quite a bit in size, so if you feel like yours doesn't look done enough at this point, you can cook for an additional 2-5 minutes at 200 degres C. Just shake and check in every couple of minutes until it's done to your liking.

260. Tomato Stuffed Squash

 Serving size: 4

 Preparation time: 10 minutes

 Cooking time: 10 minutes

 Total time: 20 minutes

Ingredients

- 1 medium/large acorn squash
- 2 tablespoons extra virgin olive oil (divided)
- 2 Italian sausage links
- 1 small onion, diced
- 2 cloves garlic, chopped
- 1 teaspoon dried oregano
- 3 tomatoes, diced
- 150 grams cooked brown rice
- 1 tablespoon dried cranberries or raisins
- 1 tablespoon toasted walnuts, chopped
- Sea salt and freshly ground pepper to taste
- Nutritional yeast and chopped fresh parsley for garnish (optional)

Instructions

- Cut each squash in half lengthwise. Scoop the seeds and strings out and discard. Brush the cut faces of the squash halves with 2 teaspoons of the olive oil. Season with salt and pepper.

- Place the halves, cut side down, in the air fryer basket or on the crisper plate. Turn the fryer on to 200°C. Cook the squash for 10 to 12 minutes until the flesh has just softened. Make the stuffing while the squash roasts.
- In a large pan over a medium-high heat, warm 1 teaspoon of the oil. Add the ground meat from the sausages and cook until the meat is browned, breaking it up with a spoon. Remove the cooked sausage to a plate. Discard the fat from the pan and wipe it out with kitchen paper.
- Turn the heat under the pan down to medium. Add 3 more teaspoons of the oil to the pan. Add the onion and sauté until translucent and fragrant, approximately 3 to 5 minutes. Add the garlic and oregano to the pan and cook for an additional 30 to 60 seconds until the garlic is aromatic.
- Add the sausage meat and diced tomatoes to the pan. Stir and sauté for another 1 to 2 minutes. Add in the rice, cranberries, and walnuts. Mix well to combine. Season with salt and pepper to taste.
- Remove the squash halves from the air fryer. Turn them over and fill the bowl of each with equal amounts of the stuffing. (There will be some extra that you can serve warm on the side). Place the squash back in the air fryer and continue to cook for another 5 to 7 minutes until the stuffing is warm and golden brown on top. The edges of the squash will start to brown and curl.
- Serve the stuffed squash halves as a main dish with a nice fall salad on the side. You can garnish the top of the squash with a little nutritional yeast and parsley. A recipe for a fall salad follows.

261. Tofu Sandwich

 Serving size: 3

 Preparation time: 15 minutes

 Cooking time: 20 minutes

 Total time: 35 minutes

Ingredients

- 1 package firm tofu drained and sliced into 3 pieces
- 3 burger buns
- toppings of your choice (lettuce, tomato, pickles...)
- Liquid Mixture
- 2 flax eggs 2 tablespoon flax seed meal+5 tablespoon water
- 30 ml. unsweetened almond milk
- 1 tablespoon apple cider vinegar
- 8-10 drops liquid smoke
- Breading Mixture
- 1/2 teaspoon smoked paprika
- 1 teaspoon garlic powder
- 1 teaspoon onion powder

- 1 teaspoon thyme
- 1/2 teaspoon black pepper
- salt to taste
- 120 grams panko bread crumbs
- 1 tablespoon nutritional yeast
- 1 tablespoon cornstarch
- Sauce
- 90 grams vegan mayo
- 1 teaspoon mustard
- 1 tablespoon bbq sauce
- 1 tablespoon agave

Instructions

- In a flat dish, mix together the ingredients for the liquid mixture and set aside.
- In another flat dish, mix together the breading ingredients.
- Dip the sliced and drained tofu into the liquid mixture, ensuring that all sides are covered. Then transfer to the breading mixture, lightly pressing the tofu into the mixture. Place in your air fryer. Complete this process until each piece of tofu is covered.
- Spray each of the pieces of tofu lightly with olive oil (optional-helpful for browning). Set your Air fryer to 200 degrees and cook for 10 minutes. Flip each piece and spray the other side of the tofu with olive oil and cook for another 10 minutes.
- While the tofu is cooking, begin mixing the ingredients for the sauce and gathering desired toppings (lettuce, tomato, pickles...etc).
- Once the tofu has finished cooking, begin forming your sandwich. Enjoy!

262. Avocado Rolls

 Serving size:
8

 Preparation time:
10 minutes

 Cooking time:
12 minutes

 Total time:
22 minutes

Ingredients

- 3 avocados diced
- 1 red onion diced
- 1 Roma tomato diced
- 3 tablespoons chopped fresh coriander leaves
- 1 teaspoon garlic powder
- Juice of 1 lime
- salt and pepper to taste
- 8 egg roll wrappers
- olive oil spray

Instructions

- In a medium bowl, add the avocado and mash to desired consistency. Add the onion, tomato, coriander, garlic powder, lime juice and salt and pepper to taste.
- Place the avocado mixture in the center of each wrapper. Using your finger, rub the edges with water. Bring the bottom

edge of the wrapper and roll it tightly over the filling. Fold in the sides and continue to roll up the wrapper and press to seal. Repeat until you have used all of the wrappers.
- Spray the basket of the air fryer with olive oil spray. Place the egg rolls in the basket and lightly spray the tops of the egg rolls with the olive oil spray. Cook at 200 degrees for 6 minutes. Then flip the egg rolls and cook for an additional 6 minutes.

263. Vegetable Skewers

 Serving size:
4

 Preparation time:
30 minutes

 Cooking time:
15 minutes

 Total time:
45 minutes

Ingredients

- Vegetable Skewers
- 4 medium red onion
- 4 medium courgettes (sliced)
- 2 red pepper
- 2 orange pepper
- 2 yellow pepper
- 2 green pepper
- olive oil (for brushing)
- Balsamic vinegar (for serving)
- For the Garlic Herb Sauce
- 40ml. olive oil
- 5 cloves garlic (chopped)
- 3 tablespoon fresh parsley (chopped)
- 3 tablespoon fresh coriander (chopped)
- 1 teaspoon fresh rosemary (chopped)
- salt (to taste)
- freshly ground black pepper (to taste)

Instructions

- Soak skewers in water for at least 10 mins before using (to prevent burning during cooking).
- Preheat air fryer to 198 degrees C.
- Thread vegetables onto the skewers.
- Place skewers in air fryer and make sure they are not touching. If air fryer basket is small, you may need to cut the ends of the skewers to fit.
- Cook for 10 mins, turning half way through the cook time. Since air fryer temperatures can vary, start with less time and then add more as needed.
- Transfer veggie kabobs to a plate and serve.

264. Roasted Vegetable Salad

 Serving size:
4

 Preparation time:
20 minutes

 Cooking time:
10 minutes

 Total time:
30 minutes

Ingredients

- 120 grams diced courgette
- 120 grams diced summer squash
- 120 grams diced mushrooms
- 120 grams diced cauliflower
- 120 grams diced asparagus
- 120 grams diced sweet red pepper
- 2 teaspoons vegetable oil
- ¼ teaspoon salt
- ¼ teaspoon ground black pepper
- 1/4 teaspoon seasoning, or more to taste
- 1 lettuce head

Instructions

- Preheat the air fryer to 180 degrees C.
- Add vegetables, oil, salt, pepper, and desired seasoning to a bowl. Toss to coat; arrange in fryer basket.
- Cook vegetables for 10 minutes, stirring after 5 minutes.
- Remove the vegetables, add the lettuce, mix well and add balsamic vinegar, olive oil and salt.

265. Paneer Cheese Balls

 Serving size:
4

 Preparation time:
10 minutes

 Cooking time:
10 minutes

 Total time:
20 minutes

Ingredients

- 130 grams Paneer crumbled
- 130 grams cheese grated
- 1 large potato (boiled and mashed)
- 1 large onion chopped finely
- 2 green chillies chopped finely
- 1 teaspoon red chilli flakes
- Salt to taste
- 4 tablespoons coriander leaves chopped finely
- 60 grams all purpose flour
- 50 ml. water
- 130 grams breadcrumbs as needed

Instructions

- Pre-heat air fryer to 180 degree C.

- Take all ingredients except flour and mix well then shape it into small balls.
- Add the all purpose flour in a bowl, add water and mix well to a smooth batter.
- Take a ball and dip in the batter. Then roll it in the bread-crumbs.
- Place it in air fryer basket and bake for 12 to 15 mins.
- Remove and serve.

266. Vegetable Filled Bread Rolls

 Serving size:
2

 Preparation time:
15minutes

 Cooking time:
5 minutes

 Total time:
20 minutes

Ingredients

- 1 tablespoon olive oil
- 1 bag broccoli slaw
- 8 white mushrooms diced
- 1 tablespoon garlic minced
- 1 tablespoon fresh ginger finely minced
- 1 can water chestnuts diced
- 20 ml. coconut aminos or soy sauce
- 1 teaspoon sesame oil
- 1/2-1 teaspoon chili flakes depending on heat preference

Egg Roll Assembly Items:

- 8 full size wonton wrappers
- 30 ml. water for sealing the edges

Instructions

- In a large pan, add olive oil. When heated, pour in broccoli slaw and cook for a few minutes until wilted. Add in diced mushrooms, garlic, ginger and diced water chestnuts.
- Once all the vegetables are wilted and tender, add in aminos or soy sauce, sesame oil, chilli flakes. Taste and add salt and pepper as neccesary. Take off heat and set aside.
- Assembling the Egg Rolls:
- Preheat the air fryer to 200 degrees C. Meanwhile, lay the egg roll wrapper so the points (corners) are on the bottom and top like a diamond. Using your finger, moisten all of the edges of the egg roll wrapper with water.
- Now, spread a spoonful of filling in the middle of the wrapper, in a horizontal line. Next, fold the bottom corner of the egg roll wrapper up and over the filling and push the filling tight into the wrapper.
- Then each side, one by one over on each other, being sure to moisten each edge with water so it sticks closed. Roll completely closed and moisten any open edges so they stay

closed. Repeat with the other egg rolls and then spray each side with cooking spray.

267. Parsnip Bake

 Serving size:
4

 Preparation time:
5 minutes

 Cooking time:
10 minutes

Total time:
15 minutes

Ingredients

- 4 medium parsnips
- 1 olive oil spray
- Salt
- Drizzle of honey (optional)

Instructions

- Preheat air fryer to 200°C.
- Cut parsnips into 2-3 inch pieces.
- Place parsnips in air fryer basket
- Spray parsnips with oil, add a pinch of salt, shake the basket and spray with oil again
- Optional: drizzle honey over the parsnips
- Set parsnips to air fry for 10-15 minutes
- The exact time will depend on how efficient your air fryer is. Check after 10 minutes, and air fry parsnips for longer if they need it.
- The parsnips are ready when they are tender and starting to turn golden brown.

268. Roasted Brussel Sprouts with Pine Nuts

 Serving size:
8

 Preparation time:
10 minutes

 Cooking time:
15 minutes

 Total time:
25 minutes

Ingredients

- 30 grams pine nuts, crushed
- 1 kg brussel sprouts
- 1 large red onion
- 1 tablespoon olive oil
- Salt
- Pepper
- 2 tablespoons lemon juice

Instructions

- Place the pine nuts in a single layer in the basket of an air fryer. Air-fry at 200 degrees C until the colour becomes golden, about 14 minutes, turning once halfway through.
- Toss the brussel sprouts, onion, oil, salt and pepper in a large bowl. Place about half of the brussel sprouts mixture in a single layer in the air fryer basket. Air-fry at 200 degrees C until browned and crispy, 14 to 16 minutes, turning once halfway through. Transfer to a serving platter. Repeat with the remaining brussel sprouts mixture. Drizzle with lemon juice; sprinkle with thyme. Crumble the cooked pinenuts over the top.

269. Mediterranean Vegetable Bowl

 Serving size:
4

 Preparation time:
10 minutes

 Cooking time:
15 minutes

Total time:
25 minutes

Ingredients

- 1 red pepper chopped
- 1 red onion chopped
- 250 grams brussel sprouts halved lengthwise
- 1 large yellow squash sliced
- 1 tablespoon olive oil
- 1 teaspoon garlic powder
- ½ teaspoon onion powder
- ½ teaspoon oregano
- 1 teaspoon salt
- ½ teaspoon black pepper

Instructions

- Place all the vegetables, olive oil and seasoning together in a large bowl and toss well to combine.
- Preheat the air fryer to 200°C. Arrange a single layer of the vegetables in the air fryer basket. Air fry for 10-15 minutes, shaking the air fryer basket once or twice during cooking to ensure even cooking.
- Serve immediately with protein of choice.

270. Hearty Carrot Roast

 Serving size:
4

 Preparation time:
5 minutes

 Cooking time:
15 minutes

 Total time:
20 minutes

Ingredients

- Olive oil
- Salt
- Pepper
- 300 grams carrots

Instructions

- Peel carrots and cut into chunks. Cut any larger pieces in half to make all pieces a similar size.
- Preheat air fryer to 200 degrees C.
- Toss carrots in about 1 teaspoon of oil.
- Place carrots in air fryer and cook for 15-18 minutes, shaking every few minutes.
- Test carrots with a fork for tenderness. They are done when it glides through the carrot easily.
- Add salt and pepper to taste and shake basket to coat.
- Serve and enjoy immediately.

271. Lemon Pepper Bites

	Serving size: 24		**Preparation time:** 10 minutes
	Cooking time: 12 minutes		**Total time:** 22 minutes

Ingredients

- 120 grams Jalapeños, diced (approximately 4 medium jalapeños)
- 12 slices bacon, cooked and diced
- 2 spring onions, diced
- 200 grams cream cheese, softened to room temperature
- 150 grams cheddar cheese, grated
- Salt and pepper to taste
- 1/4 teaspoon garlic powder
- 1/4 teaspoon onion powder
- 160 grams Panko breadcrumbs
- 3 eggs, large
- 100 grams flour
- 2 tablespoons milk

Instructions

- In a medium mixing bowl add softened cream cheese, grated cheddar, jalapeños, spring onions, chopped bacon, garlic powder, onion powder, salt and pepper and mix until incorporated.
- Line a baking sheet with wax paper. Scoop and roll the mixture into balls and place on the baking tray.
- In a small, shallow bowl add the flour. In another small, shallow bowl whisk together eggs and milk. Place breadcrumbs in a third shallow bowl.
- Roll a jalapeño ball in the flour, dip it in the egg mixture, and then roll it in the breadcrumbs. Repeat this process with all of your balls.
- Spray the basket of your air fryer with cooking spray and/or baking paper and preheat to 200°C.
- Line your air fryer basket with the bites, being sure to leave room between each one. Air Fry for 10-12 minutes, or until golden brown. Let the bites sit for a few minutes before removing them from the air fryer basket.
- Repeat with the remaining bites.
- Serve with dipping sauce of your choice if desired.

272. Beetroot Chips with Broccoli

	Serving size: 4		**Preparation time:** 10 minutes
	Cooking time: 20 minutes		**Total time:** 30 minutes

Ingredients

- 250 grams fresh beetroot, peeled and cut into chips form
- 100 grams broccoli
- 1 tablespoon extra virgin olive oil
- 1/2 teaspoon kosher salt
- Pinch of ground black pepper

Instructions

- Add the beetroot, broccoli oil, salt and pepper to a large bowl and toss to combine.
- Place the beetroot in the air fryer basket and air fry on 200 degrees C for 18-20 minutes, or until fork tender. Stir or shake them a few times while air frying.

273. Baked Green Beans

	Serving size: 4		**Preparation time:** 10 minutes
	Cooking time: 20 minutes		**Total time:** 30 minutes

Ingredients

- 300 grams fresh green beans
- 1 tablespoon olive oil
- 1/2 teaspoon kosher salt
- 1/4 teaspoon freshly ground black pepper

Instructions

- Heat an air fryer to 200°C. Meanwhile, trim the stem end from 1 pound green beans. Transfer to a large bowl. Add 1 tablespoon olive oil, 1/2 teaspoon kosher salt, and 1/4 teaspoon black pepper, and toss to combine.
- Air fry in batches if needed: Add the green beans to the air fryer basket and arrange into a single layer. Air fry until the green beans are crisp-tender, 8 minutes. If you prefer your green beans a little more tender, give the basket a toss to redistribute the beans, then cook for 2 more minutes.

274. Baked Garlic Mushrooms

	Serving size: 3		Preparation time: 2 minutes
	Cooking time: 10 minutes		Total time: 12 minutes

Ingredients

- 220 grams mushrooms , washed and dried
- 1-2 tablespoons oil
- 1/2 teaspoon garlic powder
- 1 teaspoon Worcestershire or soy sauce
- Kosher salt , to taste
- black pepper , to taste
- lemon wedges (optional)
- 1 Tablespoon chopped parsley

Instructions

- Cut mushrooms in half or quarters (depending on preferred size). Add to bowl then toss with oil, garlic powder, Worcestershire/soy sauce, salt and pepper.
- Air fry at 220°C for 10-12 minutes, tossing and shaking half way through.
- Squeeze lemon and top with chopped parsley.

275. Carrot and Broccoli Roast with Cumin

	Serving size: 4		Preparation time: 10 minutes
	Cooking time: 15 minutes		Total time: 25 minutes

Ingredients

- 380 grams broccoli
- 250 grams carrots
- 1 large pepper
- 1 large onion

- ½ teaspoon black pepper
- 1 tablespoon olive oil
- 1 teaspoon cumin
- Salt to taste

Instructions

- Wash and cut the vegetables into bite size.
- Add them to a bowl and season with salt, black pepper, cumin, and olive oil. Mix so that the veggies are covered in the seasoning.
- Add the seasoned veggies into the air fryer basket and air fry at a temperature of 175 degrees C for 15 minutes.
- Toss the veggies in the basket halfway through cooking so that all sides are crisp.
- When done, take out the basket and serve.

276. Traditional Jacked Potatoes

	Serving size: 3		Preparation time: 10 minutes
	Cooking time: 40 minutes		Total time: 50 minutes

Ingredients

- 3 russet potatoes (medium sized, scrubbed and rinsed)
- cooking spray (I used avocado oil spray)
- 1/2 teaspoon sea salt (use a bit less if you are using a finer salt, like table salt)
- 1/2 teaspoon garlic powder

Instructions

- Place your potatoes in the Air Fryer basket, and spray with cooking spray on both sides.
- Sprinkle sea salt and garlic on all sides, rotating the potatoes as you go.
- Use your hands to rub the potatoes to make sure everything gets evenly coated.
- Cook in the Air Fryer on 200 degrees C for about 40 to 50 minutes, until fork tender.

Bread

277. Banana Bread

Serving size: 8 servings	**Preparation time:** 10 minutes	**Cooking time:** 30 minutes	**Total time:** 40 minutes

Ingredients

- 80 grams plain flour
- ¼ teaspoon salt
- ¼ teaspoon baking soda
- 2 ripe bananas
- 30 grams granulated sugar
- 1 tablespoon vegetable oil
- 1 tablespoon sour cream
- ½ teaspoon pure vanilla extract
- 1 large egg
- 50 grams chopped walnuts

Instructions

- In a large bowl, whisk together flour, salt, and baking soda.
- Place bananas in a medium bowl and mash until very smooth with a fork or potato masher.
- Whisk in sugar, oil, sour cream, vanilla, and egg, making sure all ingredients are completely smooth.
- Fold into dry ingredients until just combined. Don't over-mix.
- Gently stir in walnuts if desired.
-
- Transfer the batter into a non-stick round baking tin and place the pan inside the air fryer basket. (you can also use the square, tall sided tin that came with your air fryer or any similar size air fryer-safe tin.)
- Bake at 200 degrees C for 33 to 37 minutes, or until toothpick test in the middle of the bread is clean.
- Allow to cool in the baking tin on a wire rack for at least 20 minutes before removing.

278. Bread Rolls

Serving size: 12 servings	**Preparation time:** 10 minutes	**Cooking time:** 10 minutes	**Total time:** 20 minutes

Ingredients

- 1 packet active dry yeast one packet
- 40 ml. warm water
- 250 grams plain flour
- 2 tablespoons granulated sugar
- ½ teaspoon salt
- 60 ml. milk
- 2 tablespoons unsalted butter softened
- 1 large egg

Instructions

- Add yeast to a bowl with warm water. Let the yeast sit in the warm water for about 3 to 5 minutes.
- Once the yeast has activated, add in the flour, sugar, milk, butter, and salt. Gently fold the ingredients together until they were well combined and it becomes slightly flaky.
- Turn the dough onto a floured surface and knead the dough until it is smooth and shape it into a ball.
- Place dough into a medium bowl with one tablespoon of olive or vegetable oil. Coat the ball of dough with the oil, and then wrap the bowl with cling film or a clean kitchen towel, then place in warm place until the dough rises to about double the size.
- Once the dough has doubled, punch down to release air. Divide the dough into 12 equal pieces and roll into balls. Place the rolls into a tin or directly into the basket individually, after spraying the basket with cooking spray.
- Coat the tops of the rolls with an egg wash. Air Fry at 220 degrees C for 8 to 10 minutes, until the tops of the rolls are golden brown.

279. Sourdough Bread

![serving] Serving size: 6	![prep] Preparation time: 10 minutes
![cooking] Cooking time: 20 minutes	![total] Total time: 30 minutes

Ingredients

- 130 grams bread flour
- 60 grams spelt flour
- 60 grams sourdough starter
- 1 tablespoon extra-virgin olive oil
- ½ teaspoon fine sea salt
- 40 ml. water

Instructions

- Combine bread flour, spelt flour, sourdough starter, oil, and salt in the bowl of stand mixer. Begin to knead using the dough hook. Add water until all the ingredients combine and begin to pull together; you may not need all the water. Knead on low speed for 5 minutes.
- Fold the dough into a ball. Place inside an air fryer-safe baking dish. Cover with cling film and allow to double in volume, 5 hours to overnight.
- Preheat the air fryer to 200 degrees C. Remove the vling film and score the loaf.
- Place the baking dish in the air fryer and cook until loaf is browned, about 20 minutes.
- An instant-read thermometer inserted into the centre should read at least 90 degrees C. Allow to cool before slicing.

280. Naan

![serving] Serving size: 4	![prep] Preparation time: 5 minutes
![cooking] Cooking time: 20 minutes	![total] Total time: 25 minutes

Ingredients

- 300 ml. warm water
- 1 tablespoon sugar
- 2 teaspoons active dry yeast
- 1 teaspoon salt
- 400 grams plain flour

Instructions

- Combine warm water, sugar and yeast in a bowl and let stand for 5 minutes until foamy.

- Add salt and flour and mix thoroughly.
- Knead the dough on a floured area for about 20 times and form into a tight ball. Put the dough in a well oiled bowl, cover with a damp towel, place in a warm area and allow 45 minutes to rise.
- Turn dough out onto a floured workspace and divide into 8 balls. Use a rolling pin to flatten.
- Spray each side with olive oil and cook in the air fryer for about 6 minutes on 220 degrees C.
- Remember to turn the Naan over about halfway through the cooking process and enjoy!

281. No Knead Bread

![serving] Serving size:	![prep] Preparation time:
![cooking] Cooking time:	![total] Total time:

Ingredients

- 250 grams plain flour
- 1 teaspoon salt
- 1 teaspoon instant yeast
- 50 ml. water on room temperature

Instructions

- Form the dough: In a big bowl mix the flour, salt, instant yeast and water. using a spatula or a wooden spoon, Mix it until well incorporated. The dough will be sticky and shaggy.
- Allow it to rise: You'll want to cover the bowl with cling film and let it sit on your counter or inside your unheated oven for 2 to 3 hours. During this time, the dough should double in size.
- Preheat the air fryer: Place a 6-inch round tin into the basket of your air fryer. Preheat the air fryer to 200°C for 20 minutes with the pan in it.
- Shape the dough: Meanwhile, flour your hands really well and also sprinkle a bit of flour over the dough. With your floured hands gently remove the dough from the bowl and roughly shape it into a ball. Take the ball of dough and place it over a piece of baking paper. Transfer the dough with the baking paper into a bowl and cover with a dry, clean kitchen towel until the pan has been preheated.
- Carefully, remove the tin from the air fryer basked, then lift the baking paper and drop it in the tin, with baking paper and all. You can also score the top of the dough with a sharp knife. This will not only make your bread look pretty, but it can also prevent it from cracking. Carefully cover the tin with tin foil, tightly seal the edges, and place the tin back into the air fryer basket, shut the lid, and then it's bake time.

- Bake the bread: Bake for 20 minutes then open the basket and carefully remove the foil. Close the basket and bake for another 10 minutes or until golden brown. The bread is cooked when it sounds hollow when you tap it. I turned the bread upside down after 5 minutes to allow it to brown on the bottom too.

282. Milk Bread Rolls

 Serving size:

 Preparation time:
10 minutes

 **Cooking time:**
18 minutes

 Total time:
28 minutes

Ingredients

- 600 grams plain flour
- 2 large eggs lightly beaten
- 2 tablespoons butter room temperature; plus more to sprinkle
- 2 tablespoons sugar.plus 1 tablespoon
- 1 ½ teaspoon Kosher salt
- 2 ¼ teaspoon instant yeast or 1 packet
- 1 tablespoon lukewarm milk
- 1 tablespoon milk to mix with the egg yolk
- 1 egg yolk To mix with the 1 tablespoon milk

Instructions

- Warm the milk in the microwave. The temperature should read no more than 110 degrees. Set aside. Then beat the two eggs in a separate bowl. Set aside.
- Using a sieve or flour sifter, sift 5 cups of flour into a large standing mixing bowl.
- Add the sugar, salt, and yeast. Stir in the baking machine. While the machine is running, slowly add the milk. Once the milk is added, then add the beaten eggs. Use a baking spatula to help scrape the side of the bowl so that all of the flour is incorporated.
- While mixing, add the butter and set the timer to 12 minutes and increase the speed to do 2. Knead in the machine until the timer goes off.
- Lightly sprinkle flour to a clean surface and place the dough on the floured surface. Shape the dough into a ball using the fold under method. See pictures in the post.
- Place the dough in a large clean bowl, preferably lightly oiled to avoid sticking. Cover the bowl with a clean kitchen towel and let rise for 1 hour in a warm location, or until the dough has doubled in size.
- Flour a clean surface, punch a whole in the middle of the dough, and transfer the dough to the floured surface.

- Lightly press down onto the dough to the dough and shape it into squares.
- Bake the bread on 200° C for 15 minutes.
- Brush with melted butter and enjoy.

283. Dinner Rolls

 Serving size:
8

 Preparation time:
5 minutes

 Cooking time:
5 minutes

 Total time:
10 minutes

Ingredients

- 1 bag frozen dinner rolls
- 60 grams melted butter
- 2 tablespoons Italian seasoning

Instructions

- Spread the frozen rolls onto the baking sheet or in the air fryer basket.
- In a small bowl, mix the melted butter with the herbs.
- Brush on the butter and herb mixture onto the rolls.
- Set in the air fryer at 220 degrees C, for 5 minutes.

284. Wholemeal Irish Soda Bread

 Serving size:
6

 Preparation time:
10 minutes

 Cooking time:
1 hour

 Total time:
1 hour and 10 minutes

Ingredients

- 130 grams golden raisins
- 220 ml. buttermilk
- 400 grams plain flour
- 2 teaspoons baking soda
- 2 teaspoons baking powder
- 50 grams brown sugar
- 1 teaspoon pure vanilla extract
- 1 teaspoon salt
- 1 teaspoon caraway seeds
- 1 teaspoon ground cinnamon

Instructions

- Start by soaking the raisins for about 10 to 15 minutes in the buttermilk.
- In a large bowl, mix the flour, baking powder, baking soda, salt, caraway seeds, brown sugar, and ground cinnamon. Mix

in the buttermilk, raisins, and pure vanilla extract. Mix well, combining all of the ingredients.

- Sprinkle some flour on a flat surface, then transfer your dough to that surface. Knead the dough for about 4 to 5 minutes. If you find that your dough is still sticky, add some more flour until it sticks together.
- Place the dough into the air fryer basket, make an X on the dough. This will help the steam escape, creating a moist and delicious loaf of bread.
- Set the temperature to 220 degrees C, air fryer setting for 25-30 minutes. When you can insert a toothpick into the dough's center, and it comes out clean, remove it from the air fryer.
- Plate, serve and enjoy!

285. Flatbread

Serving size: 6	**Preparation time:** 10 minutes
Cooking time: 10 minutes	**Total time:** 20 minutes

Ingredients

- 60 grams flour, plus extra for dusting
- pinch of salt
- 4 tablespoons Greek-style yoghurt
- extra virgin olive oil spray
- 1/2 teaspoon sesame seeds (optional)
- 1/2 teaspoon cumin (optional)

Instructions

- Put flour into a large bowl and stir in the salt. Add yogurt and use your hands to form a soft, shaggy dough. Don't over mix. If desired, add sesame seeds or a sprinkle of ground cumin to the flour to give your bread an extra depth of flavour.
- Pour out onto a lightly floured surface and use your hands to gently knead the dough until it just comes together in a loose ball.
- Divide the dough in half and roll each into a rough ball. The dough will be slightly sticky, so to make it easier to work with, dust your hands with a little flour if necessary. Roll out balls into discs about 5mm thick.
- Place the dough piece inside the air fryer basket, in a single layer. Spray with oil.
- Set the temperature to 200 degrees C for 6 minutes. Cook until golden brown and beginning to bubble.
- Serve.

286. Scottish Shortbread

Serving size: 10	**Preparation time:** 15 minutes
Cooking time: 10 minutes	**Total time:** 25 minutes

Ingredients

- 250 grams butter, softened
- 130 grams packed brown sugar
- 600 grams plain flour

Instructions

- Preheat air fryer to 220°C. Cream butter and brown sugar until light and fluffy. Add 3-3/4 cups flour; mix well.
- Turn dough onto a floured surface; knead for 5 minutes, adding enough remaining flour to form a soft dough.
- Roll to thickness. Cut into 3x1-in. strips; prick with a fork. Place 1 in. apart on an ungreased tray in air-fryer basket.
- Cook until cookies are set and lightly browned, 7-9 minutes. Cool in basket 2 minutes; remove to wire racks to cool completely.

287. Easy White Bread

Serving size: 10	**Preparation time:** 1 hour and 15 minutes
 **Cooking time:** 12 minutes	**Total time:** 1 hour and 25 minutes

Ingredients

- 50 ml. water warm
- 2 tablespoons sugar
- 1 1/4 teaspoon active dry yeast
- 40 ml. milk warm
- 1/2 teaspoon salt
- 1 tablespoon vegetable oil
- 350 grams flour
- 1 tablespoon butter melted

Instructions

- In a medium mixing bowl whisk warm water, sugar, and yeast together. Allow to sit for 5-10 minutes or until it appears bubbly and foamy.
- Add milk and whisk again. Add salt and vegetable oil. Whisk again. Add half of the flour at a time, combining well until it forms a ball.

- Knead the dough on a floured surface for about 5 minutes. Then place the dough in an oiled bowl, rolling it to cover all sides in oil.
- Cover the bowl with a thick kitchen towel and allow the dough to rise for about an hour. This time will depend on the temperate and humidity level of your kitchen.
- When it doubles in size, punch it down and knead it for 1 minute.
- Split dough in half and form each piece into a loaf shape. Put dough in oiled mini loaf tins. Cover with a kitchen towel and allow the dough to rise (about 30 minutes) again until it is about an inch above the pan.
- Brush each loaf with melted butter. Place tins in your air fryer basket. Air fry at 200 degrees C for 12 minutes.

288. Garlic Bread

 Serving size:
5

 Preparation time:
5 minutes

 Cooking time:
5 minutes

 Total time:
10 minutes

Ingredients

- 4-5 tablespoons unsalted butter, softened
- 3 tablespoons chopped garlic
- 70 grams parmesan cheese, or more, grated
- 1 tablespoon dried parsley
- 1 baguette, sliced

Instructions

- Mix together the softened butter, chopped garlic, parmesan cheese, and dried parsley.
- Spread the mixture onto sliced baguettes or bread of your choice.
- Place the garlic bread into your air fryer basket in a single layer.
- Air fry at 220 degrees C for 5 minutes.

289. Cloud Bread

 Serving size:
8

Preparation time:
5 minutes

Cooking time:
25 minutes

Total time:
30 minutes

Ingredients

- 6 large eggs. separated and divided
- 90 grams cream cheese. softened
- 1/4 teaspoon cream of tartar

Instructions

- Preheat the Air fryer to 170 degrees C. In one mixing bowl, add the egg whites. In a separate bowl, add the egg yolks.
- Add the cream of tartar into the egg whites. Using a stick mixer, beat together until stiff peaks form and set that aside. Add the cream cheese into the egg yolks and beat that together until combined and smooth. Fold it through the egg white mixture.
- Form 8 portions of the cloud bread mixture. Place four portions onto the air fryer basket and ai fry for 27-30 minutes, or until golden.

290. Blueberry Quick Bread

 Serving size:
4

 Preparation time:
5 minutes

 Cooking time:
30 minutes

 Total time:
35 minutes

Ingredients

- 220 ml. milk
- 250 grams of bisquick
- 50 grams protein powder
- 3 eggs
- 100 grams frozen blueberries

Instructions

- Mix all ingredients together until combined. The mixture will be thick.
- Place into a loaf tin and air fry at 220 degrees C for 30 minutes.
- To check to see if the bread is done, insert a toothpick, if the bread is done, it should come out clean

Pizza

291. Pepperoni Pizza

Serving size: 2 servings	**Preparation time:** 10 minutes	**Cooking time:** 10 minutes	**Total time:** 20 minutes

Ingredients

- plain flour
- fresh pizza dough
- non-stick cooking spray
- 100 ml. pizza sauce
- 130 grams mozzarella cheese
- 6 slices pepperoni

Instructions

- Sprinkle a clean surface with flour, and place the dough on top. Sprinkle the top of the dough with flour. Use your hands to stretch the dough out into a shape that will fit in air fryer basket.
- Preheat air fryer to 190°C. Spray air fryer basket with non-stick cooking spray.
- Transfer pizza dough to basket of air fryer.
- Spread sauce over dough, leaving a border. Sprinkle mozzarella cheese over sauce and place pepperonis on top.
- Cook pizza for 10 to 12 minutes, depending on desired level of crispiness.

292. Tofu Pizza

Serving size: 2 servings	**Preparation time:** 10 minutes	**Cooking time:** 15 minutes	**Total time:** 25 minutes

Ingredients

- 130 grams thick chopped firm tofu
- 4 cooked naans
- 1 large Onion - thinly chopped
- ½ bowl chopped sweet peppers
- 1 jalapeno - thinly chopped
- 2 tablespoons sweetcorn
- 1 tablespoon red chilli flakes
- 2 tablespoon Tandoori Masala
- 1 teaspoon Italian seasoning (optional)
- Salt - as per taste
- Red chilli powder - optional
- 3 tablespoons Ketchup
- 1 teaspoon chilli sauce
- 130 grams cheese - you can use any cheese of choice (or vegan option)

Instructions

- In a bowl, add ketchup, chilli sauce, tandoori masala, salt, pepper, and whisk everything.
- Add chopped Paneer, mix everything using a form (making sure the mixture coats each tofu cube). Set aside.
- In another bowl, add chopped onion, peppers/sweet peppers, corn, Italian seasoning, salt, and cheese. Mix everything and set aside.
- Take the cooked naan, add 2-3 tbsp of the tofu mix.
- Add 2 tbsp of veggie mix.
- Preheat the air fryer at 170 degrees C.
- Remove the air fryer basket, place prepped naan pizza (1-2).
- Air Fry for 10 minutes.
- Remove, slice, and serve.

293. 3 Types of Meat Pizza

 Serving size:
4

 Preparation time:
15 minutes

 Cooking time:
20 minutes

 Total time:
35 minutes

Ingredients

- 2 pieces of pizza dough
- pizza sauce
- 2 sausages, browned
- 4 strips bacon, fried crisp and crumbled
- 100 grams pepperoni (enough to your liking)
- 1 pepper, sliced thin
- 1 onion, sliced thin
- 50 grams sliced black olives
- 100 grams sliced mushrooms, fresh
- 2 tomatoes, sliced thin (i used small tomatoes out of the garden)
- salt & fresh ground pepper to taste
- 1 teaspoon red pepper flakes to taste, optional
- 70 grams mozzarella cheese, shredded

Instructions

- Preheat air fryer to 220 degrees C.
- Spread a thin layer of pizza sauce over dough. Then start layering with 3 meats, peppers, onions, olives, mushrooms and thinly sliced tomatoes and then topped with shredded mozzarella cheese.
- Bake for 20 minutes or until crust is golden brown around the edges.

294. Ground Beef Pizza

 Serving size:
2

 Preparation time:
5 minutes

 Cooking time:
7 minutes

 Total time:
12 minutes

Ingredients

- Buffalo mozzarella
- Pizza dough 1 12-inch dough will make 2 personal sized pizzas
- Olive oil
- Tomato sauce
- Optional toppings to finish: fresh basil, parmesan cheese, pepper flakes
- 30 grams minced beef

Instructions

- Prep: Preheat air fryer to 190°C. Spray air fryer basket well with oil. Pat mozzarella dry with paper towels (to prevent a soggy pizza).
- Cook Crust: Roll out pizza dough to the size of your air fryer basket. Carefully transfer it to the air fryer, then brush lightly with a teaspoon or so of olive oil. Cook for 3 minutes.
- Assemble: To the precooked crust, spoon on a light layer of tomato sauce and sprinkle with chunks of buffalo mozzarella, and minced beef.
- Bake: For about 7 minutes until crust is crispy and cheese has melted.
- Optionally top with basil, grated parmesan, and pepper flakes just before serving.

295. Caramelized Onion Pizza

 Serving size:
4

 Preparation time:
5 minutes

 Cooking time:
10 minutes

 Total time:
15 minutes

Ingredients

- 1 large onion, thinly sliced
- 3 tablespoons unsalted butter
- 1/2 tablespoon olive oil
- 130 grams thick cut bacon
- 2 naan bread pieces
- 1 teaspoon fresh thyme
- fresh cracked pepper
- 130 grams shredded gruyere cheese, mozzarella cheese is a good substitute

Instructions

- Preheat the air fryer to 200 grams C and line a rimmed baking sheet with foil. Arrange the bacon in a single layer on the baking sheet and bake for 15-20 minutes or until crispy. Chop the bacon and set aside.
- While the bacon is cooking, prepare the onions. Melt butter and olive oil in a non-stick pan over a medium heat, then add the onions and toss to coat. Let them sit undisturbed for 5-8 minutes, then stir occasionally until the onions turn golden brown.
- Sprinkle half the cheese over each piece of naan and bake at 200 degrees C for 4-5 minutes or until the cheese has melted.
- Then top the naan with the rest of the cheese, fresh thyme, bacon, caramelized onions, and fresh cracked pepper and bake for 5-10 minutes or until the cheese has melted and the naan is toasted.

296. Pepper Pizza

 Serving size:
4

 Preparation time:
10 minutes

 Cooking time:
20 minutes

 Total time:
30 minutes

Ingredients

- 4 peppers, halved and cored
- 1 tablespoons extra-virgin olive oil
- Kosher salt
- Freshly ground black pepper
- 50 ml. pizza sauce
- 220 grams shredded mozzarella
- 60 grams finely grated Parmesan
- 100 grams mini pepperoni
- 1 tablespoons chopped parsley

Instructions

- Preheat oven to 200°C. On a sheet tray, drizzle peppers with olive oil and season with salt and pepper.
- Spoon sauce onto each pepper half. Sprinkle with mozzarella and Parmesan and top with pepperoni. Bake for 10 to 15 minutes, until the peppers are crisp-tender and the cheese is melted.
- Garnish with parsley before serving.

297. Mozzarella Pizza

 Serving size:
2

 Preparation time:
20 minutes

 Cooking time:
15 minutes

 Total time:
35 minutes

Ingredients

- 1 large Sourdough Bread Loaf
- 40 grams unsalted butter
- 1 tablespoon dried oregano
- 1 teaspoon garlic salt
- 130 grams shredded mozzarella cheese
- 60 grams grated Parmesan Cheese
- 130 ml. marinra or pizza sauce

Instructions

- Slice your bread lengthwise and then crosswise, careful not to cut through the bread.

- Melt your butter, and then add your oregano and garlic salt. Sprinkle the melted butter mixture into the cavities of the bread.
- In a small bowl, add your two cheese, toss to mix. Fill the cavities with the cheese mixtures, add the rest of the butter mixture on top. Using foil, wrap up your bread tightly.
- Add your bread to the air fryer basket, and set the temperature to 200 degrees C, air fryer setting for 10 to 15 minutes.
- Remove the bread from the foil and air fry until the cheese is melted. Serve with marinara sauce.
- Plate, serve, and enjoy!

298. Quick Pizza

 Serving size:
2

 Preparation time:
3 minutes

 Cooking time:
7 minutes

 Total time:
10 minutes

Ingredients

- 1 pizza crust/base
- 50 ml. pizza sauce
- 50 grams mozzarella cheese
- Desired toppings
- 60 grams prosciutto

Instructions

- Preheat the air fryer to 220 degrees C.
- Meanwhile, prepare your pizza by placing pizza crust on an air fryer baking paper liner.
- Add pizza sauce, cheese, and other desired toppings to the pizza crust.
- Place the pizza in the air fryer basket and cook for 7-8 minutes, until the cheese has melted and browned.

299. Cheeseburger Pizza

 Serving size:
2

 Preparation time:
20 minutes

 Cooking time:
10 minutes

 Total time:
30 minutes

Ingredients

- 455 grams minced beef
- 1-2 tablespoons steak seasoning amount varies depending on what brand you use
- 450 grams pizza dough

- 120 grams fry sauce plus more for dipping
- 1/2 onion diced
- 120 grams shredded mozzarella
- 120 grams grated strong cheddar
- 70 grams pickle slices more or less to taste
- 70 grams shredded lettuce more to less to taste
- 1 large roma tomato diced

Instructions

- Place pizza stone into oven and preheat oven to 550 degrees F.
- Heat a large non-stick pan over a medium heat.
- Add in minced beef and steak seasoning.
- Cook, breaking up the meat as you go, until the beef is no longer pink.
- Taste and re-season, if necessary, then drain grease and set aside.
- Roll out pizza dough.
- Spread with fry sauce.
- Top with cooked beef, then diced onions.
- Sprinkle evenly with both cheeses.
- Bake on the hot pizza stones in the preheated air fryer for 10 minutes on 220 degrees C, or until the crust is cooked and the cheese has melted.
- Remove from oven and top with pickles, lettuce, and roma tomatoes.
- Cut and serve with more fry sauce for dipping!

300. Vegetable Pizza

 Serving size:
5

 Preparation time:
30 minutes

 Cooking time:
30 minutes

 Total time:
1 hour

Ingredients

Base
- 500 grams plain flour
- 2 tablespoons flax seeds
- 2-½ teaspoon dry yeast with 40 ml. warm water
- ½ teaspoon sugar to activate the yeast
- oil
- 2 teaspoon salt

Toppings
- 10 tablespoon Pizza sauce. 2 tablespoon per pizza
- 500 grams mixed vegetables (olives,baby corn,mushrooms)
- 100 grams cheese by choice

- Dried oregano flakes
- 2-3 teaspoon Olive oil
- Salt to season

Instructions

- Take a portion of the dough. Roll it into a round flat base on a crisping tray for the air fryer, or you can do it on a baking sheet and move it to the air fryer basket.
- Spread the tomato paste on the base.
- Cook the base in air fryer (pre heated) for 7 minutes at 200 degrees C . Spray oil once in between.
- Once its cooked, add the cheese and toppings.
- Season with salt and olive oil and further cooks for 7-8 minutes.

301. Sausage Pizza

 Serving size:
4

 Preparation time:
30 minutes

 Cooking time:
10 minutes

 Total time:
40 minutes

Ingredients

- 1 loaf frozen bread dough, thawed
- 130 ml. pizza sauce
- 130 grams bulk Italian sausage, cooked and drained
- 130 grams shredded part-skim mozzarella cheese
- 1 small green pepper, sliced into rings
- 1 teaspoon dried oregano
- Crushed red pepper flakes, optional

Instructions

- On a lightly floured surface, roll and stretch dough into four 4-in. circles. Cover and let rest for 10 minutes.
- Preheat air fryer to 200°C.
- Roll and stretch each piece of dough into a 6-in. circle. Place 1 crust in greased air fryer.
- Carefully spread with half the pizza sauce, half the sausage, half the cheese, a fourth of the green pepper rings and a pinch of oregano.
- Cook until crust is golden brown, 6-8 minutes.
- If desired, sprinkle with red pepper flakes. Repeat with remaining ingredients.

302. Tomato Pizza

 Serving size:
2

 Preparation time:
5 minutes

 Cooking time:
8 minutes

Total time:
13 minutes

Ingredients

- 1 thin crust pre-made cooked pizza crust
- 3 tablespoons pizza sauce
- 1 campari tomato thinly sliced
- fresh basil
- 1 teaspoon olive oil

Instructions

- Spread the pizza sauce over the prepared pizza crust. Place the tomato slices evenly apart on the crust. Add the tomato slices.
- Place in the basket of the air fryer and cook at 170°C for 5-8 minutes or until the cheese is melted.
- Remove the pizza from the air fryer and add the fresh basil and olive oil.
- Serve immediately.

303. Ham Pizza

 Serving size:
4

 Preparation time:
5 minutes

 Cooking time:
8 minutes

 Total time:
13 minutes

Ingredients

- Naan Bread
- Marinara Sauce
- Mozzarella Cheese
- Pineapple Chunks
- Ham Chunks

Instructions

- Pre-heat air fryer 200 degrees C, air fryer setting.
- Spread marinara sauce on the naan bread. If you like crust, leave a little bread showing on the edges.
- Sprinkle the mozzarella cheese on top of the marinara.
- Add the ham and pineapple.
- Place in the air fryer for 5-8 minutes or until cheese and veggies have fully cooked.
- Plate, serve, and enjoy!

304. Naan Bread Pizza

 Serving size:
2

 Preparation time:
3 minutes

 Cooking time:
7 minutes

 Total time:
10 minutes

Ingredients

- 4 pieces naan
- 50 ml. pizza sauce
- 130 grams mozzarella cheese
- 130 grams vegetables by choice

Instructions

- Place naan in single layer in the basket or on the rack of your air fryer. Work in batches if necessary.
- Air fry at 200°C for 2 minutes or until slightly crispy on the edges. Remove from air fryer carefully.
- Spread pizza sauce onto naan pieces, followed by cheese and toppings of your choice. Return to air fryer.
- Air fry at 200°C for another 5 minutes, or until cheese is melted naan are browned and crispy.

305. Cheddar Pizza

 Serving size:
2

 Preparation time:
2 minutes

 Cooking time:
6 minutes

 Total time:
8 minutes

Ingredients

- 2 slices bread
- ½ Tablespoon butter (softened or melted)
- 30 ml. pizza sauce
- 70 grams cheddar cheese
- Toppings
- 2 Slices Canadian bacon (cut into quarters)

Instructions

- Spread butter on one side of each slice of bread. Place bread in the air fryer basket, buttered side up.
- Set temperature to 200°C and air fry for 3 to 4 mins. Turn bread slices over.
- Add the toppings.
- Air fry at 200°C for 3 minutes or until cheese is melted.

306. Just Cheese Pizza

 Serving size:
2

 Preparation time:
10 minutes

 Cooking time:
10 minutes

 Total time:
20 minutes

Ingredients

- 2 slices Italian or sourdough bread
- 1 tablespoon softened butter, divided
- 3 slices deli-sliced mozzarella cheese
- 2–3 teaspoons pasta or pizza sauce
- 9 slices pepperoni
- ⅛ teaspoon Italian seasoning

Instructions

- Preheat the air fryer to 220°C.
- Place bread on a plate or baking paper for easy clean up. Butter one side of the bread and turn it over so the buttered side is down.
- Place 2 slices of mozzarella cheese on top, then evenly spread 2-3 teaspoons sauce over cheese. Add sliced pepperoni, then sprinkle with Italian seasoning. Top with the remaining slice of cheese and slice of bread.
- Butter the top of the sandwich and place it in the preheated air fryer.
- Cook for 3-4 minutes or until golden brown. Carefully turn the sandwich over and cook another 3-4 minutes or until golden brown.
- Remove and slice with a pizza cutter. Enjoy!

307. Chicken Pizza

 Serving size:
2

 Preparation time:
5 minutes

 Cooking time:
10 minutes

 Total time:
15 minutes

Ingredients

- 2 Lavash Bread cut into half
- 60 ml. BBQ Sauce
- 130 grams cooked boneless skinless chicken breast shredded
- 1 red onion sliced
- 130 grams Mozzarella cheese shredded
- coriander to garnish, if desired

Instructions

- Cut each the lavash bread in to half, so that it fits in the air fryer.
- Spread about 2 tablespoons of BBQ sauce on each lavash half.
- Sprinkle 2 tablespoons of mozzarella cheese on top of the BBQ sauce.
- Top each half with half of the cooked, shredded chicken and 1/8 of sliced red onion.
- Sprinkle the top with another 2 tablespoons of mozzarella cheese. Each lavash bread half will get 4 tablespoons of mozzarella cheese.
- Preheat your air fryer to 200 degrees C, if your air fryer has a preheat option. If not, ignore this step.
- Carefully place one lavash half in the air fryer basket.
- Air fry at 200°C for 5 minutes or until cheese is nicely melted and the crust is lightly browned and crispy . Remove from the air fryer.
- Repeat with the remaining lavash pizza halves.
- Garnish with torn coriander leaves, if desired. Serve immediately.

Pasta

308. Pasta Chips

Serving size: 6 servings	**Preparation time:** 15 minutes	**Cooking time:** 10 minutes	**Total time:** 25 minutes

Ingredients

- 1 package rigatoni noodles, cooked al dente and drained
- 3 tablespoons olive oil, divided
- 1 teaspoon garlic, minced
- 1 teaspoon kosher salt
- ½ teaspoon black pepper
- 100 grams parmesan cheese, grated

Instructions

- Preheat air fryer to 200°C.
- In a large bowl, add cooked noodles. Drizzle with 1 tablespoon of olive oil. Toss to coat.
- Add the pasta noodles to your air fryer rack/basket in a single layer.
- Air fry for 8-10 minutes, or until golden brown.
- Transfer pasta chips to a bowl.
- In a separate bowl, combine the remaining oil, garlic, salt, and pepper. Mix well.
- Pour the oil mixture over the pasta chips and toss to coat.
- Top with parmesan cheese and serve with your favorite dipping sauce, like marinara or garlic sauce.

309. Mac & Cheese

Serving size: 2 servings	**Preparation time:** 5 minutes	**Cooking time:** 20 minutes	**Total time:** 25 minutes

Ingredients

- 1 package elbow macaroni
- 130 ml. water
- 50 ml. double cream
- 130 grams mature cheddar cheese shredded and separated
- 1 teaspoon dry mustard
- ½ teaspoon kosher salt
- ½ teaspoon black pepper
- 1/4 teaspoon garlic powder

Instructions

- Combine elbow macaroni, water, cream, ¾ of the cheese, dry mustard, kosher salt, black pepper, and garlic powder in a pan that is deep enough to hold all the ingredients. Stir to combine.
- Place in air fryer basket and set the air fryer on 220 degrees C. Set the timer for 18-20 minutes and start air fryer. Halfway through cooking, open the air fryer basket and add remaining cheese and stir. Close and continue cooking.
- Once the air fryer is done cooking, open the fryer and stir the mac and cheese. Remove the pan from the basket and allow it to cool for 5-10 minutes. The mac and cheese will thicken while it cools. Serve and Enjoy

310. Pasta Bake

 Serving size: 2

 Preparation time: 10 minutes

 Cooking time: 30 minutes

 Total time: 40 minutes

Ingredients

- 250 grams cherry tomatoes
- Olive oil
- 1 block feta cheese
- 1 teaspoon oregano
- Pepper
- Salt
- 1 package pasta by choice
- 1 garlic clove
- 1 handful fresh baby spinach
- 1 teaspoon chopped basil

Instructions

- Preheat the air fryer to 200°C.
- In a baking dish (or other oven-safe dish), toss the tomatoes with ¾ of the olive oil. Place the feta in the middle, drizzle it with the remaining oil, and season with salt, pepper, and oregano. Place the baking dish in the basket of the air fryer and cook for about 30 minutes, stirring every 10 minutes, until the tomatoes have burst and the feta is browned.
- Meanwhile, cook the pasta according to the package directions. Reserve 130 ml. of the pasta water, then drain.
- Remove the feta and tomato mixture from the air fryer and stir in the garlic until everything combines into a creamy sauce.
- Stir the sauce into the cooked pasta along with the spinach, basil, and some of the reserved pasta water to loosen, if needed. Season with additional salt and pepper, as desired. Stir and enjoy!

311. Spaghetti and Meatballs

 Serving size: 4

 Preparation time: 10 minutes

 Cooking time: 15 minutes

 Total time: 25 minutes

Ingredients

- 500 grams beef
- 60 grams breadcrumbs
- 1 red onion diced
- 1 rack fresh parsley chopped
- 1 egg
- 1 teaspoon garlic salt
- 1 teaspoon oregano
- 1 package spaghetti
- 1 jar spaghetti sauce
- fresh basil optional
- Parmesan cheese optional

Instructions

- Combine the ground protein, breadcrumbs, onion, parsley, egg, garlic salt, and oregano in a bowl.
- Roll the mixture into meatballs.
- Line your air fryer basket with foil or baking paper.
- Arrange the meatballs in the air fryer basket in a single layer.
- Cook at 200 degrees C for 15 minutes.
- While the meatballs are cooking, cook the pasta according to package instructions.
- When the pasta is done cooking, toss it with ½ cup of the spaghetti sauce to coat.
- Pour half of the spaghetti sauce in a bowl and toss the cooked meatballs in the sauce to coat.
- Divide the pasta and meatballs onto 4 plates.
- Top with additional spaghetti sauce, fresh basil, and Parmesan if desired.
- Serve and enjoy!

312. Tortellini Alfredo

 Serving size: 2

 Preparation time: 5 minutes

 Cooking time: 15 minutes

 Total time: 20 minutes

Ingredients

- 1 package tortellini
- 130 ml. alfredo sauc
- 60 grams mozzarella cheese
- 150 ml. water

Instructions

- In a small air fryer safe pan, add the refrigerated tortellini and water, enough water to fill them. Since any tortellini not in the water will dry out.
- Set in the air fryer at 5 minutes for 200 degrees C.
- Then pour the alfredo sauce over the tortellini and set back in the air fryer for 3 minutes at 200 degrees C, you are just looking to heat it up.
- Then add your shredded mozzarella cheese over the top, set back in the air fryer at 200 degrees C, just long enough to melt the cheese.

313. Parmesan Pasta

 Serving size:
4

 Preparation time:
5 minutes

 Cooking time:
25 minutes

 Total time:
30 minutes

Ingredients

- 1 package uncooked bowtie pasta
- 2 Tablespoons extra-virgin olive oil
- 1 teaspoon garlic powder
- 1/2 teaspoon kosher salt
- 1/4 teaspoon black pepper
- 3 Tablespoons grated Parmesan cheese
- Homemade or store-bought marinara sauce, for serving

Instructions

- Bring a large pot of salted water to a boil. Add the pasta and cook until al dente, about 10 minutes.
- Drain pasta and add it to a bowl. Drizzle it with the olive oil, then sprinkle it with the garlic powder, salt, pepper, and Parmesan cheese and toss to combine.
- Preheat the air fryer to 200°C.
- Add a portion of the pasta chips to the air fryer and cook for 7 to 10 minutes, stopping and shaking the basket two times.
- Remove the pasta chips from the air fryer and serve them with marinara for dipping.

314. Pasta Tacos

 Serving size:
2

 Preparation time:
5 minutes

 Cooking time:
25 minutes

 Total time:
30 minutes

Ingredients

- 1 package spaghetti
- 250 grams minced beef
- 1 package taco seasoning mix
- 60 ml. water
- 130 ml. tomato sauce
- 10 taco shells
- 1 tomato
- 2 tablespoons shredded parmesan cheese

Instructions

- Preheat air fryer to 220 degrees C. Add water, and spaghetti and cook it for 4 minutes.

- Meanwhile, in 10-inch nonstick pan, cook the beef over a medium-high heat 5 to 7 minutes, stirring frequently, until thoroughly cooked; drain. Stir in taco seasoning mix and water. Heat to boiling. Reduce heat; simmer uncovered 3 to 4 minutes or until thickened.
- Stir in pasta sauce; cook over medium heat until hot. Stir in cooked spaghetti.
- Take taco shells out of the box. Spoon about spaghetti mixture into each taco shell; top with tomato and Parmesan cheese.
- Air fry them for 5 minutes at 220 degrees C.

315. Baked Feta Pasta

 Serving size:
2

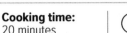 **Preparation time:**
5 minutes

 Cooking time:
20 minutes

Total time:
25 minutes

Ingredients

- Oil
- 1 onion
- 1 red pepper
- Salt
- Pepper
- 220 grams minced turkey
- 170 grams pasta
- 230 ml. pasta sauce
- 4 tablespoons grated cheese

Instructions

- Cook the pasta according to package instructions. Drain and set aside.
- While the pasta is cooking, you can prep the rest of the dish.
- Heat the oil in a pan on a medium high heat.
- Once hot, add the onions and bell pepper and cook until soft. Add in the ground turkey, season with salt and pepper and cook until browned.
- Stir in the pasta sauce and cooked pasta and toss to coat. Take off of the heat.
- Pre heat the air fryer to 200 degrees C.
- Transfer the sauce and pasta to an oven proof baking dish that will fit in your air fryer. Top with the shredded cheese.
- Cook the pasta in the air fryer for 7 to 9 minutes until the cheese has melted and the sauce is bubbling. Timings may vary slightly depending on your model of air fryer.

316. Pasta with Prosciutto

 Serving size:
2

 Preparation time:
10 minutes

 Cooking time:
10 minutes

 Total time:
20 minutes

Ingredients

- 1 tablespoon olive oil
- 3 tablespoons finely chopped onion
- 4 garlic cloves, coarsely chopped

tortellini:
- 2 large eggs
- 2 tablespoons 2% milk
- 30 grams seasoned bread crumbs
- 1 teaspoon garlic powder
- 2 tablespoons grated pecorino Romano cheese

- 130 ml. tomato puree
- 1 tablespoon chopped fresh basil
- 1/4 teaspoon salt
- 1/4 teaspoon pepper

- 1 tablespoon chopped fresh parsley
- 1/2 teaspoon salt
- 1 package refrigerated prosciutto ricotta tortellini
- Cooking spray

Instructions

- In a small saucepan, heat oil over a medium-high heat. Add onion and garlic; cook and stir until tender, 3-4 minutes. Stir in tomato puree, basil, salt and pepper. Bring to a boil; reduce heat. Simmer, uncovered, for 10 minutes. Keep warm.
- Meanwhile, preheat air fryer to 200°C.
- In a small bowl, whisk eggs and milk. In another bowl, combine bread crumbs, garlic powder, cheese, parsley and salt.
- Dip tortellini in the egg mixture, then in bread crumb mixture to coat.
- In batches, arrange tortellini in a single layer on a greased tray in air-fryer basket; spray with cooking spray. Cook until golden brown, 4-5 minutes. Turn; spray with cooking spray. Cook until golden brown, 4-5 minutes longer.

- Serve with sauce; sprinkle with additional minced fresh basil.

317. Spaghetti Squash

 Serving size:
2

 Preparation time:
15 minutes

 Cooking time:
20 minutes

 Total time:
35 minutes

Ingredients

- 1 squash
- 2 teaspoon avocado oil or your choice, *omit for oil free, see notes
- ½ teaspoon sea salt

- ¼ teaspoon black pepper optional
- ¼ teaspoon garlic powder optional
- ¼ teaspoon smoked paprika optional

Instructions

- Cut a thin slice off the ends of your squash and then cut in half, lengthwise, as evenly as possible in two halves. Place the two halves in your air fryer basket, cut side up. Then drizzle with the oil (if using) and evenly sprinkle with the seasoning.
- Cook at 200 degrees C for 20 minutes, or until a fork can easily pierce the flesh. (This may vary according to the size of your squash.)
- Once cooked, transfer to a dish and fluff up the inside with a fork. Then add the parmesan cheese and fresh parsley, if using, and enjoy.

Desserts

318. Carrot Cake

Serving size: 4 servings	**Preparation time:** 10 minutes	**Cooking time:** 25 minutes	**Total time:** 25 minutes

Ingredients

- 140 grams soft brown sugar
- 2 eggs, beaten
- 140 grams butter
- 1 orange, zest & juice
- 200 grams self-raising flour
- 1 teaspoon ground cinnamon
- 175 grams grated carrot, (approx 2 medium carrots)
- 60 grams sultanas

Instructions

- Preheat air fryer to 170 degrees C.
- In a bowl, cream together the butter and sugar.
- Slowly add the beaten eggs.
- Fold in the flour, a little bit at a time, mixing it as you go. Add the orange juice and zest, grated carrots and sultanas. Gently mix all the ingredients together.
- Grease the baking tin and pour the mixture in.
- Place baking tin in the air fryer basket and cook for 25-30 minutes. Check and see if the cake has cooked - use a cocktail stick or metal skewer to poke in the middle. If it comes out wet then cook it for a little longer.
- Remove the baking tin from the air fryer basket and allow to cool for 10 minutes before removing from the tin.

319. Minced Pie

Serving size: 6	**Preparation time:** 10 minutes	**Cooking time:** 15 minutes	**Total time:** 25 minutes

Ingredients

- 500 grams pie crust
- 350 grams jar mince meat
- 1 small egg
- 50 grams icing sugar
- Plain flour

Instructions

- Add the pie ingredients into a mixing bowl. Rub the fat into the flour and stir in sugar. Add a little extra virgin olive oil and mix with a little water at a time until you have shortcrust pastry.
- Flour a rolling pin and flour a clean worktop. Roll out your pastry and using pastry cutters, cut out to the ideal size.
- Load the pastry into muffin tins and add a dollop of mince meat in each one.
- Add another layer of pastry over the top and use your hands to press down and seal so that no mince meat will escape during cooking.
- Add an egg glaze to the top of your mince pies with a pastry brush and add into your air fryer. Air fry for 15 minutes at 180 degrees C in your air fryer oven.
- Eat warm or save for later. You can also add a sprinkling of icing sugar over your pies.

320. Grilled Peaches

 Serving size:
2

 Preparation time:
5 minutes

 Cooking time:
14 minutes

 Total time:
19 minutes

Ingredients

- 4 fresh peaches
- Leftover peach cobbler
- 1 tablespoon honey
- 1 teaspoon butter
- 1 teaspoon ground ginger
- Extra virgin olive oil spray
- Squirty cream

Instructions

- Slice your peaches and place them into the air fryer basket and spray with extra virgin olive oil. Air fry for 8 minutes at 200 degrees C.
- Place the leftover cobbler topping in a bowl and using your hands break it up until it is like breadcrumbs.
- Remove the peaches from the air fryer and place on foil.
- Sprinkle the peaches with ground ginger and drizzle with honey. Then add some thinly sliced butter. Add your layer of crumbled cobbler on top and then place back in the air fryer. Air fry for a further 6 minutes at 200 degrees C.
- When the air fryer beeps, remove it, and serve with cream.

321. Angel Cake

 Serving size:
8

 Preparation time:
20 minutes

 Cooking time:
15 minutes

 Total time:
35 minutes

Ingredients

- 9 egg whites
- 200 grams sugar
- 130 grams cake flour
- 1 ½ teaspoons cream of tartar
- 1 teaspoon vanilla extract
- 1/2 teaspoon salt

Instructions

- In a large mixing bowl, cream together the egg whites and sugar.
- Mix in the flour, cream of tartar, vanilla, and salt.
- Mix well.
- Spray a bundt cake tin with olive oil spray.

- Fill about 2/3 full.
- Set into the air fryer at 200 degrees C, air fryer setting, for 11-15 minutes.
- Let cool before removing it from the bundt pan.
- Serve with fresh berries and whipped cream.
- Plate, serve, and enjoy!

322. Churros

 Serving size:
4

 Preparation time:
10 minutes

 Cooking time:
10 minutes

 Total time:
20 minutes

Ingredients

- 250 ml. water
- 70 grams unsalted butter
- 1 tablespoon granulated sugar + 100 grams granulated sugar
- A
- of salt
- 130 grams plain flour
- 1 teaspoon vanilla extract
- Oil spray
- 1 teaspoon ground cinnamon

Instructions

- Put a silicone baking mat on a baking sheet and spray with oil spray.
- In a medium saucepan add water, butter, sugar, and salt. Bring to a boil over a medium-high heat.
- Reduce heat to medium-low and add flour to the saucepan. Stirring constantly with a rubber spatula cook until the dough comes together and is smooth.
- Remove from heat and transfer the dough to a mixing bowl. Let cool for 4 minutes.
- Add eggs and vanilla extract to the mixing bowl and mix using an electric hand mixer or stand mixer until dough comes together. The mixture will look like gluey mashed potatoes. Use your hands to press lumps together into a ball and transfer to a large piping bag fitted with a large star-shaped tip.
- Pipe churros onto the greased baking mat, into 4-inch lengths and cut end with scissors.
- Refrigerate piped churros on the baking sheet for 1 hour.
- Carefully transfer churros with a cookie spatula to the Air Fryer basket, leaving space between churros. Spray churros with oil spray. Depending on the size of your Air Fryer you have to fry them in batches.
- Air fry at 200 degrees C for 10-12 minutes until golden brown.
- In a shallow bowl combine granulated sugar and cinnamon.

- Immediately transfer baked churros to the bowl with the sugar mixture and toss to coat. Working in batches. Serve warm with Nutella or chocolate dipping sauce.

323. Apple Crisps

 Serving size:
4

 Preparation time:
10 minutes

 Cooking time:
20 minutes

Total time:
30 minutes

Ingredients

- 300 grams apples, chopped
- 1 tablespoon maple syrup
- 3 tablespoon plain flour
- 70 grams quick oats
- 40 grams brown sugar
- 2 tablespoons light butter
- ½ teaspoon cinnamon

Instructions

- In a bowl, mix together the chopped apples, lemon juice, 1 tbsp of the almond flour, maple syrup and cinnamon. Stir until well coated.
- In the baking dish of your air fryer, layer the bottom with the apple mixture.
- In a separate bowl, mix together the brown sugar, oats and remaining almond flour. Once these ingredients have been mixed well, mix in the melted butter trying to coat as much of the mixture as possible.
- Cover the apple layer with the brown sugar topping mix in the air fryer baking dish.
- Turn the air fryer to 200 degrees C for 20 minutes.
- Allow time to cool slightly before serving. You can serve with
- vanilla ice cream or frozen yogurt.

324. Snickerdoodle Poppers

 Serving size:
15

 Preparation time:
5 minutes

 Cooking time:
6 minutes

 Total time:
11 minutes

Ingredients

- 130 grams butter, softened
- 200 grams sugar
- 1 teaspoon baking soda
- 1 teaspoon cream of tartar
- ¼ teaspoon salt
- 2 eggs

- 1 teaspoon vanilla
- 500 grams plain flour
- 130 grams sugar
- 2 teaspoons ground cinnamon

Instructions

- Preheat air fryer at 200°C. In a large bowl beat butter with a mixer on medium for 30 seconds. Add 1 1/2 cups sugar, baking soda, cream of tartar, and salt. Beat for 1 to 2 minutes or until light and fluffy, scraping bowl as needed. Beat in eggs and vanilla. Beat in flour.
- In a small bowl stir together 1/4 sugar and cinnamon. Divide dough into portions and shape into balls. Roll each ball in cinnamon-sugar and flatten it.
- Place dough portions on baking paper and arrange 2 or 3 at a time, in the air-fryer basket. Cook 6 to 8 minutes or until golden. Remove with a wide spatula; cool on a wire rack.

325. Baked Apples

 Serving size:
2

 Preparation time:
5 minutes

 Cooking time:
15 minutes

 Total time:
20 minutes

Ingredients

- 2 apples
- 1 teaspoon butter, melted
- ½ teaspoon cinnamon
- 90 grams rolled oats
- 1 tablespoon butter
- 1 tablespoon maple syrup
- 1 teaspoon wholemeal
- ½ teaspoon cinnamon

Instructions

- Cut apples in half through the stem and use a knife or a spoon to remove the core, stem and seeds. Brush a teaspoon of butter evenly over the cut sides of the apples, then sprinkle over ½ teaspoon of cinnamon.
- Mix topping ingredients together in a small bowl, then spoon on top of the apple halves evenly.
- Place the apple halves carefully into the air fryer basket, then cook on 180 degrees C for 15 minutes or until softened.
- Serve warm with ice cream or cream if desired.

326. Lemon Cheesecake

 Serving size:
8

 Preparation time:
20 minutes

 Cooking time:
1 hour

 Total time:
1 hour and 20 minutes

Ingredients

- 90 grams cracker crumbs
- 2 ½ tablespoon unsalted butter
- 1 tablespoon sugar
- pinch of salt
- 450 grams cream cheese, softened
- 100 grams sugar
- 1 tablespoon plain flour
- 100 grams sour cream
- 1 teaspoon lemon juice
- ½ teaspoon vanilla extract
- 2 large eggs

Instructions

- Line the bottom of a 18 cm springform tin with baking paper. Either line the sides with baking paper as well or grease with a bit of butter or nonstick spray. Set aside.
- In a medium bowl, combine the cracker crumbs, butter, sugar, and salt and stir until the crumbs are evenly moist. Then, transfer the crumbs to the prepared pan and press the crust into the bottom, using the base of a flat-bottomed cup. Bake in the air fryer at 130°C for 10 minutes. Remove the crust from the air fryer and let cool until ready to fill. Keep the air fryer running at this temperature until you are done with preparing the filling.
- In a large bowl, using an electric mixer fitted with a whisk or paddle attachment, beat the cream cheese, sugar, and flour just until combined and no lumps remain about 1-2 minutes. Add the sour cream, lemon juice, and vanilla and stir just to combine, 30 to 60 seconds. Then, add the eggs, one at a time, and mix just until incorporated, about 30 seconds after each egg. Scrape down the bowl before you add the last egg. Do not overmix at any step.
- Pour the filling into the prebaked crust and spread evenly. Place in the air fryer and bake at 130°C for 20 minutes, then, without removing the cheesecake from the air fryer or opening the air fryer basket, lower the temperature to 110°C and bake for an additional 40 minutes.
- When the time is up, turn off the air fryer and leave the basket closed for 30 minutes. Then, remove the cake from the air fryer and let it cool to room temperature for about 2-3 hours. Once cooled, refrigerate the cake overnight for at least 8 hours.
- Before serving, remove the cake from the pan, cut, and serve. Store in an airtight container in the fridge for up to 3 days or freeze for up to 3 months.

327. Raspberry Cheesecake

 Serving size:
2

 Preparation time:
10 minutes

 Cooking time:
10 minutes

 Total time:
20 minutes

Ingredients

- 1 packet cream cheese
- 2 eggs
- 100 grams sugar
- ½ teaspoon vanilla
- 2 tablespoons sour cream
- 1 packet frozen raspberries
- 100 grams sugar
- 2 tablespoons water
- 1 tablespoon cornstarch/ cornflower (+1 tablespoon water)

Instructions

- Preheat the air fryer to 200°C.
- Mix together the eggs, sugar and vanilla. Add your sour cream and cream cheese. Beat until smooth. You can use a blender, hand mixer or do it by hand.
- Pour into the ramekin and put in a pan with a half-inch of water. Bake for 7 minutes.
- Check the cheesecake, it should be a little brown on top and firm. If not, put back in for a few minutes.
- Let cool and serve with raspberry compote.
- Combine raspberries, sugar, and 2 tablespoons of water in a small saucepan. Bring to a boil and mash the raspberries using your spoon.
- While boiling combine cornstarch and water, then pour into the raspberry mixture.
- Let simmer for 5 minutes or until sauce has thickened.

328. Dark Chocolate Brownies

 Serving size:
4

 Preparation time:
10 minutes

 Cooking time:
15 minutes

 Total time:
25 minutes

Ingredients

- 70 grams plain flour
- 6 tablespoon unsweetened cocoa powder

- 100 grams sugar
- 50 grams unsalted butter melted
- 2 large eggs
- 1 tablespoon vegetable oil
- ½ teaspoon vanilla extract
- ¼ teaspoon salt
- ¼ teaspoon baking powder

Instructions

- Prepare your 18 inch baking pan by generously greasing with butter on the bottom and all sides. Set aside.
- Preheat your air fryer by setting the temperature to 220 degrees C and allowing it to run for about 5 minutes while you prepare your brownie batter.
- Add your plain, cocoa powder, sugar, butter, eggs, vegetable oil, vanilla extract, salt, and baking powder into a large bowl and stir until thoroughly combined.
- Add it to the prepared baking pan and smooth out the top.
- Place in your preheated Air Fryer and bake for 15 minutes or until a toothpick entered in the centre comes out mostly clean.
- Remove and allow to cool in the pan before taking out and cutting.

329. Baked Pears

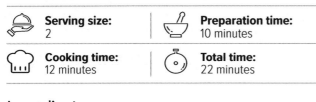

Serving size: 2	Preparation time: 10 minutes
Cooking time: 12 minutes	Total time: 22 minutes

Ingredients

- 2 pears
- 3 tablespoons butter
- 3 tablespoons powdered sugar
- ½ teaspoon ground cinnamon
- ¼ teaspoon ground nutmeg

Instructions

- Add butter to an 16 cm baking dish and place in your air fryer basket.
- Preheat the air fryer to 160°C.
- Halve pears and remove and core with a small spoon.
- When the air fryer finishes preheating, add the sugar, cinnamon and nutmeg to the melted butter and stir to combine.
- Place the pear halves cut side down into the butter spice mixture. Spoon some of the mixture over the top of the pear halves.
- Air fry at 160°C for 10 minutes.

- Turn the pears over so they are cut side up, spoon some of the melted butter mixture over the pears.
- Air fry pears for 2-4 more minutes to slightly caramelize the tops.
- To serve, drizzle with "caramel sauce" remaining in the pan and a scoop of vanilla ice cream or yogurt on the side.

330. Baked Apples with Walnuts

Serving size: 1	Preparation time: 5 minutes
Cooking time: 20 minutes	Total time: 25 minutes

Ingredients

- 1 apple (any kind)
- 2 tablespoons walnuts
- 2 tablespoons raisins
- 1 tablespoon melted butter, unsalted
- Your choice of all-spice (ground), ground cinnamon, or ground nutmeg

Instructions

- Start by coring out the apple. If you want to use the top again, make sure you cut it off, then core it.
- In a small bowl, mix your filling, raisins, and walnuts. Feel free to mix with oats; they taste amazing. Then mix in your butter.
- Scoop the filling into the apple, and sprinkle some of the spices on top.
- Set your apple into an air fryer-safe pan and cook for 20 minutes at 200 degrees C, air fryer setting.
- Remove from the air fryer.
- Plate, serve and enjoy!

331. Chocolate and Raspberry Cake

Serving size: 12	Preparation time: 15 minutes
Cooking time: 20 minutes	Total time: 35 minutes

Ingredients

- 180 grams dark chocolate, broken into pieces
- 180 grams butter, cubed
- 260 grams caster sugar
- 3 large eggs
- 80 grams plain flour

- 50 grams cocoa powder
- 100 grams milk chocolate, roughly chopped into small chunks
- 200 grams raspberries
- ice cream to serve

Instructions

- To install the grill plate, slide it into the front of the base so it hooks in, then press down on the back until it clicks into place. Close the lid, set temperature to 170°C and time to 25 minutes.
- Line crisper basket with a whole piece of baking paper. Cut the paper in corners to ensure it fits.
- Place chocolate and butter in a small saucepan. Gently melt over a low heat, stir until smooth. Allow to cool slightly.
- In a large bowl, beat the sugar and eggs with a whisk until thick and creamy, then gently fold in melted chocolate mixture. Sift the flour and cocoa over mixture and fold in with a spoon. Finally fold in the chopped chocolate and raspberries. Pour mixture into lined crisper basket.
- When the unit beeps to signify it has preheated, place crisper basket on grill plate in. Close lid and cook for 20-25 minutes. The brownies should be soft.
- Leave to cool in crisper basket before lifting out, using the baking paper like a sling. Cut into squares, serve warm with ice cream or allow to fully cool.

332. Apple Caramel Relish

	Serving size: 8		**Preparation time:** 10 minutes
	Cooking time: 20 minutes		**Total time:** 30 minutes

Ingredients

- 90 ml. warm water
- 1 teaspoon active dry yeast
- ½ teaspoon white sugar
- 240 grams plain flour
- 100 grams caster sugar
- ¼ teaspoon salt
- 50 ml. milk, at room temperature
- 2 tablespoons vegetable oil
- 1 egg, lightly beaten
- 50 grams chopped apple
- ½ teaspoon ground cinnamon
- 40 grams caramel sauce
- 1 tablespoon hot water, or more as needed
- Salt

Instructions

- Stir together warm water, yeast, and 1/2 teaspoon sugar; let stand until foamy, about 5 minutes.

- Stir together flour, half of the sugar, and 1/4 teaspoon salt in a medium bowl. Add yeast mixture, milk, oil, and egg; stir until a soft dough comes together. Turn dough out onto a lightly floured surface and knead until smooth, 1 to 2 minutes (dough will be sticky). Pat dough into squares.
- Toss together apple and cinnamon in a small bowl, and sprinkle over 1/2 of the dough. Fold the side with no apples over the apples and knead until apples are dispersed, about 30 seconds. Transfer dough to a lightly greased bowl, cover, and let rise in a warm place until doubled in volume, about 1 hour.
- Lightly flour a piece of baking paper; set aside. Turn dough out onto a lightly floured surface. Cut into 8 pieces. Pat each portion of dough with floured hands into oval; fritters do not have to be uniformly shaped. Transfer fritters to the prepared baking paper, cover loosely with plastic wrap, and let stand until doubled in volume, about 30 minutes.
- Preheat the air fryer to 180 degrees C. Preheat the oven to 100 degrees C. Place a wire rack over a rimmed baking sheet.
- Place 2 to 3 fritters in a single layer in the preheated air fryer basket and cook until golden brown, about 5 minutes. Remove cooked fritters to the prepared baking sheet and keep warm in the preheated oven. Repeat with remaining fritters.
- Whisk together caramel sauce and 1 tablespoon hot water, adding more water if necessary, to make a smooth drizzling consistency. Drizzle hot fritters with caramel sauce and sprinkle with sea salt, allowing baking sheet to catch caramel drips and excess salt.

333. Cannoli

	Serving size: 12		**Preparation time:** 10 minutes
	Cooking time: 6 minutes		**Total time:** 16 minutes

Ingredients

- 350 grams ricotta cheese
- 100 grams caster sugar
- 1/2 teaspoon orange zest
- 1/4 teaspoon salt
- flour for working surface
- 1 package refrigerated pie crust
- 1 egg white, beaten
- 120 grams chocolate chips, optional

Instructions

- Place ricotta in a strainer lined with cheese cloth (or kitchen paper) and press until the excess liquid has all drained away. Place strained ricotta, sugar and zest, and salt in a bowl, mix together and add to piping bag or a zip-top plastic bag. Set in your fridge.

- Roll out pie crust on lightly floured surface. Cut out 12 moulds. Wrap circles around cannoli moulds (see above tip) brushing edges with some egg white to seal. Lightly brush entire wrapper with egg white, roll in turbinado sugar to coat
- Add a few at a time to lightly coated air fryer basket, not touching. Cook at 200 degrees for 5-7 minutes. Carefully remove with tongs, let cool for 1 minutes before removing cannoli moulds. Let cool completely. Repeat with remaining shells.
- Pipe ricotta mixture into cannoli shells on each end, dip in chocolate chips if desired. Dust with powered sugar and serve.

334. White Chocolate Pudding

 Serving size:
6

 Preparation time:
10 minutes

 Cooking time:
15 minutes

 Total time:
25 minutes

Ingredients

- 300 grams bread
- 1 egg
- 150 ml. double cream
- ½ teaspoon vanilla extract
- 150 grams caster sugar
- 150 grams chocolate chips

Instructions

- Spray the inside of a baking dish that fits inside the air fryer with cooking spray.
- Put bread cubes into a baking dish. If using chocolate chips, sprinkle them over the bread.
- In another bowl, mix the egg, whipped cream, vanilla and sugar.
- Pour the egg mixture over the bread cubes and let stand for 5 minutes.
- Put the baking dish inside the air fryer basket. Cook in the air fryer at 200 degrees C for 15 minutes, or until the bread pudding is cooked through.

335. Lemon Curd

 Serving size:
9

 Preparation time:
10 minutes

 Cooking time:
35 minutes

 Total time:
45 minutes

Ingredients

- 350 grams plain flour
- 1/3 teaspoon baking powder
- pinch fine salt
- 2 tablespoons raw sugar
- 300 ml buttermilk
- 80 grams lemon curd
- olive oil cooking spray
- to serve: jam and whipped cream

Instructions

- Sift flour, baking powder, salt and sugar into a large bowl. Make a well in the centre; pour in combined buttermilk and lemon curd. Using a flat-bladed knife, gently stir until dough just comes together.
- Turn dough out onto a lightly floured work surface. Using your hands, knead mixture briefly. Pat out until dough is 3cm thick.
- Using a floured cutter, cut 5.5cm rounds from dough. Press scraps of dough together until 3cm thick. Repeat cutting to get a total of 9 scones. Brush top of scones with any buttermilk left in the carton or 1 tablespoon of milk.
- Preheat air fryer to 180°C for 3 minutes.
- Spray the air fryer basket with cooking spray. Taking care, place scones, side by side, in the basket. Reset the temperature to 160°C cook for 17 minutes.
- Serve warm scones with jam and cream.

336. Almond Cookies

 Serving size:
32 cookies

 Preparation time:
15 minutes

 Cooking time:
7 minutes

 Total time:
22 minutes

Ingredients

- 210 grams refined coconut oil
- 300 grams coconut sugar
- 2 eggs
- 150 grams almond flour
- 80 grams starch
- 80 grams coconut flour
- 50 grams starch
- 1 teaspoon baking soda
- 1 teaspoon salt
- 150 grams chocolate chips

Instructions

- In a large mixing bowl with an electric hand or stand mixer, beat together the oil, coconut sugar and vanilla until light and fluffy.
- Beat in the eggs until well combined.
- Add the dry ingredients (almond flour through salt) in a medium mixing bowl and stir until combined.

- Add this to the wet mixture and beat until combined.
- Stir in chocolate chips until combined.
- Preheat the air fryer to 160 °C. Place a piece of baking paper on top of the basket.
- Form dough into 38-gram balls.
- Place in the air fryer, and make sure there is a space between them.
- Cook for 5-7 minutes or until lightly browned. They are delicious hot out of the oven but you can detect the starch. That goes away after sitting overnight.
- Let sit for 5 minutes or until soft enough to remove to a cooling rack.
- Store cooled cookies in an airtight container for up to 5 days. The baked cookies can be frozen for up to 3 months. Or you can roll the dough into balls, flatten them slightly with your palm, and freeze those for up to 3 months. Add 1 minute to the baking time.

337. Peanut Butter Banana Sandwiches

	Serving size: 1		Preparation time: 5 minutes
	Cooking time: 5 minutes		Total time: 10 minutes

Ingredients

- 2 tablespoons peanut butter creamy or chunky
- 4 slices bread any type
- 1 large banana sliced

Instructions

- Start by spreading the peanut butter to one side of the bread.
- Then place the bananas on top of the peanut butter.
- Use the other slice of bread, and place it over the bananas.
- Place the bread in the air fryer basket, set the temperature for 200 degrees C, air fryer setting, and air fry for 5 minutes.
- Plate, serve, and enjoy!

338. Crème Brulé

	Serving size: 4		Preparation time: 20 minutes
	Cooking time: 30 minutes		Total time: 50 minutes

Ingredients

- 100 ml. milk
- 2 egg yolks
- 60 grams light cream
- 3 tablespoon caster sugar
- 1 teaspoon vanilla extract

Instructions

- Add the milk, light cream, egg yolks and a few drops of vanilla extract to a bowl and whip uniformly.
- Heat to simmer in a pan on low and stir in 1⅔ tbsp of sugar to dissolve.
- Once the sugar has dissolved, pour into ramekins. Preheat the air fryer to 200°C.
- Cook for 25-30 mins. Using an oven mitt, test that it is set by gently shaking.
- Bring to room temperature.
- Sprinkling the remainder of the sugar evenly across the top.
- Caramelise the layer of sugar using a small culinary torch.
- Enjoy!

339. Butter Cake

	Serving size: 4		Preparation time: 5 minutes
	Cooking time: 15 minutes		Total time: 20 minutes

Ingredients

- cooking spray
- 7 tablespoons butter, at room temperature
- 100 grams caster sugar
- 2 tablespoons white sugar
- 1 egg
- 300 grams plain flour
- 1 pinch salt, or to taste
- 6 tablespoons milk

Instructions

- Preheat an air fryer to 180 degrees C. Spray a small fluted tube tin with cooking spray.
- Beat butter and add 2 tablespoons sugar together in a bowl using an electric mixer until light and creamy. Add egg and mix until smooth and fluffy. Stir in flour and salt. Add milk and mix batter thoroughly.
- Transfer batter to the prepared tin; use the back of a spoon to level the surface.
- Place the tin in the air fryer basket. Set the timer for 15 minutes. Bake until a toothpick inserted into the cake comes out clean.
- Turn cake out of tin and allow to cool, about 5 minutes.

340. Cherry Crumble

Serving size: 4

Preparation time: 10 minutes

Cooking time: 7 minutes

Total time: 17 minutes

Ingredients

- 300 grams cherry pie filling
- 100 grams butter
- 140 grams oats
- 60 grams brown sugar

Instructions

- Start by spraying an air fryer-safe dish (which is oven safe) with olive oil, and then pour the cherry pie filling into it.
- Then in a small bowl, mix together the butter, quick oats, and brown sugar.
- Pour the topping over the cherry pie filling. Set the pan into the air fryer and set the temperature to 200 degrees C, for 7 minutes. (air fryer setting) Let cool slightly before serving.
- Plate, serve, and enjoy!

341. Donut Sticks with Powdered Sugar

Serving size: 6

Preparation time: 15 minutes

Cooking time: 5 minutes

Total time: 20 minutes

Ingredients

- 250 grams refrigerated crescent roll dough
- 130 grams caster sugar
- 2 tablespoons cinnamon
- 40 grams butter

Instructions

- Unroll crescent roll dough to form a rectangle and seal seams together.
- With a pizza cutter, slice the dough in half. Then, slice crosswise into strips.
- In a bowl, add melted butter. In a large, plastic storage bag, mix together ground cinnamon and sugar.
- Dip a strip of dough into melted butter. Don't drench it, but be sure to coat it well. Place in the basket of your air fryer.
- Cook for 4-5 minutes at 200 degrees C or until browned.

- Remove from air fryer and place in storage bag of cinnamon sugar mixture. Seal the bag and shake to coat.
- Repeat with remaining strips of dough.

342. Cookie Fries

Serving size: 24

Preparation time: 20 minutes

Cooking time: 10 minutes

Total time: 30 minutes

Ingredients

- 130 grams plain flour
- 3 tablespoons caster sugar
- 60 grams butter
- 60 grams strawberry jelly
- 1/8 teaspoon chipotle pepper
- 50 grams lemon curd

Instructions

- Combine flour and sugar in a medium bowl. Cut in butter with a pastry blender until mixture resembles fine crumbs and starts to cling. Form the mixture into a ball and knead until smooth.
- Preheat an air fryer to 190 degrees C.
- Roll dough, and cut the dough into fries.
- Arrange fries in a single layer in the air fryer basket. Cook until lightly browned, 3 to 4 minutes. Let cool in the basket until firm enough to transfer to a wire rack to cool completely. Repeat with remaining dough.
- To make strawberry "ketchup," press jam through a fine mesh sieve using the back of a spoon. Stir in ground chipotle. Whip the lemon curd to make it a dippable consistency for the "mustard."
- Serve sugar cookie fries with the strawberry ketchup and lemon curd mustard.

343. French Toast Sticks with Powdered Sugar

Serving size: 4

Preparation time: 5 minutes

Cooking time: 5 minutes

Total time: 10 minutes

Ingredients

- 3 large eggs
- 60 ml. milk
- 1 teaspoon vanilla extract
- ½ teaspoon cinnamon
- Pinch salt
- 8 slices brioche bread

Instructions

- Preheat the air fryer 200°C and line the air fryer with baking paper if needed.
- In a large shallow bowl, whisk together the eggs, milk, vanilla, cinnamon and a pinch of salt.
- Dip each piece of bread into the egg mixture and then turn it over to coat both sides. Place the French toast sticks in the air fryer and repeat with as many pieces as will fit in the air fryer at once, about 8-12 pieces.
- Cook for 5-6 minutes, or until the French toast is golden brown and puffed.
- Serve the French toast sticks warm with maple syrup and powdered sugar, if desired.

344. Peanut Butter and Jelly S'mores

 Serving size: 2

 Preparation time: 5 minutes

 Cooking time: 1 minute

 Total time: 6 minutes

Ingredients

- 1 chocolate-covered peanut butter cup
- 2 chocolate cracker squares, divided
- 1 teaspoon seedless raspberry jam
- 1 large marshmallow

Instructions

- Preheat the air fryer to 200 degrees C.
- Place peanut butter on 1 cracker square. Top with jelly and marshmallow. Carefully place in air fryer basket.
- Cook in preheated air fryer until marshmallow is lightly browned and softened, about 1 minute. Immediately top with remaining cracker square.

345. Raspberry Crisp

 Serving size: 4

 Preparation time: 10 minutes

 Cooking time: 15 minutes

 Total time: 25 minutes

Ingredients

- 150 grams raspberries
- 1 teaspoon cornstarch/ cornflour
- 2 teaspoon caster sugar
- 100 grams rolled oats
- 100 grams walnuts
- 1 teaspoon cinnamon
- 1 teaspoon chia seeds
- 2 tablespoon light butter

Instructions

- Preheat air fryer to 200°C.
- Mix together raspberries, cornstarch and 1 teaspoon of sugar. Pour into an air fryer cake pan. Set aside.
- In a food processor, combine oats, walnuts, cinnamon, chia seeds, butter and remaining sugar. Pulse until mixture resembles a coarse crumb.
- Sprinkle the crumb topping over the berries.
- Bake in the air fryer for 15 minutes or until topping is golden brown. Let it cool for a few minutes before serving.

346. Pumpkin Cookies

 Serving size: 24 cookies

 Preparation time: 20 minutes

 Cooking time: 5 minutes

Total time: 25 minutes

Ingredients

- 130 grams plain flour
- 1 teaspoon ground cinnamon
- 1/2 teaspoon salt
- 1/2 teaspoon ground nutmeg
- 1/2 teaspoon baking soda
- 100 grams brown sugar
- 1 stick unsalted butter, room temperature
- 1 large egg
- 1 teaspoon pure vanilla extract
- 70 grams canned pumpkin
- 200 grams old-fashioned oats
- 130 grams dried cranberries

Instructions

- Start by combining the flour, cinnamon, salt, nutmeg, and baking soda in a large mixing bowl.
- Add in the butter.
- Mix in the egg, vanilla extract, and canned pumpkin.
- Add the old fashioned oats and cranberries.
- Mix well.
- Be careful to scrape the sides of the bowl.
- Spray either your air fryer pan or your basket with olive oil spray. (or if you see the blog post about baking paper)
- I used an ice cream scooper to scoop my cookie dough. If you do not have one, add 2 tablespoons of cookie dough.
- Set in your air fryer oven (I used the middle shelf) and set the timer for 5 minutes at 200 degrees C. Continue to air fry your cookies, until all of the dough is used up.
- Plate, serve, and enjoy!

347. Raspberry Hand Pies

 Serving size:
4

 Preparation time:
10 minutes

 Cooking time:
5 minutes

 Total time:
15 minutes

Ingredients

- 1 package refrigerated pie crust
- 140 grams raspberry pie filling
- olive oil spray
- sparkling sugar

Instructions

- Start by rolling out the dough.
- Use your biscuit cutter, and cut out the circles. Repeat until you use all of your dough.
- Scoop about 1 tablespoon of pie filling in the centre. Place another circle on top, and then use your fork tines to create the crust. Spray with olive oil.
- Place the pastry on either a greased air fryer tray or in a greased air fryer basket.
- Sprinkle with sparkling sugar.
- Set in the air fryer basket or tray for 5 minutes at 220 degrees C, air fryer setting.
- Plate, serve, and enjoy!

348. Blueberry Scones

 Serving size:
16

 Preparation time:
10 minutes

 Cooking time:
6 minutes

 Total time:
16 minutes

Ingredients

- 130 grams butter
- 200 grams plain flour
- 100 grams sugar
- 2 teaspoons baking powder
- 1 egg
- 100 grams blueberries
- 4 tablespoons milk

Instructions

- In a medium bowl, combine the butter, flour, sugar, and baking powder. Stir until it become crumbly.
- Add in the egg, and the milk, one tablespoon at a time, until the dough forms.
- Stir in the blueberries.
- Roll the dough, and then cut it.
- Place in air fryer basket on baking paper, or lightly brushed with olive oil.
- Cook at 220 degrees C for 5-6 minutes, until they are golden.

349. British Chocolate Fudge

 Serving size:
8

 Preparation time:
20 minutes

 Cooking time:
25 minutes

 Total time:
45 minutes

Ingredients

Brownie Ingredients:
- 130 grams butter
- 150 grams semisweet chocolate chips
- 2 tablespoons unsweetened cocoa powder
- 220 grams caster sugar
- 60 grams brown sugar
- 1 tablespoon vanilla
- 1/2 teaspoon salt
- 4 large eggs
- 300 grams plain flour

Frosting Ingredients:
- 5 tablespoons butter melted
- 5 tablespoons unsweetened cocoa powder
- 2 tablespoons milk
- 1 teaspoon vanilla extract
- 2 tablespoons powdered sugar

Instructions

- Start by melting the butter (I used a microwave-safe bowl) and microwaved it until melted.
- Mix in the chocolate chips.
- Mix until the chocolate chips are melted.
- Mix in the unsweetened cocoa powder, sugar, and the rest of the ingredients in. Mix well.
- Spread into an air fryer safe pan, and bake at 220 degrees C for 20-25 minutes.
- Let cool before you frost the brownies,
- Plate, serve, and enjoy!

350. Coconut Oat Cookies

 Serving size:
6

 Preparation time:
2 minutes

 Cooking time:
6 minutes

Total time:
8 minutes

Ingredients

- 60 grams unsweetened apple sauce
- 1 tablespoon ground flax
- 1 tablespoon oat flour
- 1/2 teaspoon baking powder
- pinch salt
- 1 tablespoon coconut sugar
- 60 grams rolled oats
- 1 teaspoon vanilla extract
- 2 tablespoons tahini
- 3 tablespoons dairy free chocolate chips
- 3 tablespoons coconut flakes

Instructions

- In a large bowl combine the apple sauce and ground flax.
- Add the oat flour, baking powder and salt. Stir to incorporate.
- Add the coconut sugar, rolled oats, coconut flakes and vanilla extract. Stir well to be sure the oats are well incorporated.
- Pour the tahini in batter and stir well.
- Add the chocolate chips and stir to ensure they are distributed well.
- Cut a piece of baking paper to fit in the air fryer basket. Cut a few holes to ensure airflow.
- Use a small cookie scoop to scoop out 6 cookies and press them down so they are flat.
- Bake in 200 degrees C air fryer for 6 minutes.
- Allow to cool slightly before serving.

351. Oat Cookies

 Serving size:
12

 Preparation time:
15 minutes

 Cooking time:
15 minutes

 Total time:
30 minutes

Ingredients

- 90 grams oat flour
- 60 grams wheat flour
- 2 tablespoons coconut oil
- 50 grams brown sugar
- ¼ teaspoon baking soda
- 1 teaspoon vanilla essence

Instructions

- Measure and keep all the ingredients ready.
- Take coconut oil and brown sugar in a bowl.
- Mix it completely till combined and sugar is dissolved.
- Add vanilla essence to it and mix.
- Then add oats flour, wheat flour, and baking soda to it.
- Bring together to form a dough.
- Take a small ball of dough and flatten them a little in your hands.
- Prepare the same for the rest of the dough.
- Preheat the air fryer at 160°C for three minutes.
- Place the cookies in the air fryer basket and bake at the same temperature for 12-15 minutes till it is done.

352. Lime Tarts

 Serving size:
15

 Preparation time:
5 minutes

 Cooking time:
5 minutes

 Total time:
10 minutes

Ingredients

- 1 package filo tarts
- 400 ml. sweetened condensed milk
- 60 ml. lime juice
- 2 tablespoons lime zest
- 2 tablespoons powdered sugar
- 4 egg yolks (only yolks)

Instructions

- In a small mixing bowl, add the sweetened condensed milk, lime juice, zest, powdered sugar, egg yolks.
- Mix well, until all of the eggs are blended in.
- Then fill the shells with the filling.
- As you fill the tarts place them in your air fryer tray or basket.

- Place the tray into the air fryer.
- Set the temperature to 200 degrees C, for 5 minutes.
- Let them cool about 10 minutes, before adding whipped cream (if desired).

353. Mock Cherry Pie

 Serving size:
4

 Preparation time:
5 minutes

 Cooking time:
25 minutes

Total time:
30 minutes

Ingredients

- 2 frozen pie filling crusts
- 2 premade cherry filling
- 1 egg yolk
- 2 tablespoons milk

Instructions

- Start by leaving your frozen pie crusts out for about 10 minutes, just so the dough is pliable.
- Then fill the bottom pie crust with the cherry filling.
- You can either cover it with the pie crusts and then cut out holes (this is the easiest way), or you can press the dough with the tool shown in the list of items used in this recipe.
- Mix the egg yolk and milk, and brush it on the top of the pie crust.
- Place the uncooked prepared pie into the air fryer and set the temperature to 200 degrees C for 10 minutes. Then open it, and check it out.
- Let cool before slicing.
- Plate, serve, and enjoy!

354. Lemon Glazed Muffins

 Serving size:
12

 Preparation time:
20 minutes

 Cooking time:
15 minutes

 Total time:
25 minutes

Ingredients

Lemon Poppy Seed Muffins:
- 60 grams caster sugar
- 1 tablespoon lemon zest
- 1 tablespoon lemon juice
- 130 grams plain flour
- 1 teaspoon baking powder
- 1/4 teaspoon baking soda
- 1/2 teaspoon salt
- 60 grams sour cream
- 1 egg
- 1 teaspoon vanilla extract

- 40 grams melted butter
- 1 tablespoons poppy seeds

Lemon Glaze:
- 140 grams powdered sugar
- 2 tablespoons of milk
- 1 tablespoon lemon juice

Instructions

- In a small mixing bowl, mix the sugar, lemon zest, lemon juice, flour, baking powder, baking soda, and salt well.
- Mix the sour cream, egg, vanilla extract, and melted butter in another mixing bowl.
- Fold the dry ingredient into the wet ingredients.
- Then fold in the poppy seeds.
- Either grease the mini muffin tin with olive oil or use mini muffin paper liners and pour the batter about 3/4 the way to the top.
- Set in the air fryer for 12 minutes at 200 degrees C.
- When the time is up, place a toothpick in the center of the muffin and if it comes out clean, remove it from the air fryer. If not, add a couple of minutes.
- Let cool slightly before serving.
- Drizzle the lemon glaze, over the muffins.
- Plate, serve and enjoy!

355. Apple Pie

 Serving size:
6

 Preparation time:
5 minutes

 **Cooking time:**
20 minutes

 Total time:
25 minutes

Ingredients

- 1 box premade pie crusts
- 1 canned apple pie filling
- 1 tablespoon unsalted butter
- 1 teaspoon sugar
- 1 teaspoon cinnamon

Instructions

- To begin, unfold the pie crust. Use a rolling pin to flatten it out if necessary.
- Place one pie crust circle into the bottom of the pie plate, lightly pressing it down. Then, pour the apple filling over the crust, and spread it evenly.
- Top with the second crust and trim excess edges. Cut a few slits in the top of the pie to release steam while it's cooking.
- In a microwave safe bowl, melt the butter, then brush the top of the crust with the melted butter. You can also use an egg wash to help the pie turn golden while it's cooking.

- Combine the sugar and cinnamon together, and sprinkle a dash of the cinnamon sugar on top and place in the air fryer basket. Use the air fry feature and cook at 190 degrees C for about 18-23 minutes. The pie crust should be golden brown on top, and cooked on the bottom.
- Once it is cooked, you can sprinkle a little bit of brown sugar, white sugar, powdered sugar, or another dash of the cinnamon and sugar mixture.
- Serve chilled or warm, topped with ice cream or whipping cream.

356. Orange Sponge Cake

 Serving size:
6

 Preparation time:
20 minutes

 **Cooking time:**
42 minutes

 Total time:
1 hour and 2 minutes

Ingredients

Cake Batter:
- 4 egg yolks
- 50 grams caster sugar
- 1 tablespoon vegetable oil
- 40 ml. water
- 3 tablespoon Juice from fresh orange
- 160 grams all purpose flour
- 1½ teaspoon baking powder
- ½ teaspoon salt kosher
- Orange zest reserve 1 teaspoon zest and set aside

Egg White Mixture:
- 4 egg whites
- 1 teaspoon vinegar
- 40 grams sugar

Condensed Milk Frosting:
- 1 can condensed milk chilled
- Remaining orange juice
- 1 teaspoon orange zest

Instructions

- Mix together the egg yolks and sugar. Mix together until well combined. Should be light and fluffy.
- Add the oil, water, and orange juice. Mix.
- Using a sieve, sift the flour, baking soda and salt on top of the egg yolk mixture. Mix until lumps are no longer visible.
- Add the zest and mix well.
- In a separate bowl, beat the egg white, vinegar, and sugar until stiff peak.
- Fold in the egg white mixture to the batter one scoop at a time until all is used and combined.

- Preheat the air fryer. Line the pan with baking paper and slowly pour batter into the pan.
- Bake the cake in a preheated air fryer on 220 degrees C for 42 minutes or until the toothpick comes out clean when inserted, and removed from the middle.
- Let the cake cool completely.
- In a medium bowl, pour the condensed milk, orange zest, and orange juice.
- Using an electric mixture, on high speed, mix the milk for 4 minutes.
- Once the cake is completely cooled, turn the cake upside down in the same pan, remove the paper, then frost the cake. See notes for frosting methods.
- Refrigerate for at least 1 hour before cutting and serving.
- Serve as desired and enjoy!

357. Coffee Cake

 Serving size:
8

 Preparation time:
20 minutes

 Cooking time:
20 minutes

 Total time:
40 minutes

Ingredients

Cake:
- 260 grams plain flour
- 40 grams caster sugar
- 2 teaspoons baking powder
- 1/2 teaspoon salt
- 30 grams melted butter
- 40 ml. milk
- 1 teaspoon vanilla
- 1 egg

Topping:
- 40 grams plain flour
- 50 grams caster sugar
- 2 teaspoon ground cinnamon
- 30 grams melted butter

Instructions

- Start by making the batter for the cake, mix all of your dry ingredients, and then mix in the wet ingredients. Mix well.
- Find the largest pan that will fit in your air fryer. Spray it with non-stick cooking spray.
- Pour the batter into the pan.
- Then make the topping, mix it all in a small bowl. Mix well, then sprinkle it on top of the cake.
- Place the pan in the air fryer and set the temperature to 220 degrees C for 25-35 minutes.
- Note: The exact time of your air fryer will depend on the wattage and how thick the cake is: the thicker, the longer. If you

need additional time, add it. You want the toothpick to come out clean in the middle.
- Let cool slightly before slicing.
- Plate, serve, and enjoy!

358. Banana Fritters

 Serving size: 20

 Preparation time: 5 minutes

 Cooking time: 7 minutes

 Total time: 12 minutes

Ingredients

- 4 ripe bananas mashed
- 130 grams flour
- 2 teaspoon baking powder
- 1/2 teaspoon baking soda
- 1/4 teaspoon salt
- 1/2 teaspoon cinnamon
- 1 teaspoon vanilla extract
- 2 tablespoons brown sugar or to taste
- 30 ml. milk

Instructions

- Preheat the air fryer to 200 degrees C for 5 minutes.
- In a bowl, mash the bananas with a fork.
- In a separate bowl, whisk together the flour, baking soda, baking powder and salt to combine.
- Add the mashed bananas, brown sugar, cinnamon, milk and vanilla extract to the bowl with the dry ingredients. Mix everything together until fully combined.
- Place an air fryer baking paper liner inside of the air fryer and spray it with propellant-free coconut oil cooking spray.
- Use a tbsp or cookie scoop to transfer the dollops of banana fritter batter to the air fryer, leaving space in between them so they don't stick together after cooking. You'll have to cook them in separate batches until you've finished all of the batter.
- Cook at 220 degrees C for 7-8 minutes or until the fritters are a dark, golden brown colour. Do not turn over.
- Remove the banana fritters from the air fryer and immediately top with powdered sugar or honey and serve.

359. Berry Crumble

 Serving size: 2

 Preparation time: 10 minutes

 Cooking time: 15 minutes

 Total time: 25 minutes

Ingredients

- 150 grams frozen blueberries
- 2 teaspoons plain flour
- 1 teaspoon lemon juice
- 1 pinch salt

Topping:
- 3 tablespoons quick-cooking oats
- 1½ tablespoons plain flour
- 1½ tablespoons brown sugar
- ½ teaspoon ground cinnamon
- 1½ tablespoons salted butter, softened

Instructions

- Preheat an air fryer to 180 degrees C.
- Combine blueberries, flour, lemon juice, and salt in a small bowl. Toss to coat, then divide the mixture between two ramekins.
- Combine oats, flour, brown sugar, and cinnamon for the topping in a small bowl. Mix in softened butter using a fork until mixture is crumbly. Sprinkle over the blueberries.
- Place the ramekins in the air fryer basket and cook until the blueberries are warmed throughout and topping is golden brown, 12 to 14 minutes.

360. Baked Cherries with Nuts

 Serving size: 4

 Preparation time: 10 minutes

 Cooking time: 19 minutes

 Total time: 29 minutes

Ingredients

- Cherry Filling
- 220 grams cherries, halved, fresh or frozen
- 1 tablespoon sugar, or Monkfruit sweetener
- 1 teaspoon cornstarch, or arrowroot
- ¼ teaspoon almond extract
- Crumble Topping
- 30 grams oat flour, or almond flour
- 6 tablespoon rolled oats, not quick oats
- 2 tablespoon almonds, finely chopped
- 2 tablespoon coconut sugar, or brown sugar, or Monkfruit sweetener
- 2 tablespoon butter, melted
- 1 pinch sea salt

Instructions

- In a small bowl, combine halved cherries (fresh or frozen) with sweetener, cornstarch, and almond extract.
- In another bowl, melt butter, then combine with remaining topping ingredients.
- Divide cherry filling evenly between four small ramekins. Top with crumble topping, pressing down gently.
- Cover with foil, wrapping ramekins completely.
- Arrange in air fryer basket. Air fry at 200°C. for 14-16 minutes or until cherries are bubbling.
- Carefully remove foil. Ramekins will be hot!
- Cook for 3 minutes at 200°C. more to brown the crisp topping. Use oven mitts to remove the ramekins from the air fryer, as they will be hot.
- Let cool slightly, then serve warm plain, or with ice cream, whipped cream or whipped coconut milk.

361. Pecan Pie

 Serving size:
8

 Preparation time:
5 minutes

 Cooking time:
30 minutes

 Total time:
35 minutes

Ingredients

- 130 ml. light corn syrup
- 130 grams brown sugar
- 40 grams butter melted
- 2 teaspoons vanilla
- ½ teaspoon salt
- 3 large eggs
- 220 grams chopped pecans
- 1 pie crust

Instructions

- Prepare the crust and place into a pie plate that will fit into your basket or rack oven. Air fry the crust at 200 degrees C for 3-4 minutes, then remove until the filling is ready
- In a medium bowl, pour in the corn syrup, brown sugar, melted butter, vanilla, and salt. Stir all of the ingredients together so the sugar is mixed into the liquids.
- Whisk or beat the eggs, and add whisked eggs to the bowl. Next, add the pecans and stir into the egg mixture. Once it is well combined, pour into the prepared crust.
- Place in the air fryer basket, or on the rack, and air fry at 200 degrees C for about 30-35 minutes, until the top of the pie is golden brown and crispy.

362. Banana Pastry

 Serving size:
4

 Preparation time:
10 minutes

 Cooking time:
10 minutes

 Total time:
20 minutes

Ingredients

- 2 sheets, puff pastry
- 2 large bananas
- 500 grams Nutella
- 1 egg

Instructions

- Thaw pastry (if frozen) and put on a sheet of baking paper.
- Score into three equal sections. Starting about 3 to 4 cm from the bottom, score and cut the side panels on an angle making 1 to 1½ cm strips.
- Cut and remove the two bottom triangles and the two top triangles.
- Spread about 200 grams of Nutella on the middle panel, starting 1 cm from the top down to the last bottom strips at the side. The bottom 3 to 4 cm should also be free from Nutella.
- Thinly slice the banana and lay one layer over the top of Nutella. Then add a second layer of banana over the first just covering where you can see Nutella.
- Fold the top over the filling and press into place, cut away the first two top strip.
- Starting from the top, cross over each strip to the opposite side and one down. Press into place. Repeat, alternating from side to side, forming a crisscross pattern. Stop once you have reached the last 4.
- Cut about half of the bottom middle panel away, then fold that over the filling. Crisscross the first two strips over that, and then the last two go straight across
- Preheat the air fryer for 2 minutes at 180°C on the manual mode setting.
- Whisk the egg and baste the danish
- Spray the bottom of the air fryer basket with non-stick cooking spray, place the danish in the air fryer and cook at 180°C for 10 minutes on the Manual setting.
- Allow to stand for a couple of minutes before transferring to a cooling rack.
- Melt 100g of Nutella in the microwave till it resembles melted chocolate. Add to a piping bag, cut off a small amount of the tip and pipe over the top of the danish in a zigzag motion.

363. Pumpkin Pie

 Serving size:
16

 Preparation time:
10 minutes

 Cooking time:
35 minutes

 Total time:
45 minutes

Ingredients

- 1 package refrigerated pie crust, I recommend Pillsbury
- 1 can pure pumpkin puree
- 1 can evaporated milk
- 50 grams brown sugar
- 50 grams white sugar
- 2 tablespoons plain flour

- 1 teaspoon ground cinnamon
- 1/2 teaspoon ground nutmeg
- 1/2 teaspoon ground ginger
- 1/4 teaspoon ground cloves
- 1/2 teaspoon salt
- 3 large eggs room temperature

Instructions

- Pie Crust
- Preheat the air fryer to 200 degrees C for about 5 minutes. Place pie crust into two pie pans. Cut off any excess crust, leaving a bit of crust around the edges. Fold the remaining pie crust edges in toward the pie, and pinch or crimp the edges to create a decorative look.
- Press a sheet of tin foil over the pastry – the tin foil should be pressed into every nook of the crust and make sure it is larger than the crust so it can easily be removed later. Fill the foil with beans, pie weights, or rice. Blind bake the crust for 10 minutes at 200 degrees C.
- Remove the foil containing the beans, weights, or rice. Prick the bottom of the crust with a fork about 10 times to help keep the crust from puffing up. Bake at 200 for another 5 minutes.
- Pie
- While the crust is baking, use an electric mixer to combine the pumpkin, evaporated milk, brown sugar, white sugar, flour, cinnamon, nutmeg, ginger, salt, cloves. Once the batter is combined, mix in eggs until combined, but do not over mix.
- Transfer the batter into a container that allows you to easily pour from it, such as a liquid measuring cup. Leave the crust in the air fryer while you carefully pour the pumpkin batter into the pie plate. Use no more than half of the mixture in each pie. Do not overfill the crust.
- If you have an air fryer with a rack that allows you to cook both pies at the same time, you may get both of the pies ready to bake, otherwise bake them one at a time.

- Set the temperature to 220 degrees C and bake the pie for 20 minutes. The middle should be just set, and not move when slightly shaken. If the center still has a liquid or moveable texture, bake at additional 5 minute intervals until done.
- Cool the pies at room temperature for an hour, maximum 2 hours. Simply remove the basket from the air fryer, the pie can sit in the air fryer basket while it cools, this may be easier than removing the hot pie from the air fryer basket.
- Cool the pies in the fridge for at least 2 hours to firm up. Store loosely covered in the fridge for 3-4 days.

364. Air Fried Oreos

 Serving size:
12

 Preparation time:
10 minutes

 Cooking time:
15 minutes

 Total time:
25 minutes

Ingredients

- 1 large egg
- 40 ml. milk
- 1 teaspoon pure vanilla extract
- 130 grams pancake and baking mix, plus more if needed

- 2 tablespoons sugar
- Nonstick cooking spray
- 12 chocolates sandwich cookies, such as Oreos

Instructions

- Cut 2 sheets of baking paper to fit the basket of an air fryer without hanging over the edges and set aside. Preheat the air fryer to 220 degrees C.
- Whisk together the egg, milk and vanilla in a medium bowl. Add the pancake mix and sugar and whisk until smooth. The batter should be the consistency of thick cake batter to allow it to coat the cookie and hold its shape. If necessary, adjust the consistency by adding more pancake mix 1 tablespoon at a time.
- Line the basket of the air fryer with a piece of baking paper and spray lightly with cooking spray.
- Dip 6 cookies in the batter, letting the excess drip back into the bowl. Arrange the cookies on the baking paper in a single layer without touching. (Make sure to place a cookie on each of the four corners so the baking paper doesn't fly up during cooking.)
- Air fry at 200 degrees C until the battered coating is golden brown and puffed, about 7 minutes. Remove and repeat with the remaining sheet of baking paper and cookies.
- Dust the fried Oreos with icing sugar just before serving.

365. The Best Colorful Cake

 Serving size:
8

 Preparation time:
20 minutes

 Cooking time:
15 minutes

 Total time:
25 minutes

Ingredients

- 220 grams self raising flour
- 130 grams sugar
- 1/2 teaspoon baking soda
- 1 teaspoon baking powder
- 30 grams unsalted butter, room temperature
- 3 large egg whites
- 3 teaspoons pure vanilla extract
- 60 grams sour cream
- 60 ml. milk
- 50 grams sprinkles (colourful)
- 1/2 teaspoon salt
- 130 grams buttercream frosting

Instructions

- In a large mixing bowl, add the flour, sugar, baking soda, baking powder, mix well. Then in another bowl, add your wet ingredients, the butter, eggs, vanilla extract, sour cream, and milk. Mix well. Mix in your sprinkles.
- Pour your cake batter into a prepared tin (spared with cooking spray or baking spray) and pour the batter in about 2/3 way full. Set into the air fryer and bake at 220 degrees C, air fryer setting, for 12 to 15 minutes, or until a toothpick comes out clean.
- Let the cake cool before frosting and decorating the cake.
- Once cake is cool, frost the cake, and decorate.
- Plate, serve, and enjoy!

366. Jelly Donuts

 Serving size:
8

 Preparation time:
5 minutes

 Cooking time:
5 minutes

 Total time:
10 minutes

Ingredients

- 1 package Pillsbury Grands (Homestyle)
- 60 grams seedless raspberry jelly
- 1 tablespoon butter, melted
- 60 grams plain sugar

Instructions

- Preheat air fryer to 200 degrees C.
- Place Grand Rolls inside the air fryer in a single layer and cook for 5-6 minutes until golden brown.
- Remove the rolls from the air fryer and set aside.
- Place sugar into a wide bowl with a flat bottom.
- Baste butter on all sides of the donut and roll in the sugar to cover completely. Complete with all remaining donuts.
- Using a long cake tip, pipe 1-2 tablespoons of raspberry jelly into each donut.

367. Lava Cakes

 Serving size:
3

 Preparation time:
5 minutes

 Cooking time:
10 minutes

Total time:
15 minutes

Ingredients

- 6 tablespoon unsalted butter cut into pieces
- 200 grams semi-sweet chocolate bar broken into pieces
- 1 large egg
- 1 egg yolk from a large egg
- 3 Tablespoon white sugar
- ½ teaspoon vanilla extract
- 3 tablespoon plain flour
- pinch of salt

Instructions

- Grease 3 6-ounce ramekins and set aside.
- Melt butter and chocolate in a microwave-safe bowl in for about 1 minute until melted, stirring every 30 seconds. Set aside.
- In a separate large bowl, use an electric beater and beat egg, egg yolk, vanilla extract, and sugar together until well blended.
- Then add flour, the chocolate mixture, and a pinch of salt and stir until combined. Pour the mixture into the ramekins, filling each one about halfway.
- Place in the air fryer basket and air fry on 200 degrees C for 8-10 minutes.
- Once done air frying, use a clean thick dish towel to remove ramekins from the air fryer basket. Allow cake to cool in a ramekin for about 1 minute. Use a butter knife to loosen the cake from the ramekin and turn over onto a plate.
- Serve with fresh whipped cream, fresh berries, or topped with powdered sugar and enjoy.

368. Cookie Cake

 Serving size:
8

 Preparation time:
15 minutes

Cooking time:
10 minutes

Total time:
25 minutes

Ingredients

- 60 grams butter softened
- 60 grams plain sugar
- 60 grams light brown sugar
- 1 egg
- 1 teaspoon vanilla
- 1/2 teaspoon baking soda
- 1/4 teaspoon salt
- 300 grams plain flour
- 130 grams chocolate chips or chocolate chunks

Instructions

- Preheat air fryer to 220 degrees C. Grease two glass or metal pans that will fit in your air fryer.
- Cream together butter, sugar, and brown sugar. Add egg and vanilla. Mix in baking soda, salt, and flour. Stir in chocolate chips or chocolate chunks.
- Press cookie dough into the bottom of greased pan. One at a time, bake 10-12 minutes until lightly browned around the edges.

369. Cinnamon Sugar Fries

 Serving size:
4

 Preparation time:
5 minutes

 Cooking time:
15 minutes

 Total time:
20 minutes

Ingredients

- 2 sweet potatoes
- 1 tablespoon butter, melted
- 1 teaspoon butter, melted and separated from the above
- 2 tablespoons sugar
- 1/2 teaspoon cinnamon

Instructions

- Preheat your air fryer to 220 degrees C.
- Peel and cut the sweet potatoes into skinny fries.
- Coat fries with 1 tablespoon of butter.
- Cook fries in the preheated air fryer for 15-18 minutes. They can overlap but should not fill your air fryer more than 1/2 full.

- Remove the sweet potato fries from the air fryer and place them in a bowl.
- Coat with the remaining butter and add in sugar and cinnamon. Mix to coat.
- Enjoy immediately.

370. Pumpkin Pie Twists

 Serving size:
8

Preparation time:
5 minutes

 Cooking time:
6 minutes

 Total time:
11 minutes

Ingredients

- 1 can Pillsbury crescent rolls
- 60 grams pumpkin puree
- 2 teaspoons pumpkin pie spice
- 1/8 teaspoon salt
- 3 tablespoons unsalted butter, melted
- Icing
- 60 grams plain sugar
- 2 tablespoons melted butter
- 2 and 1/4 teaspoons milk

Instructions

- Roll out crescent roll dough and press down on any perforated lines.
- Cut dough into quarters by making one cut length-wise and then again width-wise. Cut into eighths if needed for smaller air fryers.
- Add pumpkin puree, half of the pumpkin pie spice, and salt, then mix to combine.
- Spread the pumpkin puree on top of crescent roll dough.
- Place the 2 of the crescent dough sheets on top of the other two, pumpkin side down. Make sure the corners and sides match up as well as possible.
- Using a dough or pizza cutter, cut each pumpkin twist sheet into 4 long strips, making a total of 8.
- Preheat air fryer to 220 degrees C for 2-3 minutes.
- Twist each strip 1-2 times on the bottom and 1-2 times on the top.
- Baste melted butter on top of the pumpkin pie twists and sprinkle with remaining pumpkin pie spice.
- Place the pumpkin twists into the air fryer evenly in one layer and not touching. Cook for 6 minutes.
- Meanwhile, make the icing by whisking the icing sugar, melted butter, and milk in a bowl.
- Remove Air Fryer Pumpkin Pie Twists from the air fryer and drizzle with icing.
- Enjoy immediately or store in a fridge for up to 3 days.

371. Apple Peanut Butter Wedges

 Serving size:
6

 Preparation time:
10 minutes

 Cooking time:
12 minutes

 Total time:
22 minutes

Ingredients

- 4 medium apples
- 130 grams plain flour
- 3 tablespoons Apple Pie Spice
- 3 large eggs
- 1 teaspoon vanilla extract
- 60 grams granulated sugar
- 2 teaspoons ground cinnamon

Instructions

- Peel the apples and cut into 1/2 inch wedges.
- In a bowl, whisk flour and apple pie spice.
- Pour the flour mixture into a gallon sized plastic zipper bag, followed by the apple slices. Zip closed with air, and shake vigorously to coat apples.
- Place a wire rack over the top of a baking sheet. Dump the apples onto the rack allowing the extra flour mixture to fall through and collect on the baking sheet.
- In a medium bowl whisk the eggs and vanilla together. Coat the apples in the egg mixture.
- To the extra flour mixture leftover on the baking sheet, dredge the egg dipped apple slices in the flour mixture again.
- Lay prepared apple slices in the air fryer basket without overlapping the slices and spray with canola oil. Air fry for 12 minutes at 220 degrees C, turning over half way through and spraying the other side with canola oil.
- In another medium bowl mix the sugar and cinnamon with a whisk. Sprinkle over warm apple slices.

372. Classic British S'mores

 Serving size:
4

 Preparation time:
1 minute

 Cooking time:
3 minutes

 Total time:
4 minutes

Ingredients

- 8 cracker squares or digestive biscuits
- 4 marshmallows
- 4 squares of milk chocolate

Instructions

- Heat air fryer to 200 degrees C. Place cracker halves or digestive biscuits in air fryer basket.
- Top each biscuit with a whole marshmallow. Air fry for 3-4 minutes or until marshmallows are golden brown.
- Remove from the air fryer and immediately place a chocolate square on top, or for extra gooey chocolate place the square on top of the marshmallow still in air fryer and air fry for another 30 seconds.
- Top with another cracker half or digestive biscuit. Enjoy immediately!

373. Donuts with Chocolate Glaze

 Serving size:
6

 Preparation time:
15 minutes

 Cooking time:
15 minutes

 Total time:
30 minutes

Ingredients

- 1 package Grand Flakey Biscuits
- 130 grams powdered sugar
- 3 1/2 tablespoons cocoa powder
- 1 teaspoon vanilla
- 3 1/2 tablespoons water
- Sprinkles optional

Instructions

- Open the biscuits and then use a small donut cutter to make a hole.
- Place the biscuit donuts in the air fryer on the lower rack at 220 degrees C and then cook for 3-4 minutes.
- Turn over the donuts and then air fry for another 1 minute.
- Once cool enough to handle dip the donuts into the chocolate glaze and top as desired.
- Chocolate Glaze
- In a bowl combine the chocolate glaze ingredients and mix until combined.

374. Cinnamon Bread Twists

 Serving size:
4

 Preparation time:
1o minutes

 Cooking time:
20 minutes

 Total time:
30 minutes

Ingredients

- For the Bread Twists Dough
- 120 grams plain Flour
- 1 teaspoon baking powder
- 1/4 teaspoon Kosher Salt
- 150 grams fat free Greek yogurt

- For Brushing on the Cooked Bread Twists
- 30 grams light butter
- 30 grams plain sugar
- 1-2 teaspoons ground cinnamon, to taste

Instructions

- Mix the flour, baking powder, and salt together before adding the Greek yogurt. Use a fork to stir everything together until a crumbly dough begins to form. Some dry flour should remain in the bowl.
- Transfer the crumbly dough onto a flat surface and work the dough into one smooth ball of dough. Portion the dough into six 45-gram pieces. Roll the pieces of dough between your palms or on the flat surface to form thin strips.
- Fold one end of each strip over to form a ribbon shape and transfer to an air fryer basket sprayed with cooking spray. Once all six bread twists are in the basket, spray the top with cooking spray and close the lid.
- Air fry at 220°C for 15 minutes.
- Towards the end of cooking, microwave the light butter and mix in the granulated sugar and cinnamon. Brush the cinnamon sugar butter on top of the bread twists as soon as they come out of the air fryer. Serve warm.

375. Glazed Air Fryer Donuts

 Serving size:
12

 Preparation time:
30 minutes

 Cooking time:
4 minutes

 Total time:
34 minutes

Ingredients

- 250 ml milk, lukewarm (about 100°F)
- 2 1/2 teaspoon active dry yeast, or instant yeast
- 50 grams plain sugar, plus 1 teaspoon
- 1/2 teaspoon salt
- 1 egg
- 60 grams unsalted butter, melted

- 375 grams plain flour
- Oil Spray, Coconut oil works best
- Glaze
- 6 tablespoons unsalted butter
- 240 grams powdered sugar
- 2 teaspoons vanilla extract
- 4 tablespoons hot water, or as needed

Instructions

- In the bowl of a stand mixer. fitted with the dough hook, gently stir together lukewarm milk, 1 teaspoon of sugar, and yeast. Let it sit for 10 minutes until foamy.
- Add sugar, salt, egg, melted butter and 2 cups of flour to the milk mixture. Mix on a low speed until combined, then with the mixer running, add the remaining cup of flour slowly, until the dough no longer sticks to the bowl. Increase the speed to medium-low and knead for 5 minutes, until the dough is elastic and smooth.
- Place the dough into a greased bowl and cover with cling film. Let rise in a warm place until doubled. Dough is ready if you make a dent with your finger and the indention remains.
- Turn the dough out onto a floured surface, punch it down and gently roll out. Cut out 10-12 donuts
- Transfer donuts and donut holes to lightly floured baking paper and cover loosely with greased cling film. Let donuts rise until doubled in volume, about 30 minutes. Preheat Air Fryer to 220 degrees C.
- Spray air fryer basket with oil spray, carefully transfer donuts to the basket in a single layer. Spray donuts with oil spray and cook at 220 degrees C until golden brown, for about 4 minutes. Repeat with remaining donuts and holes.
- While the donuts are in the air fryer, melt butter in a small saucepan over a medium heat. Stir in powdered sugar and vanilla extract until smooth. Remove from heat and stir in hot water one tablespoon at a time until the icing is somewhat thin, but not watery. Set aside.
- Dip hot donuts and donut holes in the glaze using to forks to submerge them. Place on a wire rack set over a rimmed baking tray to allow excess glaze to drip off. Let sit until glaze hardens, about 10 minutes.

376. British Apple Hand Pies

 Serving size:
6

 Preparation time:
8 minutes

 Cooking time:
10 minutes

 Total time:
18 minutes

Ingredients

- 2 package pie crusts, refrigerated
- ½ can apple pie filling
- 1 large egg

- 3 teaspoons turbinado sugar
- Caster sugar
- Caramel sauce

Instructions

- Remove pie crusts from packaging and allow to come to room temperature, per package instructions.
- Cut the pie crusts into 5-inch circles using a cookie cutter.
- Place two slices of apples from the apple pie filling onto the pie crusts on the bottom half of the crust. With a little water on the tip of your finger, moisten the outside edges of the pie crust. Fold dough over filling to form half-moons; pinch the edges of the crust together, then crimp edges with a fork to seal.
- In a small bowl, whisk together the egg with a splash of water. Brush the pies with the egg wash all over the tops.
- Sprinkle ½ teaspoon of the sugar over each pie.
- Make three slits in the crust on the top of the pies.
- Preheat the air fryer at 220 degrees C for 5 minutes. Spray the air fryer basket with nonstick cooking spray.
- Place 2 pies in the basket at a time and air fry for about 10 minutes or until the crust is golden brown and filling is bubbling. Carefully remove and transfer to a wire rack to cool.
- Repeat with remaining pies. (If your air fryer basket is large, you can cook more than 2 at a time as long as they are not touching at all.)
- Serve with caramel sauce for dipping!

377. British Pumpkin Hand Pies

	Serving size: 7		**Preparation time:** 10 minutes
	Cooking time: 12 minutes		**Total time:** 22 minutes

Ingredients

- 1 box premade pie crusts (2 pie crusts)
- 1 can of pumpkin pie mix
- 3 eggs
- 60 ml. condensed milk
- 1 pouch of white cookie icing (optional)

Instructions

- Roll out premade pie crust on a cutting board.
- Use a round cookie cutter or sandwich cutter to cut out circles in the pie crust.
- In a large bowl, mix canned pumpkin pie mix, 2 eggs and condensed milk.
- In half of the pie crust circles add approximately a tablespoon of pumpkin pie mix in the middle.
- Place the other pie crust circles on top and seal the edges together with a fork or sandwich sealer.

- Use a fork to whisk 1 egg in a small bowl. Egg wash each hand pie using a pastry brush.
- Arrange the hand pies on the air fryer rack or air fryer basket, keeping them from touching.
- Bake the hand pies in the air fryer for 12-15 minutes at 220 degrees C.
- Remove and place on a cooling rack.
- Add white cookie icing on top (optional).
- Serve warm.

378. Beignets

	Serving size: 20		**Preparation time:** 10 minutes
	Cooking time: 15 minutes		**Total time:** 25 minutes

Ingredients

- 250 grams plain flour, plus more for working the dough (see Cook's Note)
- 6 tablespoons granulated sugar
- 2 1/4 teaspoons instant yeast
- 1/2 teaspoon kosher salt
- 1 large egg, plus 1 large egg yolk
- 60 ml. lukewarm whole milk
- 3 tablespoons unsalted butter, melted, plus more for brushing the bowl
- 1 teaspoon pure vanilla extract
- Nonstick cooking spray

Instructions

- Combine the flour, sugar, yeast and salt in the bowl of a stand mixer. fitted with the dough hook and mix to combine. Add the egg, egg yolk, milk, butter and vanilla and mix on low to combine. Increase the speed to medium high and knead until the dough forms a loose ball around the hook and is smooth and elastic, should take about 3 minutes.
- Transfer the dough to a floured surface and lightly knead by hand just enough to bring it together into a smooth ball. Brush a medium bowl with melted butter and add the dough, turning to coat. Cover and let rise in a warm area until it has doubled in size, expect it to take 1 hour to 1 hour 15 minutes.
- Punch the dough down and roll out on a lightly floured surface to a square slightly larger than 10 inches by 10 inches. Trim the edges with a sharp knife or pizza cutter to make an even square. Cut the square in a 4 by 5 grid pattern to make 20 rectangles. Loosely cover the dough and let rise right on the countertop for about 15 minutes.

- Preheat air fryer to 220 degrees C. Spray the basket with cooking spray and add half the beignets. Spray the beignets lightly with cooking spray. Cook until puffed and golden, for about 6 minutes.
- Remove and repeat with the remaining beignets. Dust the beignets with icing sugar and serve warm.

379. Smores Pie

 Serving size:
4

 Preparation time:
2 minutes

 Cooking time:
6 minutes

 Total time:
8 minutes

Ingredients

- 6 premade mini pie crusts
- 12 snack bars (broken in half)
- 150 grams mini marshmallows

Instructions

- Pre heat your air fryer to 220 degrees C.
- Place 4 broken pieces of bar into each mini crust.
- Top with mini marshmallows, you want enough to completely cover your snack bars.
- Air fry at 220 degrees C for 5-7 minutes, depending on how toasty you want your marshmallows.
- Serve immediately & Enjoy!

380. Twix Cheesecake

 Serving size:
8

 Preparation time:
30 minutes

 Cooking time:
55 minutes

 Total time:
1 hour and 25 minutes

Ingredients

- Cookie Crust
- 250 grams plain flour
- 130 grams powdered sugar
- 1 ½ sticks butter melted
- Cheesecake
- 400 grams cream cheese softened
- 1 teaspoon lemon juice
- 2 eggs
- 50 grams double cream
- Half a packet jelly instant cheesecake pudding
- 300 grams powdered sugar
- Topping
- 1 jar caramel ice cream topping
- 1 chocolate almond bark melting chocolate
- 60 grams double cream

Instructions

- Crust
- Add the flour and powdered sugar in a bowl and blend well. Melt the butter in the microwave, and pour into the flour/powdered sugar mixture. Stir the butter into the flour.
- Line the bottom of a 7 inch spring-form tin with baking paper and press the flour mixture firmly into the bottom of the pan.
- Place the pan in the Air Fryer at 350 degrees, and set the time for 6 minutes.
- Cheesecake
- While the crust is baking, place the softened cream cheese in the mixing bowl of a stand mixer, and blend until smooth.
- Add the lemon juice, and eggs, and mix just until the eggs are blended. Add the cream to the instant pudding, and mix until smooth.
- Add the pudding to the mixing bowl. Add the powdered sugar and mix on low until smooth. Scrape down the sides of the bowl, and mix until completely blended.
- Remove the tin from the Air Fryer and pour the cheesecake mixture into the spring form tin.
- Set the time for 55 minutes, and bake the cheesecake at 220 degrees C.
- After about 10 minutes, open the Air Fryer, and cover the cheesecake loosely with foil. Place it back in the Air Fryer and finish cooking.
- When the cheesecake is done, leave it in the Air Fryer for 30 minutes, (with the Air Fryer turned off) and then remove the cheesecake. Place it on a wire rack to cool.
- When the cheesecake is cooled, cover with foil, and place in the fridge to set overnight for the best results. The next day, remove the cheesecake from the fridge, spoon the caramel topping on top, and place it back in the fridge.
- Topping
- Place the cream in a dish, and heat in the microwave, just until hot. Do not boil. Place three squares of Chocolate Almond Bark in the hot cream, and stir to melt the chocolate. If the chocolate doesn't completely melt, place it back in the microwave for 15 seconds, and stir until the chocolate is completely melted and smooth.
- Remove the cheesecake from the fridge and remove it from the tin. Place the cheesecake on a serving plate.
- Pour the hot Ganache (melted chocolate) over the cheesecake and allow it to run down the sides, and onto the serving plate. Place the cheesecake back in the fridge to set the chocolate a bit and until its time to serve. Serve on dessert plates, and enjoy!

381. Bread Pudding

 Serving size:
4

 Preparation time:
5 minutes

 Cooking time:
15 minutes

 Total time:
20 minutes

Ingredients

- 500 grams cubed white bread (cut into cubes), refer notes for bread choices
- 50 grams golden raisins
- Egg mixture
- 2 large eggs
- 130 ml. whole milk
- 40 grams double cream (or use whole milk)
- 5 tablespoons sugar
- 2 tablespoons melted butter
- 1 teaspoon vanilla extract
- 1/2 teaspoon ground cinnamon
- 1/8 teaspoon salt
- For serving
- Icing sugar, for dusting
- Vanilla ice cream, for serving

Instructions

- Add eggs into a bowl, whisk to combine, add remaining egg mixture ingredients (except butter) and whisk until sugar is dissolved. Stir in HOT melted butter (this helps in butter not clumping up when mixed with cold milk).
- Grease a 6-inch round cake tin with non-stick cooking spray, spread half the bread cubes, sprinkle half the raisins on top and pour about half the egg mixture evenly on top.
- Repeat process with remaining bread, raising and egg mixture. (Using the back of a spoon, gently press the bread into the liquid).
- Pre heat air fryer to 200°C for 15 minutes. When hot, place the baking tin inside the air fryer basket and bake for about 15 minutes (the top will be deep golden brown and a knife inserted in the middle comes clean).
- Rest for a few minutes, dust the top with icing sugar. Serve topped with a scoop of vanilla ice cream.

382. Strawberry Chimichangas

 Serving size:
6

 Preparation time:
20 minutes

 Cooking time:
5 minutes

 Total time:
25 minutes

Ingredients

- 200 grams cream cheese, room temperature
- 60 grams sour cream
- 40 grams plain sugar, divided
- 1 teaspoon lemon zest
- 1 teaspoon vanilla extract
- 160 grams strawberries, diced
- 6 flour tortillas
- 1 tablespoon cinnamon

Instructions

- In a small mixing bowl, beat the cream cheese, sour cream, ¼ sugar, lemon zest and vanilla.
- Fold in the strawberries.
- Lay out a tortilla and spoon 2 tablespoons of filling on one side.
- Fold that edge over, then fold in the sides. Roll up tightly without allowing filling to come out.
- Spray the air fryer basket with nonstick cooking spray. Add the chimichangas and spray them.
- Place the basket in the air fryer and set for 220°C. Set the timer for 5 minutes, turn them over at 3 minutes.
- Combine ½ sugar and the cinnamon together in a dish. Remove the chimichangas from the air fryer and roll in the cinnamon sugar.
- Serve immediately.

383. Coconut Macaroons

 Serving size:
36

 Preparation time:
15 minutes

 Cooking time:
55 minutes

 Total time:
1 hour and 40 minutes

Ingredients

- 1 packet sweetened flaked coconut
- 100 ml. sweetened condensed milk
- ¾ teaspoon kosher salt
- ½ teaspoon vanilla extract
- 2 large egg whites, at room temperature
- 300 grams bittersweet chocolate, chopped

Instructions

- Preheat an air fryer to 160 degrees C for 10 minutes. Cut a piece of baking paper to fit the air fryer basket, leaving 1 inch on each side to use as handles.

- Mix coconut, condensed milk, salt, and vanilla together in a large bowl.
- Beat egg whites in a medium bowl with an electric mixer with a whisk attachment on a medium-high speed until stiff peaks almost form, about 90 seconds. Fold egg whites into the coconut mixture.
- Working in batches, spoon level tablespoons of the coconut mixture into rounds and place on the baking paper, about 6 at time. Carefully transfer the paper with coconut rounds into the air fryer basket.
- Cook until golden brown and set, 9 to 10 minutes. Remove the baking paper from basket, transfer macaroons to a wire rack, and repeat the process with remaining coconut mixture using the same piece of baking paper.
- Microwave chocolate in a medium microwave-safe bowl on high power for 30 seconds, then stir. Continue microwaving and stirring in 30 second increments, until melted and smooth, about 90 seconds total.
- Dip flat bottoms of macaroons into melted chocolate and transfer to a baking paper-lined baking sheet to set. Let rest until chocolate firms, about 30 minutes.

384. Roasted Bananas

Serving size: 1		**Preparation time:** 2 minutes	
Cooking time: 7 minutes		**Total time:** 9 minutes	

Ingredients

- 1 banana, sliced
- avocado oil cooking spray

Instructions

- Line air fryer basket with baking paper.
- Preheat the air fryer to 190 degrees C.
- Place banana slices into the basket, making sure that they are not touching; cook in batches if necessary. Mist banana slices with avocado oil.
- Cook in the air fryer for 5 minutes. Remove basket and turn over the banana slices carefully (they will be soft).
- Cook until banana slices are browning and caramelized, an additional 2 to 3 minutes. Carefully remove from basket.

385. British Banana Cake

Serving size: 8		**Preparation time:** 5 minutes	
Cooking time: 35 minutes		**Total time:** 40 minutes	

Ingredients

- Dry ingredients
- 130 grams plain flour
- 1/2 teaspoon baking powder
- 1/2 teaspoon baking soda
- 1/4 teaspoon salt
- Wet ingredients
- 130 grams plus 2 tablespoons mashed banana (about 1 very large)
- 60 grams packet golden brown sugar
- 60 grams plain yogurt (refer notes to use Greek yogurt)
- 1 tablespoon vegetable oil
- 1 large egg
- 1 teaspoon vanilla extract

Instructions

- Pre heat air fryer to 220°C for 5 minutes (the air fryer will run empty during this time, this helps to kick start the baking process). Prepare cake batter in the mean time (if you are a beginner to baking, then we recommend this preheating process when you are in about step 3 or 4 of prepping the cake batter).
- Grease a round cake tin with non-stick cooking spray and set aside.
- Add all dry ingredients into a small bowl and whisk until combined.
- Add all wet ingredients into a larger bowl, whisk until smooth and combined. Stir in the dry ingredients and mix with a rubber spatula, until combined well.
- Transfer batter to the prepared pan, smooth top and sprinkle chopped walnuts on top.
- Set air fryer to 220°C for 35 minutes. When ready, place the cake tin into the air fryer basket and bake until done and brown.
- Check by inserting a knife into the middle of the cake and it needs to come out clean.
- Place the cake pan on a wire rack to cool completely.

Snacks

386. Crispy Lavash

Serving size: 3 servings	Preparation time: 15 minutes	Cooking time: 10 minutes	Total time: 25 minutes

Ingredients

- 130 grams plain flour
- 1 teaspoon white sesame seeds
- 1 teaspoon nigella seeds
- 1 tablespoon olive oil
- 120 ml. water
- 1 teaspoon salt
- 1 teaspoon red chilli powder

Instructions

- Preheat air fryer to 200 degrees C.
- In a food processor on stand mixer, add the flour, salt, and red chilli powder. Turn on the food processor, add the oil and slowly drizzle in the water until a ball forms.
- Divide the dough into two dough balls. Place them on the counter, cover with a towel and rest for few minutes.
- Lightly flour a clean countertop. Take one dough ball and use a rolling pin to roll out thinly in desired shape. Sprinkle with sesame seeds, and nigella seeds.
- Use a pizza cutter to make the dough into the desired shape.
- Line the bottom of your air fryer with foil.
- Air fry the chips for 10 minutes until they get a golden brown colour.

387. Large Broccoli Nuggets

Serving size: 3	Preparation time: 5 minutes	Cooking time: 10 minutes	Total time: 15 minutes

Ingredients

- 30 grams almond flour
- 250 grams broccoli flouretes
- 130 grams cheddar cheese
- 2 egg whites

Instructions

- Preheat the air fryer to 200 degrees C.
- Spray air fryer basket with cooking spray.
- Add cooked broccoli into the bowl and using a masher mash broccoli into the small pieces.
- Add remaining ingredients to the bowl and mix well to combine.
- Make small nuggets from broccoli mixture and place into the air fryer basket.
- Cook broccoli nuggets for 15 minutes. Turn halfway through.
- Serve and enjoy.

388. Mixed Nuts

 Serving size:
8

 Preparation time:
5 minutes

 Cooking time:
15 minutes

 Total time:
20 minutes

Ingredients

- 200 grams mixed nuts
- 1 teaspoon chipotle chilli powder
- 1 teaspoon ground cumin
- 1 tablespoon butter
- 1 teaspoon pepper
- Salt

Instructions

- In a bowl, combine all of the ingredients, coating the nuts well.
- Set your Air Fryer to 200°C and allow to heat for 5 minutes.
- Place the mixed nuts in the fryer basket and roast for 4 minutes, shaking the basket halfway through the cooking time.

389. Cheese Crisps

 Serving size:
4

 Preparation time:
5 minutes

 Cooking time:
15 minutes

 Total time:
20 minutes

Ingredients

- 100 grams parmesan cheese
- 100 grams cheddar cheese
- 1 teaspoon Italian seasoning
- 100 ml. marinara sauce

Instructions

- Start by preheating your air fryer to 200 degrees C. Place a piece of baking paper in the cooking basket.
- Mix the cheese with the Italian seasoning.
- Add about 1 tablespoon of the cheese mixture (per crisp to the basket, making sure they are not touching. Bake for 6 minutes or until browned to your liking.
- Work in batches and place them on a large tray to cool slightly. Serve with the marinara sauce. Bon appétit!

390. Cashew Bowls

 Serving size:
4

 Preparation time:
5 minutes

 Cooking time:
5 minutes

 Total time:
10 minutes

Ingredients

- 200 grams cashews
- 1 teaspoon ranch seasoning
- 1 teaspoon sesame oil

Instructions

- Preheat the air fryer to 200 degrees C.
- Mix up cashew with ranch seasoning and sesame oil and put in the preheated air fryer.
- Cook the cashew for 4 minutes.
- Then shake well and cook for minute more.

391. Cheese Straws

 Serving size:
6

 Preparation time:
10 minutes

 **Cooking time:**
30 minutes

 Total time:
40 minutes

Ingredients

- 130 grams plain flour
- Salt
- Pepper
- ¼ teaspoon paprika
- ½ teaspoon celery seeds
- 250 grams cheddar cheese
- 1 stick butter

Instructions

- Start by preheating your air Fryer to 170 degrees C. Line the air fryer basket with baking paper.
- In a mixing bowl, thoroughly combine the flour, salt, black pepper, paprika, and celery seeds.
- Then, combine the cheese and butter in the bowl of a stand mixer. Slowly stir in the flour mixture and mix to combine well.
- Then, pack the dough into a cookie press fitted with a star disk. Pipe the long ribbons of dough across the baking paper. Then cut into strips.
- Bake in the preheated air fryer for 1 minute.
- Repeat with the remaining dough. Let the cheese straws cool on a rack. You can store them between sheets of baking paper in an airtight container. Bon appétit!

392. Radish Chips with Sage

 Serving size: 6

 Preparation time: 5 minutes

 Cooking time: 35 minutes

 Total time: 40 minutes

Ingredients

- 300 grams radish
- ½ teaspoon sage
- 2 teaspoons avocado oil
- Salt

Instructions

- In the mixing bowl mix up radish, sage, avocado oil, and salt.
- Preheat the air fryer to 200 degrees C.
- Put the sliced radish in the air fryer basket and cook it for 35 minutes.
- Shake the vegetables every minutes.

393. Courgette Rolls

 Serving size: 4

 Preparation time: 5 minutes

 Cooking time: 15 minutes

 Total time: 20 minutes

Ingredients

- 3 courgettes
- 1 tablespoon olive oil
- 130 grams goat cheese
- Black pepper

Instructions

- Preheat your Air Fryer to 170°C.
- Coat each courgette strip with a light brushing of olive oil.
- Combine the sea salt, black pepper and goat cheese.
- Scoop a small, equal amount of the goat cheese onto the center of each strip of courgette. Roll up the strips and secure with a toothpick.
- Transfer to the air fryer and cook for minutes until the cheese is warm and the courgette slightly crispy.
- If desired, add some tomato sauce on top.

394. Carrot and Tortilla Dip

 Serving size: 6

 Preparation time: 10 minutes

 Cooking time: 15 minutes

 Total time: 25 minutes

Ingredients

- 250 grams carrots
- ¼ teaspoon cayenne pepper
- 4 tablespoons butter
- 1 tablespoon chives
- Pepper
- Salt

Instructions

- Add all ingredients into the air fryer baking dish and stir until well combined.
- Place dish in the air fryer and cook at 170 degrees C for 15 minutes.
- Transfer the cooked carrot mixture into the blender and blend until smooth.
- Serve and enjoy.

395. Turmeric Popcorn

 Serving size: 4

 Preparation time: 5 minutes

 Cooking time: 11 minutes

 Total time: 16 minutes

Ingredients

- 200 grams cauliflower florets
- 1 teaspoon ground turmeric
- 2 eggs, beaten
- 2 tablespoons almond flour
- 1 teaspoon salt
- Cooking spray

Instructions

- Cut the cauliflower florets into small pieces and sprinkle with ground turmeric and salt.
- Then dip the vegetables in the eggs and coat in the almond flour. Preheat the air fryer to 200 degrees C.
- Place the cauliflower popcorn in the air fryer in one layer and cook for 7 minutes.
- Give a good shake to the vegetables and cook them for 4 minutes more.

396. Sweet Potato Tots

 Serving size:
25

 Preparation time:
5 minutes

 Cooking time:
31 minutes

 Total time:
36 minutes

Ingredients

- 2 sweet potatoes, peeled
- 1/2 tsp cajun seasoning
- Salt

Instructions

- Add water in large pot and bring to boil. Add sweet potatoes in pot and boil for minutes. Drain well.
- Grate the boiled sweet potatoes into a large bowl using a grater.
- Add cajun seasoning and salt in grated sweet potatoes and mix until well combined.
- Spray air fryer basket with cooking spray.
- Make small tot of sweet potato mixture and place in air fryer basket.
- Cook at 160 degrees C for 8 minutes. Turn tots to another side and cook for 8 minutes more.
- Serve and enjoy.

397. Crispy Potatoes with Rosemary

 Serving size:
8

 Preparation time:
10 minutes

 Cooking time:
30 minutes

 Total time:
40 minutes

Ingredients

- 2 tablespoons olive oil
- 2 teaspoons chopped fresh rosemary leaves
- 1 teaspoon salt
- ½ teaspoon pepper
- ½ teaspoon garlic powder
- 2 red potatoes, cut into 1-inch pieces

Instructions

- In a large bowl, mix oil, rosemary, salt, pepper and garlic powder. Add potatoes; toss to coat.
- Using a slotted spoon, place potato mixture into air fryer basket. Set to 200°C; cook 25 to 30 minutes, shaking basket every 10 minutes, until potatoes are tender and browned.

398. Spiced Chicken Wings

 Serving size:
4

 Preparation time:
10 minutes

 Cooking time:
20 minutes

 Total time:
30 minutes

Ingredients

- Nonstick cooking spray, for the basket
- 1 kg. chicken wings, split at the joint and tips removed
- Kosher salt
- 4 tablespoons unsalted butter
- 30 grams hot sauce, such as Frank's Red Hot
- Ranch or blue cheese dressing, for serving

Instructions

- Spray the basket of a 3.5-quart air fryer with cooking spray and set aside. Pat the chicken wings dry and sprinkle generously with salt. Place the wings in the fryer basket so they are not touching (if necessary to fit, line up the drumettes standing upright along the sides).
- Set the air fryer to 200 degrees C and cook for 12 minutes, then turn the wings with tongs and cook for 12 minutes more. Turn the wings again, increase the heat to 200 degrees C and cook until the outsides are extra-crispy, about 6 minutes more.
- Meanwhile, warm the butter in a microwave-safe bowl in the microwave until melted, about 1 minute. Whisk in the hot sauce.
- Toss the wings with the butter mixture to coat in a large bowl and serve with dressing on the side.

399. Feta Brussels Sprouts

 Serving size:
4

 Preparation time:
10 minutes

 Cooking time:
20 minutes

 Total time:
30 minutes

Ingredients

- 300 grams Brussels sprouts, trimmed and cut off the ends
- 1 teaspoon kosher salt
- 1 tablespoon lemon zest
- Non-stick cooking spray
- 130 grams feta cheese, cubed

Instructions

- Firstly, peel the Brussels sprouts using a small paring knife. Toss the leaves with salt and lemon zest; spritz them with a cooking spray, coating all sides.
- Bake at 200 degrees C for 8 minutes; shake the cooking basket halfway through the cooking time and cook for 7 more minutes.
- Make sure to work in batches so everything can cook evenly. Taste and adjust the seasonings. Serve with feta cheese.

400. Pepper Chips

 Serving size:
4

 Preparation time:
5 minutes

 Cooking time:
20 minutes

 Total time:
25 minutes

Ingredients

- 1 egg, beaten
- 130 grams parmesan, grated
- 1 teaspoon sea salt
- 1/2 teaspoon red pepper flakes, crushed
- 200 grams peppers, deveined and cut into strips
- 2 tablespoons grapeseed oil

Instructions

- In a mixing bowl, combine together the egg, parmesan, salt, and red pepper flakes; mix to combine well.
- Dip peppers into the batter and transfer them to the cooking basket. Brush with the grapeseed oil.
- Cook in the preheated air fryer at 200 degrees C for 4 minutes. Shake the basket and cook for a further 3 minutes.
- Work in batches.
- Taste, adjust the seasonings and serve.

401. Broccoli Chips

 Serving size:
4

 Preparation time:
10 minutes

 **Cooking time:**
15 minutes

 Total time:
25 minutes

Ingredients

- 200 grams broccoli florets
- 1/2 teaspoon onion powder
- 1 teaspoon granulated garlic

- 1/2 teaspoon cayenne pepper
- Sea salt and ground black pepper, to taste
- 2 tablespoons sesame oil
- 4 tablespoons parmesan cheese, preferably freshly grated

Instructions

- Start by preheating the air fryer to 170 degrees C.
- Blanch the broccoli in salted boiling water until al dente, about 3 to 4 minutes. Drain well and transfer to the lightly greased air fryer basket.
- Add the onion powder, garlic, cayenne pepper, salt, black pepper, and sesame oil.
- Cook for 6 minutes, tossing halfway through the cooking time.

402. Baby Corns with Garlic

 Serving size:
4

 Preparation time:
10 minutes

 Cooking time:
20 minutes

Total time:
30 minutes

Ingredients

- 250 grams baby corns, boiled
- 130 grams flour
- 1 teaspoon garlic powder
- ½ teaspoon carom seeds
- ¼ teaspoon chilli powder
- Pinch of baking soda
- Salt to taste

Instructions

- In a bowl, combine the flour, chilli powder, garlic powder, baking soda, salt and carom seeds. Add in a little water to create a batter-like consistency.
- Coat each baby corn in the batter.
- Pre-heat the air fryer at 200 degrees C.
- Cover the air fryer basket with tin foil before laying the coated baby corns on top of the foil.
- Cook for 10 minutes.

403. Pickle Chips

 Serving size:
5

 Preparation time:
5 minutes

 Cooking time:
20 minutes

 Total time:
25 minutes

Ingredients

- 50 grams cornmeal
- 60 grams plain flour
- 1 teaspoon cayenne pepper
- 1/2 teaspoon shallot powder
- 1 teaspoon garlic powder
- 1/2 teaspoon porcini powder
- Kosher salt and ground black pepper, to taste
- 2 eggs
- 300 grams pickle slices, pat dry with kitchen towels

Greek Yogurt Dip:

- 100 grams Greek yogurt
- 1 clove garlic, chopped
- 1/4 teaspoon ground black pepper
- 1 tablespoon fresh chives, chopped

Instructions

- In a shallow bowl, mix the cornmeal and flour; add the seasonings and mix to combine well. Beat the eggs in a separate shallow bowl.
- Dredge the pickle slices in the flour mixture, then, in the egg mixture. Press the pickle slices into the flour mixture again, coating evenly.
- Cook in the preheated air fryer at 200 degrees C for 5 minutes; shake the basket and cook for 5 minutes more. Work in batches.
- Meanwhile, mix all the sauce ingredients until well combined. Serve the fried pickles with the Greek yogurt dip and enjoy.

404. Cashew Dip

 Serving size:
6

 Preparation time:
5 minutes

 Cooking time:
8 minutes

 Total time:
11 minutes

Ingredients

- 90 grams cashews, soaked in water for 4 hours and drained
- 3 tablespoons coriander, chopped
- 2 garlic cloves, chopped
- 1 teaspoon lime juice
- A pinch of salt and black pepper
- 2 tablespoons coconut milk

Instructions

- In a blender, combine all the ingredients, pulse well and transfer to a ramekin.
- Put the ramekin in your air fryer's basket and cook at 170 degrees C for 8 minutes.
- Serve as a party dip.

405. Quick Popcorn

 Serving size:
4

 Preparation time:
5 minutes

 Cooking time:
20 minutes

 Total time:
25 minutes

Ingredients

- 2 tablespoons dried corn kernels
- 1 teaspoon sunflower oil
- Kosher salt, to taste
- 1 teaspoon red pepper flakes, crushed

Instructions

- Add the dried corn kernels to the air fryer basket; brush with sunflower oil.
- Cook at 200 degrees C for 15 minutes, shaking the basket every 5 minutes.
- Sprinkle with salt and red pepper flakes.

406. Roasted Parsnip

 Serving size:
5

 Preparation time:
5 minutes

 **Cooking time:**
55 minutes

 Total time:
1 hour

Ingredients

- 6 large parsnips
- 1 tablespoon maple syrup
- 1 tablespoon coconut oil
- 1 tablespoon dried parsley flakes

Instructions

- Melt the duck fat or coconut oil in your air fryer for 2 minutes at 200°C.
- Rinse the parsnips to clean them and dry them. Chop into cubes. Transfer to the fryer.
- Cook the parsnip cubes in the fat/oil for 35 minutes, tossing them regularly.
- Season the parsnips with parsley and maple syrup and allow to cook for another 5 minutes or longer to achieve a soft texture throughout.

407. Green Tomatoes

 Serving size:
2

 Preparation time:
5 minutes

 Cooking time:
10 minutes

Total time:
15 minutes

Ingredients

- 2 medium green tomatoes
- 1 egg
- 50 grams blanched finely ground flour
- 100 grams parmesan cheese, grated

Instructions

- Slice the tomatoes, about a half-inch thick.
- Crack the egg into a bowl and beat it with a whisk. In a separate bowl, mix together the flour and parmesan cheese.
- Dredge the tomato slices in egg, then dip them into the flour cheese mixture to coat. Place each slice into the fryer basket. They may need to be cooked in multiple batches.
- Cook at 200 degrees C for 7 minutes, turning them halfway through the cooking time, and then serve warm.

408. Fish Sticks with Basil

 Serving size:
4

 Preparation time:
5 minutes

 Cooking time:
10 minutes

 Total time:
15 minutes

Ingredients

- 1 box fish sticks frozen
- 1 tablespoon dried basil

Instructions

- Preheat air fryer to 200 degrees C for 5 minutes.
- Pour frozen fish sticks into air fryer basket in one layer, so they aren't overlapping
- Cook for 5 minutes, gently shake the basket or turn pieces over. Then continue cooking for 4-5 minutes until they're as crispy on the outside as you'd like.
- Add dried basil all over the fish sticks.

409. Avocado Wedges

 Serving size:
4

 Preparation time:
5 minutes

 Cooking time:
8 minutes

 Total time:
11 minutes

Ingredients

- 4 avocados, peeled, pitted and cut into wedges
- 1 egg, whisked
- 130 grams almond meal
- A pinch of salt and black pepper
- Cooking spray

Instructions

- Put the egg in a bowl, and the almond meal in another.
- Season avocado wedges with salt and pepper, coat them in egg and then in the almond meal.
- Arrange the avocado bites in your air fryer's basket, grease them with cooking spray and cook at 200 degrees C for 8 minutes.

410. Tofu with Lemon

 Serving size:
4

 Preparation time:
5 minutes

 Cooking time:
15 minutes

Total time:
20 minutes

Ingredients

- 200 grams tofu, drained and pressed
- 1 tablespoons arrowroot powder
- 1 tablespoons tamari
- For sauce:
- 2 teaspoon arrowroot powder
- 2 tablespoon erythritol
- 40 ml. water
- 40 ml. lemon juice
- 1 teaspoon lemon zest

Instructions

- Cut tofu into cubes. Add tofu and tamari into the zip-lock bag and shake well.
- Add 1 tablespoon arrowroot into the bag and shake well to coat the tofu. Set aside for 15 minutes.

- Meanwhile, in a bowl, mix together all the sauce ingredients and set aside.
- Spray air fryer basket with cooking spray.
- Add tofu into the air fryer basket and cook at 170 degrees C for 10 minutes. Shake halfway through.
- Add cooked tofu and sauce mixture into the pan and cook over medium-high heat for 3-5 minutes.

411. Muffins from Mexico

 Serving size:
4

 Preparation time:
5 minutes

 Cooking time:
15 minutes

 Total time:
20 minutes

Ingredients

- 130 grams minced beef
- 1 teaspoon taco seasonings
- 150 grams Mexican blend cheese, shredded
- 1 teaspoon keto tomato sauce
- Cooking spray

Instructions

- Preheat the air fryer to 170 degrees C.
- Meanwhile, in the mixing bowl mix up minced beef and taco seasonings. Spray the muffin moulds with cooking spray.
- Then transfer the beef mixture into the muffin moulds and top them with cheese and tomato sauce.
- Transfer the muffin moulds in the preheated air fryer and cook them for 15 minutes.

412. Beef Bites

 Serving size:
2

 Preparation time:
5 minutes

 Cooking time:
15 minutes

 Total time:
20 minutes

Ingredients

- 1 teaspoon cayenne pepper
- 200 grams beef loin, chopped
- 1 tablespoon coconut flour
- 1 teaspoon nut oil
- ¼ teaspoon salt
- 1 teaspoon apple cider vinegar

Instructions

- Sprinkle the beef with apple cider vinegar and salt.
- Then sprinkle it with cayenne pepper and coconut flour. Shake the meat well and transfer in the air fryer.
- Sprinkle it with nut oil and cook at 200 degrees C for 15 minutes.
- Shake the beef popcorn every 5 minutes to avoid burning.

413. Avocado and Tomato Egg Rolls

 Serving size:
4

 Preparation time:
5 minutes

 Cooking time:
10 minutes

 Total time:
15 minutes

Ingredients

- 10 egg roll wrappers
- 3 avocados, peeled and pitted
- 1 tomato, diced
- Salt and pepper, to taste

Instructions

- Pre-heat your Air Fryer to 200°C.
- Put the tomato and avocados in a bowl. Sprinkle on some salt and pepper and mash together with a fork until a smooth consistency is achieved.
- Spoon equal amounts of the mixture onto the wrappers. Roll the wrappers around the filling, enclosing them entirely.
- Transfer the rolls to a lined baking dish and cook for 5 minutes.

414. Herbs and Tomatoes

 Serving size:
2

 Preparation time:
5 minutes

 Cooking time:
30 minutes

 Total time:
35 minutes

Ingredients

- 2 large tomatoes
- 1 teaspoon oregano
- 1 teaspoon basil
- 1 teaspoon thyme
- 1 teaspoon rosemary
- 1 teaspoon sage

Instructions

- Spray both sides of each tomato half with a small amount of cooking spray.
- Coat the tomatoes with a light sprinkling of pepper and herbs of your choice.
- Place the tomatoes in the basket, cut-side-up. Cook at 200 degrees C for 20 minutes, or longer if necessary.
- Serve hot, at room temperature, or chilled as a refreshing summer snack. Optionally, you can garnish them with grated Parmesan and chopped parsley before serving.

415. Deviled Eggs

 Serving size:
3

 Preparation time:
5 minutes

 Cooking time:
25 minutes

 Total time:
30 minutes

Ingredients

- 6 eggs
- 6 slices bacon
- 2 tablespoons mayonnaise
- 1 teaspoon hot sauce
- 1/2 teaspoon Worcestershire sauce
- 2 tablespoons onions, chopped
- 1 tablespoon pickle relish
- Salt and ground black pepper, to taste
- 1 teaspoon smoked paprika

Instructions

- Place the wire rack in the air fryer basket; lower the eggs onto the wire rack.
- Cook at 170 degrees C for 15 minutes.
- Transfer them to an ice-cold water bath to stop them cooking. Peel the eggs under cold running water; slice them into halves.
- Cook the bacon at 200 degrees C for 3 minutes; flip the bacon over and cook an additional 3 minutes; chop the bacon and reserve.
- Mash the egg yolks with the mayo, hot sauce, Worcestershire sauce, onions, pickle relish, salt, and black pepper. Add the reserved bacon and spoon the yolk mixture into the egg whites.
- Garnish with smoked paprika.

416. Ricotta Balls

 Serving size:
4

 Preparation time:
5 minutes

 Cooking time:
25 minutes

 Total time:
30 minutes

Ingredients

- 250 grams ricotta, grated
- 2 eggs, separated
- 2 tablespoons chives, finely chopped
- 2 tablespoons fresh basil, finely chopped
- 4 tablespoons plain flour
- Salt
- Pepper
- 1 teaspoon orange zest, grated
- For coating
- 40 grams friendly bread crumbs
- 1 tablespoon vegetable oil

Instructions

- Pre-heat your Air Fryer at 200°C.
- In a bowl, combine the yolks, flour, salt, pepper, chives and orange zest. Throw in the ricotta and incorporate with your hands.
- Mould equal amounts of the mixture into balls.
- Mix the oil with the bread crumbs until a crumbly consistency is achieved.
- Coat the balls in the bread crumbs and transfer each one to the fryer's basket.
- Put the basket in the fryer. Air fry for 8 minutes or until a golden brown colour is achieved.
- Serve with a sauce of your choosing, such as ketchup.

417. Onion Dip

 Serving size:
8

 Preparation time:
5 minutes

Cooking time:
25 minutes

 Total time:
30 minutes

Ingredients

- 200 grams onion, chopped
- 1/2 teaspoon baking soda
- 6 tablespoon butter, softened
- Pepper
- Salt

Instructions

- Melt butter in a pan over medium heat.
- Add onion and baking soda and sauté for 5 minutes.
- Transfer onion mixture into the air fryer baking dish.
- Place in the air fryer and cook at 200 degrees C for 25 minutes.
- Serve and enjoy.

418. Okra with Sesame

 Serving size:
4

 Preparation time:
5 minutes

 Cooking time:
4 minutes

 Total time:
9 minutes

Ingredients

- 250 grams okra
- 1 egg
- 1 teaspoon sesame seeds
- 1 tablespoon sesame oil
- Pepper
- Salt

Instructions

- In a bowl, whisk together egg, pepper, and salt.
- Add okra into the whisked egg. Sprinkle with sesame seeds.
- Preheat the air fryer to 200 degrees C.
- Stir okra well. Spray air fryer basket with cooking spray.
- Place okra pieces into the air fryer basket and cook for 4 minutes.
- Serve and enjoy.

419. Prawn and Cabbage Egg Rolls

 Serving size:
3

 Preparation time:
10 minutes

 Cooking time:
15 minutes

 Total time:
15 minutes

Ingredients

- 1 tablespoon toasted sesame oil
- 1 teaspoon grated ginger
- 3 garlic cloves, chopped
- 2 large spring onions, chopped
- 170 grams chopped green cabbage
- 70 grams shredded carrots
- 2 tablespoons reduced sodium soy sauce
- 1/2 tablespoon unseasoned rice vinegar
- 300 grams large peeled raw shrimp, chopped
- 6 egg roll wrappers
- Olive oil spray
- Sweet chili sauce, duck sauce or spicy mustard, for dipping (optional)

Instructions

- In a large pan, heat sesame oil over a medium-high heat. Add the shrimp and sauté, until shrimp is almost cooked through, 1 to 2 minutes.
- Add ginger, garlic and spring onions. Sauté until fragrant, about 30 seconds. Add cabbage and carrots, soy sauce and vinegar.
- Cook on high heat until vegetables are tender crisp, about 2 to 3 minutes. Transfer to a colander to drain and let cool.
- One at a time, place an egg roll wrapper on a clean surface, points facing top and bottom like a diamond. Spoon half from mixture onto the bottom third of the wrapper.
- Dip your finger in a small bowl of water and run it along the edges of the wrapper. Lift the point nearest you and wrap it around the filling.
- Fold the left and right corners in toward the centre and continue to roll into a tight cylinder. Set aside and repeat with remaining wrappers and filling.
- Spray all sides of the egg rolls with oil using your fingers to evenly coat.
- In batches, cook 200 degrees C for 5 to 7 minutes, turning halfway through until golden brown.
- Serve immediately, with dipping sauce on the side, if desired.

420. Buffalo Sauce Cauliflower

 Serving size:
2

 Preparation time:
5 minutes

 Cooking time:
15 minutes

 Total time:
20 minutes

Ingredients

- ½ head cauliflower
- 100 grams buffalo sauce (we used Frank's Red Hot Buffalo Wing Sauce, 120 ml)
- 30 ml. olive oil
- 1 teaspoon garlic powder
- ½ teaspoon salt
- To serve: creamy dip (like ranch or bleu cheese) and celery stalks

Instructions

- Cut cauliflower into bite-sized florets. In a large bowl, gently stir together cauliflower and all remaining ingredients.

- Cook: Lightly grease your air fryer basket or rack. Arrange cauliflower in a single layer (working in batches if they don't all fit in a single layer). Cook at 190°C for 12 to 15 minutes, or until fork tender and slightly browned.
- Serve: Serve warm with your favorite dipping sauce and celery sticks.

421. Chicken Taquitos with Special Chicken Sauce

 Serving size:
6

 Preparation time:
15 minutes

 Cooking time:
20 minutes

 Total time:
35 minutes

Ingredients

- 1 teaspoon vegetable oil
- 2 tablespoons diced onion
- 1 clove garlic, chopped
- 2 tablespoons chopped green chilles
- 2 tablespoons Mexican-style hot tomato sauce
- 130 grams shredded rotisserie chicken
- 2 tablespoons Neufchatel cheese
- 130 grams shredded Mexican cheese blend
- 1 pinch salt and ground black pepper to taste
- 6 corn tortillas
- 1 serving avocado oil cooking spray

Instructions

- Heat oil in a pan. Add onion and cook until soft and translucent, 3 to 5 minutes. Add garlic and cook until fragrant, about 1 minute. Add green chilles and Mexican tomato sauce; stir to combine. Add chicken, Neufchatel cheese, and Mexican cheese blend. Cook and stir until cheeses have melted and mixture is completely warmed, about 3 minutes. Season with salt and pepper.
- Heat tortillas in a pan or directly on the grates of a gas stove until soft and pliable. Place 3 tablespoons of chicken mixture down the centre of each tortilla. Fold over and roll into taquitos.
- Preheat an air fryer to 200 degrees C.
- Place taquitos in the air fryer basket, making sure they are not touching, and mist with avocado oil. Cook in batches if necessary. Cook until golden brown and crispy, 6 to 9 minutes. Turn taquitos over, mist with avocado oil, and air fry for an additional 3 to 5 minutes.

422. Grill Cheese Sandwich

 Serving size:
1

 Preparation time:
5 minutes

 Cooking time:
10 minutes

 Total time:
15 minutes

Ingredients

- 2 slices of bread
- 15 grams butter
- 50 grams cheddar cheese

Instructions

- Lay cheese in between the bread. Butter the outside of the bread.
- Lay the sandwich in air fryer basket. If needed, use two toothpicks to secure the sandwich together by sticking it through the sandwich.
- Air Fry at 200°C for about 3-5 minute.
- Turn the sandwich and increase the heat to 200°C to finish and crisp the bread. Finish air frying for about 5 minutes or until the sandwich is to your preferred texture. Check on the sandwich often to make sure it doesn't burn (different breads will toast quicker or slower than others). Allow to cool a bit before biting into the yummy grilled cheese sandwiches for the cheese to melt.

423. Chicken Tenders with Special Chicken Sauce

 Serving size:
4

 Preparation time:
10 minutes

 Cooking time:
50 minutes

 Total time:
1 hour and 5 minutes

Ingredients

- Chicken tenders
- 500 grams chicken tenders
- Kosher salt
- Freshly ground black pepper
- 100 grams plain flour
- 100 grams panko breadcrumbs
- 2 large eggs
- 100 ml. buttermilk
- Cooking spray
- Honey mustard
- 90 grams mayonnaise
- 3 tablespoons honey
- 2 tablespoons Dijon mustard
- 1/4 teaspoon hot sauce (optional)
- Pinch of kosher salt
- Freshly ground black pepper

Instructions

- Season chicken tenders on both sides with salt and pepper. Place flour and breadcrumbs in two separate shallow bowls. In a third bowl, whisk together eggs and buttermilk. Working one at a time, dip chicken in flour, then egg mixture, and finally in breadcrumbs, pressing to coat.
- Working in batches, place chicken tenders in basket of air fryer, being sure to not overcrowd
- it. Spray the tops of chicken with cooking spray and cook at 200° for 5 minutes. Flip chicken over, spray the tops with more cooking spray and cook 5 minutes more. Repeat with remaining chicken tenders.
- Make sauce: In a small bowl, whisk together mayonnaise, honey, dijon, and hot sauce, if using. Season with a pinch of salt and a few cracks of black pepper.
- Serve chicken tenders with honey mustard.

424. Spicy Chicken Tenders

	Serving size: 4		**Preparation time:** 10 minutes
	Cooking time: 10 minutes		**Total time:** 20 minutes

Ingredients

- 60 grams mayonnaise
- 1-2 tablespoons hot sauce
- 1 tablespoon chopped dill pickles
- 2 teaspoons wholegrain mustard
- 1 clove garlic, peeled and chopped
- 40 grams plain flour
- 3 large eggs, beaten
- 2 tablespoons Dijon mustard
- 200 grams cornflakes, crushed into a coarse meal
- 60 grams cornmeal
- 1 tablespoon Cajun seasoning, divided
- 1 ½ teaspoons kosher or sea salt, divided + more for serving
- ¾ teaspoon ground black pepper, divided
- 1 kg. chicken tenderloins or boneless skinless chicken breasts, cut into 12 strips

Instructions

- In a small bowl, whisk together the remoulade ingredients. Cover and place in the fridge.
- Preheat the air fryer to 200 degrees. Coat the basket with cooking spray.
- Set up 3 shallow bowls, one with the flour, one with the eggs and Dijon mustard and one with the crushed cornflakes and cornmeal.

- Distribute the Cajun seasoning, salt and black pepper into each bowl and thoroughly whisk each to combine.
- Dip each chicken tender into the flour mixture, then the egg mixture, then the cornflake mixture, thoroughly dredging on all sides, and place on a plate. Repeat with the remaining chicken tenders.
- Coat each tender with cooking spray. Cook in batches in the air fryer for 7-10 minutes.
- Dust the chicken strips with more salt, if desired. Serve immediately with remoulade.

425. British Quiche

	Serving size: 2		**Preparation time:** 10 minutes
	Cooking time: 10 minutes		**Total time:** 20 minutes

Ingredients

- 1 egg
- 60 ml double cream
- 5 broccoli florets
- 1 tablespoon cheddar cheese, grated

Instructions

- Whisk together egg and cream. Lightly grease a ceramic quiche dish. Distribute broccoli florets on the bottom. Pour in the egg mixture. Top with grated cheddar cheese.
- Air fry at 162 degrees C for 10 minutes.

426. Bacon Quiche

	Serving size: 1		**Preparation time:** 10 minutes
	Cooking time: 15 minutes		**Total time:** 25 minutes

Ingredients

- 1 Pie crust dough
- 130 grams swiss cheese
- 2 tablespoons cooked bacon crumbles
- 1 large egg
- 1 tablespoon double cream
- Salt
- Pepper

Instructions

- Remove the pie crust from the fridge about 15 minutes before preparing the quiche.

- Unroll the dough and place your tart pan on top of the crust. Cut a circle.
- Press the crust into the tart pan, tucking the edges down along the sides and cutting off any excess dough so that the crust is even with the top of the pan.
- Place the tart pan into the basket of the air fryer and cook at 200°C for 5 minutes.
- Sprinkle cheese into the bottom of the tart pan and then sprinkle bacon over the top of the cheese.
- Whisk together egg and cream until smooth. Take a moment to whisk some extra air into the egg mixture.
- Carefully pour egg mixture over the fillings in the crust. The egg mixture should reach the top edge of the crust. Do not overfill.
- Place the prepared quiche back into the air fryer's basket and cook at 200°C for another 10 minutes or until the egg is set in the centre.
- Allow to cool for 1-2 minutes, and then carefully pop the quiche from the tart pan. Use a spatula to remove the quiche from the bottom plate of the tart pan and serve immediately or set it on a cooling rack to cool. Plate, serve, and enjoy!

427. Parmesan Chicken Fingers

 Serving size: 4   **Preparation time:** 9 minutes

 Cooking time: 9 minutes   **Total time:** 18 minutes

Ingredients

- 8 chicken tenders
- 2 ½ tablespoons olive oil or calorie controlled cooking spray
- 75 grams panko breadcrumbs
- 50 grams grated Parmesan cheese
- ¾ teaspoon Herbes de Provence
- salt to taste

Instructions

- Preheat the air fryer to 180 degrees C.
- Add the chicken and olive oil to a bowl, and mix until the chicken is coated with the oil.
- Mix together the panko breadcrumbs, Parmesan, herbs, and salt on a rimmed plate.
- Coat each tender on both sides with the breadcrumb mixture.
- Place in the air fryer basket and cook for 9 – 12 minutes, turning halfway through.

428. Mozzarella Sticks

 Serving size: 2   **Preparation time:** 6 minutes

 Cooking time: 6 minutes   **Total time:** 12 minutes

Ingredients

- 10 frozen mozzarella sticks
- marinara sauce for dipping

Instructions

- Preheat the air fryer to 200 degrees C.
- Place the frozen mozzarella sticks in the air fryer cook for 6-8 minutes.
- Pinch slightly (and carefully since they're hot). They are done when the cheese inside is soft and there is give to the mozzarella stick.
- Remove them from the air fryer and enjoy with a marinara sauce for dipping.

429. British Taquitos

 Serving size: 2   **Preparation time:** 10 minutes

 Cooking time: 10 minutes   **Total time:** 20 minutes

Ingredients

- 6 taquitos (any flavour)
- 90 grams sour cream
- 1 tablespoon pepper
- 1 tablespoon all spice

Instructions

- Preheat your air fryer to 200 degrees C.
- Place the taquitos inside the air fryer and cook for about 5 minutes.
- Remove taquitos from the air fryer.
- Meanwhile, mix pepper, sour cream, and all spice together. Serve with taquitos

430. Classic Onion Rings

 Serving size: 2   **Preparation time:** 10 minutes

 Cooking time: 10 minutes   **Total time:** 20 minutes

Ingredients

- 1 large sweet (Vidalia) onion, sliced into ½-inch rings
- 2 large eggs
- 60 grams buttermilk
- 60 grams plain flour
- ½ teaspoon kosher salt
- ½ teaspoon black pepper
- ½ teaspoon garlic powder
- 60 grams panko breadcrumbs

Instructions

- Peel the onion and cut into thick slices.
- Separate the slices and place them on a plate. Set aside.
- In a wide, shallow bowl, lightly beat the eggs with the buttermilk until well combined. In a second bowl, combine the flour, salt, pepper, and garlic powder. Place the panko breadcrumbs in a third bowl.
- Dip each onion ring into the flour, then the buttermilk mixture, and then dredge it through the breadcrumbs, pressing to adhere. Set aside on a baking tray and repeat with remaining rings. Spray the rings with an oil sprayer.
- Preheat the air fryer to 200 degrees C.
- Transfer the rings into the air fryer basket in a single layer, nesting the smaller ones inside the larger ones but leaving a little space between each ring. Don't overcrowd the basket, and work in batches if necessary.
- Air fry for 9-12 minutes, or until golden brown and crispy.
- Sprinkle with salt if desired, and serve.

431. Bacon Wrapped Asparagus

 Serving size:
2

 Preparation time:
10 minutes

 Cooking time:
12 minutes

 Total time:
22 minutes

Ingredients

- 1 bunch of asparagus
- 1 pound of bacon (regular sliced not thick)

Instructions

- Wash and trim the ends of your asparagus.
- Preheat your air fryer to 200 degrees C.
- Wrap one slice of bacon around one stalk of asparagus.
- Lay your bacon-wrapped asparagus in your air fryer. If possible lay the ends of your bacon down flat to help keep them from curling. Leave space between your stalks so the air can circulate around them.

- I tried to do my first batch with my thicker stalks and they cooked for 12 minutes. Then in my second batch, I cooked my thinner ones for 10 minutes.
- Serve and enjoy.

432. British Pub Chips

 Serving size:
2

 Preparation time:
5 minutes

 Cooking time:
2 minutes

 Total time:
7 minutes

Ingredients

- 4 potatoes
- 130 grams cheddar cheese
- 3 onions
- 20 slices pickled jalapeno peppers
- 3 strips of bacon
- 40 ml. dipping sauce of your choice

Instructions

- Preheat the air fryer to 200 degrees C.
- Cut the potatoes into the desired shape and bake them for 7 minutes.
- Chop the rest of the ingredients, add it over the potatoes and bake for another 7 minutes.
- Remove from the air fryer and serve with the dipping sauce of your choice.

433. Avocado Chips

 Serving size:
2

 Preparation time:
5 minutes

 Cooking time:
10 minutes

 Total time:
15 minutes

Ingredients

- 4 avocados
- 100 grams panko breadcrumbs
- 60 grams plain flour
- 2 eggs
- 1/2 teaspoon garlic powder
- 1/2 teaspoon salt
- Sriracha-ranch sauce
- 90 ml. ranch dressing
- 1 teaspoon sriracha sauce

Instructions

- Preheat air fryer to 200 degrees C.
- Wash the avocados to clean them, then cut each avocado in half and then slice it into wedges. Use a big spoon to scoop out the wedges to keep them intact.
- Set up 3 bowls. Put the panko breadcrumbs in the first bowl and add the garlic powder and salt in. Mix to combine.
- Place the flour and eggs separately into the other two bowls. Whisk the eggs.
- Dip each avocado wedge into the breading in this order: egg, flour, egg, panko.
- Place the breaded avocado wedges into your air fryer basket in a single layer and cook for 4-6 minutes, flipping halfway through.
- While cooking, mix together dipping sauce. Combine the sriracha and ranch dressing and mix well.
- Enjoy immediately!

434. Toad in the Hole

 Serving size:
2

 Preparation time:
10 minutes

 Cooking time:
20 minutes

 Total time:
30 minutes

Ingredients

- 8 frozen turkey breakfast sausages
- 2 large eggs
- 140 ml. 2% milk
- 120 grams plain flour
- 1 teaspoon onion powder
- 1 teaspoon stone-ground mustard
- 1/8 teaspoon salt
- 1/8 teaspoon pepper

Instructions

- Preheat air fryer to 200°C. Cut sausages in half widthwise. Arrange in a greased 6-in. round baking tin. Place tin on the tray in air-fryer basket. Cook until lightly browned, 6-8 minutes, turning once.
- Meanwhile, in a large bowl, whisk eggs, milk, flour, onion powder, mustard, salt and pepper. If desired, stir in bacon; pour over sausages. Cook until puffed and golden brown, 10-15 minutes. Serve immediately and, if desired, garnish with parsley.

435. Shepherd's Pie

 Serving size:
4

 Preparation time:
20 minutes

 Cooking time:
10 minutes

Total time:
30 minutes

Ingredients

- 4 boneless skinless chicken breasts
- ¼ teaspoon salt plus extra for sprinkling
- ¼ teaspoon black pepper plus extra for sprinkling
- 1 jar chicken gravy
- 200 grams frozen mixed vegetables thawed
- ½ teaspoon onion powder
- 200 grams prepared mashed potatoes
- 2 tablespoons butter melted

Instructions

- Coat air fryer basket with cooking spray. Sprinkle chicken with salt and pepper, place in basket, and air fry 5 minutes. Turn chicken over and continue to cook 5 to 6 more minutes or until no pink remains in centre. Remove to a cutting board, let cool slightly, and cut into chunks.
- Meanwhile, in a pan over a medium heat, combine gravy, vegetables, onion powder, 1/4 teaspoon salt, and 1/4 teaspoon pepper. Cook 5 to 7 minutes or until heated through. When chicken is ready, stir that in and spoon mixture evenly into 4 ramekins.
- Top each ramekin with half of the mashed potatoes and drizzle melted butter on top.

436. Yorkshire Puddings

 Serving size:
4

 Preparation time:
5 minutes

 Cooking time:
15 minutes

 Total time:
20 minutes

Ingredients

- 1 tablespoon olive oil
- 50 grams plain flour
- 1 small egg
- 150 ml. milk
- Salt
- Pepper

Instructions

- Preheat your Air Fryer to 200 degrees C.
- Mix the plain flour and the seasoning in a bowl. Pour in the egg (a bit at a time) stirring gradually with a fork until the egg is all added.
- Add the milk a bit at a time and stir regularly until you have a mixture that is the thickness of a thick batter. Beat well until it forms bubbles on the top.
- Place a little olive oil in your Yorkshire Pudding tins and place in the Air Fryer for 5 minutes or until smoking. Pour your mixture (1/2 way up your Yorkshire pudding tin) and place back in the Air Fryer and cook at 200 degrees C for 15 minutes.

437. Chips

 Serving size:
4

 Preparation time:
10 minutes

 Cooking time:
20 minutes

 Total time:
30 minutes

Ingredients

- 5 large potatoes
- 3 tablespoons olive oil
- Salt
- Vinegar

Instructions

- Add Potatoes to a bowl of water and soak 10 minutes.
- Drain. Rinse the potatoes and pat dry with kitchen towel.
- Add the chips to the air fryer in a single layer and add oil.
- Toss through to coat the chips. Add the seasoning.
- Preheat air fryer to 180 degrees C. Set timer for 20 minutes, shaking midway.
- Check if the chips are cooked. If they aren't cook for a further 5 minutes and continue to do so until they're fully cooked.

438. Mashed Peas

 Serving size:
4

 Preparation time:
5 minutes

 Cooking time:
10 minutes

 Total time:
15 minutes

Ingredients

- 1 packet frozen peas
- 40 ml double cream
- 1 tablespoon butter
- Salt
- Black pepper

Instructions

- Bring a shallow pan of lightly salted water to a boil over a medium-high heat. Add frozen peas, and cook for 3 minutes, or until tender.
- Drain peas, and transfer to a blender or large food processor. Add cream, butter, salt and pepper to peas, and process until blended, but still thick with small pieces of peas. Adjust seasonings to taste, and serve immediately.

439. Bubble & Squeak

 Serving size:
2

 Preparation time:
5 minutes

 Cooking time:
12 minutes

 Total time:
17 minutes

Ingredients

- 500 grams mashed potatoes
- 200 grams cabbage
- 100 grams meat of your choice
- 40 grams cheddar cheese
- 2 teaspoons thyme
- Salt
- Pepper

Instructions

- Load into a mixing bowl all your ingredients. Mix well with your hands and form it into a ball.
- Load into your air fryer cake pan or baking pan and air fry for 8 minutes at 180 degrees C, followed by a further 4 minutes at 200 degrees C.

440. Pasta Chips

 Serving size:

 Preparation time:
30 minutes

 Cooking time:
10 minutes

 Total time:
40 minutes

Ingredients

- 150 grams whole wheat bow tie pasta
- 1 tablespoon olive oil
- 1 ½ teaspoon Italian seasoning blend
- ½ teaspoon salt

Instructions

- Cook the pasta for half the time featured on the package. Toss the drained pasta with the olive oil, nutritional yeast, Italian seasoning, and salt.
- Place about half of the mixture in your air fryer basket if yours is small; larger ones may be able to cook it in one batch.
- Cook on 200°C for 5 minutes. Shake the basket and cook 3 to 5 minutes more or until crunchy.
- Note: These will crisp up more as they cool.

441. Mini Pizzas

 Serving size:
1

 Preparation time:
10 minutes

 Cooking time:
20 minutes

 Total time:
30 minutes

Ingredients

- 1 pack white rolls, 12
- 1 can marinara or pizza sauce
- 250 grams grated mozzarella cheese
- ¼ red onion diced
- 150grams mix coloured peppers chopped, using red, green and orange
- 5-6 black olives sliced
- ¼ teaspoon dry oregano
- Salt
- Pepper

Instructions

- Cut the dinner rolls in half lengthwise. Place the bottom half of the bread on to the prepared baking tray. Apply some butter, followed by you favorite pizza or marinara sauce (homemade or shop-bought) and ½ of the mozzarella cheese.
- Add the toppings (onion, pepper and olives), sprinkle some salt, black pepper and oregano and remaining cheese.
- Transfer to the air fryer and bake at 220° C for 5-7 mins or until the cheese is melted and then again after covering. bake the other half bake for another 5 minutes. Brush with more garlic butter and sprinkle some fresh parsley. Serve immediately on its own or with some more marinara for dipping!!

442. Cucumber Sandwiches

 Serving size:
2

 Preparation time:
5 minutes

 Cooking time:
10 minutes

Total time:
15 minutes

Ingredients

- 90 grams cream cheese
- 3 tablespoons mayonnaise
- 2 teaspoons fresh dill
- 1 teaspoon fresh chives
- ¼ teaspoon garlic powder
- Salt
- Pepper
- 1 english cucumber
- 1 loaf sliced bread

Instructions

- Assemble the ingredients in the middle of a slice of bread and place another slice on top, to form a sandwich.
- Preheat the air fryer to 200 degrees C.
- Add the sandwich and bake it for 8 minutes.
- Remove the sandwich and cut it into small pieces.

443. Scotch Egg

 Serving size:
6

 Preparation time:
15 minutes

 Cooking time:
20 minutes

Total time:
30 minutes

Ingredients

Dipping Sauce:
- 3 tablespoons Greek yogurt
- 2 tablespoons mango chutney
- 1 tablespoon mayonnaise
- ⅛ teaspoon salt
- ⅛ teaspoon pepper
- ⅛ teaspoon curry powder
- ⅛ teaspoon cayenne pepper (Optional)

Scotch Eggs:
- 500 grams pork sausage
- 6 eggs, hard-boiled and shelled
- 40 grams plain flour
- 2 eggs, lightly beaten
- 120 grams panko breadcrumbs
- cooking spray

Instructions

- Combine yogurt, chutney, mayonnaise, salt, pepper, curry powder, and cayenne in a small bowl. Refrigerate until ready to use.
- Divide pork sausage into 6 even portions. Flatten each portion into a thin patty. Place one egg in the middle and wrap the sausage around the eggs, sealing all sides. Set eggs aside on a plate.
- Preheat air fryer to 200 degrees C.
- Place flour into a small bowl and beaten eggs into another small bowl. Place panko breadcrumbs onto a plate. Dip each sausage-wrapped egg into flour, then dip into beaten egg, letting the excess drip off. Roll in breadcrumbs and place onto a plate.
- Spray basket of the air fryer with cooking spray and place eggs into the basket. Do not overcrowd; cook in batches if necessary. Cook for 12 minutes, turning eggs over halfway through. Repeat with remaining eggs. Serve with dipping sauce.

444. Chip Butties

 Serving size:
1

 Preparation time:
5 minutes

 Cooking time:
20 minutes

 Total time:
25 minutes

Ingredients

- 2 slices of white bread (or a white bap)
- Butter
- Salt
- Frozen Chips

Instructions

- Cook the frozen chips in the air fryer, according to the instructions provided on the packet.
- Butter your bread or roll on both inside surfaces (as thick as you like).
- Place the chips on one side of the bread and salt them.
- Preheat the air fryer at 200 degrees C and bake the sandwich for 5 minutes.

445. Sausage in the Air Fryer

 Serving size:
2

 Preparation time:
5 minutes

 Cooking time:
12 minutes

 Total time:
17 minutes

Ingredients

- 6 sausages
- Spray oil

Instructions

- Preheat air fryer to 180°C for 5 minutes.
- Prick each sausage a few times with a sharp knife.
- Spray the base of the air fryer with a couple of squirts of spray oil to prevent sausages from sticking.
- Use a pair of tongs to carefully place sausages in (do not allow them to touch for even cooking).
- Put the timer on for 12 minutes.

446. Kidney Pie

 Serving size:
2

 Preparation time:
5 minutes

 Cooking time:
1 hour and 35 minutes

Total time:
1 hour and 40 minutes

Ingredients

- 500 grams beef steak
- 1 can ale
- 1 large onion
- 1 tablespoon tomato puree
- 1 tablespoon olive oil
- 1 tablespoon plain flour
- 2 oxo cubes
- Salt
- Pepper

Instructions

- Place. in a large pan. the onion, stewing steak, tomato puree and the olive oil. Cook on a medium heat until the beef is sealed.
- In a jug add the can of ale and double the quantity of liquid with warm water. Place it in the pan along with the OXO cubes and the salt and pepper. Stir the ingredients and then bring to the boil on a high heat. Reduce the temperature to low and simmer for an hour.
- In a small bowl mix together a tablespoon of plain flour with 3 tablespoons of warm water. This will provide you with a thi-

ckening agent for your pie. Pour it into the pan slowly (a bit at a time) and mix well.

- Take the meat off the heat and put to one side.
- Roll out your shortcrust pastry and line your ramekins or mini pot pie dishes. Dust them with flour first though to stop them sticking. Add your pie filling and then add extra pastry for the top. Stab with a fork so that they have chance to breathe.
- Cook in the air fryer for 10 minutes at 200c and then a further 6 minutes at 170c in order for them to cook in the middle.
- Serve with homemade mash.

447. Mini Sausage Rolls

 Serving size:
12

 Preparation time:
5 minutes

 Cooking time:
10 minutes

Total time:
15 minutes

Ingredients

- 3 sausages
- 3 sheets puff pastry
- 1 tablespoon sesame seeds
- 1 eggs

Instructions

- Turn the air fryer on to 180°C for 15 mins
- Use a knife and chopping board to remove the skin from the sausages
- Add egg to a small bowl, pierce the yoke and whisk
- Place a sheet of puff pastry (thawed) onto the chopping board and place 1 of the sausages on top
- Roll the pastry around the sausage, then use a pastry brush to coat the top of the pastry where the 2 bits of pastry will meet
- Continue to roll the pastry around the sausage and again brush one side of where the pastry joins with the egg
- Repeat for each sausage
- Brush the top of the length of the long rolled sausage with egg
- Sprinkle the top with sesame seeds
- Use a knife to cut the excess pastry off each end
- Then cut the long sausage roll into 4 smaller rolls
- Spray the Air Fryer Basket with oil (or use baking paper) then place raw sausage rolls into Air Fryer (work in batches)
- Cook sausage rolls in Air Fryer for 7- 9 mins until pastry is golden and crispy
- Serve with sauce

448. Cheese and Pineapple

 Serving size:
4

 Preparation time:
10 minutes

 Cooking time:
10 minutes

Total time:
20 minutes

Ingredients

- 1 whole Pineapple peeled and cut into slices
- 4 tablespoons unsalted butter melted
- 90 grams parmesan cheese

Instructions

- Place the cut pineapple into a large bowl.
- Pour the melted butter into the bowl, and toss the pineapple until all of the pieces are well coated with the butter.
- Grate the parmesan cheese and put it over the pineapple.
- Place the coated pineapple slices into the air fryer basket.
- Cook at 200 degrees C for about 10 minutes.

449. Turkey Croquettes

 Serving size:
6

 Preparation time:
20 minutes

 Cooking time:
10 minutes

 Total time:
30 minutes

Ingredients

- 220 grams mashed potatoes (with added milk and butter)
- 100 grams grated Parmesan cheese
- 100 grams grated Swiss cheese
- 1 shallot, finely chopped
- 2 teaspoons chopped fresh rosemary or 1/2 teaspoon dried rosemary, crushed
- 1 teaspoon chopped fresh sage or 1/4 teaspoon dried sage leaves
- 1/2 teaspoon salt
- 1/4 teaspoon pepper
- 250 grams finely chopped cooked turkey
- 1 large egg
- 2 tablespoons water
- 130 grams panko breadcrumbs
- Butter-flavoured cooking spray
- Sour cream, optional

Instructions

- Preheat air fryer to 220°C. In a large bowl, combine mashed potatoes, cheeses, shallot, rosemary, sage, salt and pepper; stir in turkey. Mix lightly but thoroughly. Shape into 12 1-inch thick patties.
- In a shallow bowl, whisk egg and water. Place breadcrumbs in another shallow bowl. Dip croquettes in egg mixture, then in breadcrumbs, patting to help the coating adhere.
- Working in batches, place croquettes in a single layer on a greased tray in air-fryer basket; spray with cooking spray. Cook until golden brown, 4-5 minutes. Turn; spray with cooking spray. Cook until golden brown; 4-5 minutes. If desired, serve with sour cream.

Instructions

- Boil a pot of water.
- Add the green beans and cook until tender for 5 minutes.
- Heat the butter in a large pan over a high heat. Add the garlic and pine nuts and sauté for 2 minutes or until the pine nuts are lightly browned.
- Transfer the green beans to the pan and turn until coated.
- Serve!

450. Grandma's Beans

Serving size: 4		**Preparation time:** 5 minutes	
Cooking time: 10 minutes		**Total time:** 15 minutes	

Ingredients

- 200 grams green beans
- 120 grams butter
- 2 cloves garlic
- 130 grams pine nuts

BONUS!

Thanks! Find your gift here!

My Mediterranean Air fryer cookbook in PDF.
An extensive collection of air fryer meals to have even more
Ideas, or make a gift. Send the Pdf to friends and family with
a single Click on Whatsapp or Social Network. Enjoy!

INDEX

Chicken Schnitzel with Mozzarella, 12
Chicken with Peas and Carrots, 14
Chicken Pizza, 104
Crispy Chicken with Pickles, 18
Lemon Chicken with Thyme and Broccoli, 23
Mozzarella and Parmesan Chicken, 24
Parmesan Chicken, 18
Pesto Chicken, 24
Pineapple and Pepper Chicken, 19
Salsa Verde Chicken Kebobs, 12
Shepherd's Pie, 148
Spicy Chicken Breasts, 15
Sweet Chicken Breasts, 15
Tarragon Chicken, 15

CHICKEN DRUMSTICKS
Curry Chicken, 21
Drumsticks with Cheddar Cheese Sause, 13
Hot Chicken Drumsticks, 21
Southern Drumsticks, 24
Spicy Chicken Drumsticks, 22

CHICKEN THIGHS
Asiago Chicken Thighs, 26
Chicken Bites with English Mustard, 13
Chicken Honey, 14
Chicken Souvlaki, 20
Chicken Thighs with 5 Different Spices, 21
Chicken with Black Beans, 21
Sweet Chili Chicken Fillets, 18
Spicy Chicken Tenders, 145

CHICKEN WINGS
Chicken Wings with Cayenne Spice and Potatoes, 11
Chicken Wings with Sesame Seeds, 12
 Spiced Chicken Wings, 137
Spicy Wings, 26

CHIPS, CRISP, AND NACHOS
British Pub Chips, 147
British Taquitos, 146
Chip Butties, 151
Crispy Lavash, 134
Pasta Chips, 105
Pasta Chips, 149
Pasta Tacos, 107
Pickle Chips, 138
Polenta Fries, 80
Quick Popcorn, 139
Vegetable Tacos, 79

CHOCOLATE
British Chocolate Fudge, 119
Dark Chocolate Brownies, 112
White Chocolate Pudding, 115

CORN
Baby Corns with Garlic, 138
Corn Cakes, 71
Corn in Turmeric, 72

COURGETTE
Cabbage Steaks, 87
Courgette Chips, 83
Courgette Rolls, 136
Mayo Carrot Courgette Dish, 74
Parmesan Courgette, 85
Roasted Rosemary Squash, 82
Spaghetti Squash, 108
Tomato Stuffed Squash, 88

DESSERTS, SWEETS
Apple Caramel Relish, 114
Banana Pasty, 124
Beignets, 130
Berry Crumble, 123
Bread Pudding, 132
Cannoli, 114
Cherry Crumble, 117
Churros, 110
Cinnamon Bread Twists, 128
Cinnamon Sugar Fries, 127
Classic British S'mores, 128
Crème Brulé, 116
Donut Sticks with Powdered Sugar, 117
Donuts with Chocolate Glaze, 128
Glazed Air Fryer Donuts, 129
Jelly Donuts, 126
Lemon Curd, 115
Peanut Butter and Jelly S'mores, 118
Snickerdoodle Poppers, 111
Strawberry Chimichangas, 132

DUCKS
Chinese Duck Breast, 27
Crispy Duck Breast, 28
Duck Breast with Tomato Sauce, 26
Juicy Duck Breast, 27
Spicy Duck Leg, 27
Whole Duck with Potatoes, Carrots and Celery, 28

EGGS
Deviled Eggs, 142
Egg and French Beans Mixture, 10
Eggs with Baby Spinach and Plum Tomatoes, 3
Ramekins with Mushrooms, Baby Spinach and Eggs, 4
Scotch Egg, 150
Yorkshire Pudding, 148

FISH

Air Fried Salmon with Broccoli, 57
Apple Cod Fillet, 61
Barramundi with Lemon Butter Garlic Sauce, 55
Beer Cod Fillet, 62
Blackened Fish, 67
British Seafood Bomb, 64
Broiled Tilapia, 68
Cajun Salmon, 62
Celery and Garlic Turbot, 65
Cod Fennel Platter, 67
Cod with Basil Vinaigrette, 60
Cod with Soy Sauce, 59
Crisped Filet with Crumb Tops, 66
Crispy Salmon, 54
Fish Tacos, 57
Grilled Halibut, 65
Haddock with Pepper and Lemon, 58
Lemon Fish Cakes, 66
Parmesan Tilapia, 67
Salmon Balls, 58
Salmon with Thyme, 53
Sesame Fish Fillets, 56
Sockeye Fish, 67
Thai Cod, 61
Trout Frittata, 69
Tuna Patties, 63
Tuna Tacos, 58
White Fish Fillets with Chips, 56 Wine Baked Cod, 62

FRUIT MEALS

Apple Chips, 78
Apple Crips, 111
Apple Fritters, 6
Apple Peanut Butter Wedges, 128
Baked Apples, 111
Baked Apples with Walnuts, 113
Baked Cherries with Nuts, 123
Baked Pears, 113
Banana Fritters, 123
Cheese and Pineapple, 152
Grilled Peaches, 110
Pepper Pineapple with Sugar Glaze, 78
Raspberry Crisp, 118
Roasted Bananas, 133

GRAIN, BEANS, LEGUMES

Air-Fried Falafel, 80
Chickpea-Fig with Arugula, 77

LAMB

Cashew Lamb Rack, 50
Honey and Pork Dish, 48
Lamb Steaks with Potatoes and Mushrooms, 51
Mediterranean Lamb Chops, 34
Mediterranean Lamb Chops, 52
Rosemary and Garlic Lamb Chops, 51
Thyme Lamb Chops, 51

MEATBALLS

Beef Rolls, 9
Greek Meatballs with Basil, 33
Italian Meatballs, 34
Kofta Kabobs with Cheese Sauce, 34
Meatballs with Tomato Sauce, 43
Muffins from Mexico, 141
Peppercorn Meatloaf, 44
Spaghetti and Meatballs, 106
Spicy Meatloaf with Tomato Basil Sauce, 45
Spicy Pork Kebabs, 40

MORE BEEF MEALS

Beef Bites, 141
Beef Quesadillas, 42
Beef Schnitzel, 42
British Beef Roast, 48
Chipotle Steak, 46
Liver Muffins with Eggs, 42
Liver Souffle, 44
Roast beef, 43
Sweet Beef and Vegetables, 41

MORE PORK MEALS

Crispy Roast Pork, 36
Pork Rack with Macadamia Nuts, 40
Pork Tenderloins with Honey Garlic Sauce, 34
Pulled Pork with Bacon and Cheddar, 39
Stuffed Pork Loins with Bacon, 37
Tangy Pork Roast, 39

MORE VEGETABLES

Baked Green Beans, 92
Balsamic Vegetables, 71
Beetroot Chips with Broccoli, 92
Bubble & Squeak, 149
Butterbean Pork Ratatouille, 50
Creole Vegetables, 75
Grandma's Beans, 153
Mashed Peas, 149
Mediterranean Vegetable Bowl, 91
Okra with Sesame, 143
Parsnip Bake, 91
Radish Chips with Sage, 136
Ratatouille, 86
Roasted Parsnip, 139
Roasted Vegetable Salad, 90
Tempura Vegetables with Sesame Sauce, 79
Three Cheese Vegetable Frittata, 85
Vegetable Croquettes, 70
Vegetable Skewers, 89
Vegetable Pizza, 102
Veggie Sushi, 71
Winter Vegetable Delight, 83

MUFFIN, CUPCAKES, COOKIES
Air Fried Oreos, 125
Almond Cookies, 115
Blueberry Scones, 119
Coconut Macaroons, 132
Coconut Oat Cookies, 120
Cookie Fries, 117
Egg Muffins, 8
Lemon Glazed Muffins, 121
Oat Cookies, 120
Pumpkin Cookies, 118

MUSHROOMS
Baked Garlic Mushrooms, 93
Filled Mushrooms with Cheddar and Bacon, 84
Fried Portobello Mushrooms, 77
Mushrooms with Pesto, 78

NUGGETS, FINGERS, STRIPS, AND BITES
British Chicken Nuggets, 16
Chicken Fingers with Parmesan Cheese, 14
Chicken Lemon, 16
Chicken Tenders with Special Chicken Sauce, 23
Cod Nuggets, 68
Crispy Fish Fingers, 55
Fish Nuggets, 53
Fish Sticks with Basil, 140
Mozzarella Sticks, 146
Parmesan Chicken Fingers, 146
Paprika Fish Nuggets, 66
Traditional British Fish & Chips, 54

NUTS
Cashew Bowls, 135
Cashew Dip, 139
Mixed Nuts, 135
Walnuts and Green Beans, 77

OAT
Air Fryer Granola with Sour Cream and Blueberries, 7
Oats with Cream Cheese, 9

OMELET
Fluffy Omelet, 7
Ramekins Eggs Omelet and Bacon, 4
Tofu and Plum Tomatoes Omelet, 7

ONION
Buttered Onion Rings, 72
Caramelized Onion Pizza, 100
Classic Onion Rings, 146
Onion Chicken, 22
Onion Dip, 142

PANCAKES, TOASTS
British Blueberry Pancakes, 4
British French Toast, 6
French Toast Sticks with Powdered Sugar, 117
French Toast Sticks with Strawberry Marmalade, 7
Grilled Tomato Toast, 4
Savory French Toast, 8
Waffles with Orange Marmalade, 5

PASTA, NOODLE
Baked Feta Pasta, 107
Mac & Cheese, 105
Parmesan Pasta, 107
Pasta Bake, 106
Tortellini Alfredo, 106

PEPPERS
Pepper Chips, 138
Pepper Pizza, 101
Pepper Tortilla, 74
Pepper with Tofu, and Spices, 73
Peppers Filled with Cheese, 81

PIES, CAKES
Angel Cake, 110
Apple Pie, 121
British Banana Cake, 133
British Apple Hand Pies, 129
British Pumpkin Hand Pies, 130
Butter Cake, 116
Chocolate and Raspberry Cake, 113
Carrot Cake, 109
Coffee Cake, 122
Cookie Cake, 127
Lime Tarts, 120
Lava Cakes, 126
Lemon Cheesecake, 112
Minced Pie, 109
Mock Cherry Pie, 121
Orange Sponge Cake, 122
Pumpkin Pie Twists, 127
Pumpkin Pie, 125
Pecan Pie, 124
Raspberry Hand Pies, 119
Raspberry Cheesecake, 112
Smores Pie, 131
The Best Colorful Cake, 126
Twix Cheesecake, 131

PIZZA
3 Types of Meat Pizza, 100
Ground Beef Pizza, 100 Mini Pizzas, 150
Quick Pizza, 101
Pepperoni Pizza, 99

PORK CHOPS
Bacon Wrapped Pork Chops, 38
Breaded Pork Chops, 37
Crispy Pork Chops, 35
Herbed Pork Chops, 38
Juicy Pork Chops, 49
Mustard Pork Chops, 40
Sweet and Tender Pork Chops, 49
Pork Chops with Onions and Apples, 35

PORK RIBS
BBQ Ribs, 41
Char Siew Pork Ribs, 37
Ginger Beef Ribs, 46
Pork Ribs with Honey, 36

POTATOES
Baked Potatoes with Olives and Cream Cheese, 73
Chips, 149
Crispy Potatoes with Rosemary, 137
Eggs with Yellow Potatoes, 2
Filled Hash Browns, 5
Olives with Sweet Potatoes, 76
Potato Chips, 84
Sweet Potatoes Hash, 2
Sweet Potato Tots, 137
Traditional Jacket Potatoes, 93
Yellow Potatoes Hash, 2

PRAWNS, SCALLOPS, CRABS, SHRIMP
Almond Shrimps, 60
Breaded Scallops, 57
British Prawn Recipe, 54
British Crab Legs, 68
Cajun Shrimp, 59
Cajun Shrimps, 66
Calamari, 57
Chili Clams, 61
Chinese Shrimp Medley, 64
Chipotle Crab Cakes, 63
Clams with Herbed Butter, 65
Coconut Shrimps, 59
Crab Croquettes, 56
Garlic Lobster with Herbs, 69
Garlic Sriracha Prawns, 62
Garlic Scallops, 61
Greek Fried Mussels, 63
Hot Prawns, 55
Prawn and Cabbage Egg Rolls, 143
Rainbow Prawns, 65
Shrimp Bake, 64
Shrimp Risotto, 60

SANDWICHES, WRAPS
Cucumber Sandwiches, 150
Feta and Pesto Tomato Sandwiches, 85
Grilled Cheese Sandwich, 144
Ham and Cheese Sandwich, 50
Peanut Butter Banana Sandwiches, 116
Tuna Sandwich, 55

SAUSAGES
Bacon-Wrapped Sausages, 38
Eggs with English Sausages, 3
Mini Sausage Rolls, 152
Onion and Sausage Balls, 49
Sausage in the Air Fryer, 151
Sausage Pizza, 102
Toad in the Hole, 148
Traditional English Breakfast, 8

TOFU
Crispy Tofu, 70
Paprika Tofu, 76
Tofu Enchiladas with Cheese, 87
Tofu Pizza, 99
Tofu Sandwich, 88
Tofu with Lemon, 140

TOMATO
Almonds, Cheese and Tomatoes, 78
Green Tomatoes, 140
Herbs and Tomatoes, 141
Lemony Tomatoes, 76
Tomato Pizza, 103

TURKEY
Candied Turkey Breast, 30
Cheese Turkey Breast, 31
Coconut Turkey Fingers, 30
Garlic Herb Turkey Breast, 28
Lemon Turkey Breast, 29
Maple Turkey Breast, 32
Olive Bried Turkey Breast, 29
Rosemary Turkey Breast with Potatoes, 29
Sweet Turkey Bake, 31
Turkey Breast, 28
Turkey Nuggets with Thyme, 31
Turkey Croquettes, 152

WHOLE CHICKEN
Chicken Taquitos with Special Chicken Sauce, 144 Christmas Chicken, 19
Easter Chicken, 20
Portuguese Whole Chicken, 11

COOKING TIME CHARTS

Beef in the Air Fryer

Burger	16 to 20 Mins	370' F 188°C	(4 oz.)
Flie! Mignon	18 Mins	400°F 204°C	(8 oz.)
Flank Steak	12 Mins	400'F 204°C	(1.5 lbs.)
London Broil	20 to 28 Mins	400'F 204°C	(2 lbs.)
Meatballs	7 Mins	380"F 193°C	1-inch}
Meatballs	10 Mins	380"F 193°C	(3-inch)
Rlbeye, bone ln	10 to 15 Mins	400'F 204°C	1-inch, 8 oz.}
Sirloin steaks	9 to 14 Mins	400'F 204°C	1-inch,12 oz.}
Beef Eye Round Roast	45 to 55 Mins	390"F 199°C	(4lbs.)

Vegetables in the Air Fryer

Asparagus	5 Mins	400°F 204°C	(sliced 1-inch)
Beest	40 Mins	400°F 204°C	(whole)
Broccoli	6 Mins	400'F 204°C	(florets)
Brussels Sprouts	15 Mins	380"F 193°C	(halved)
Carrots	15 Mins	380"F 193°C	(sllced½-inch)
Cauliflower	12 Mins	400°F 204°C	(florets)
Com on the cob	6 Mins	390"F 199°C	
Eggplant	15 Mins	400°F 204°C	(1½-inch cubes)

Fennel	15 Mins	370°F 188°C	(quartered)
Green Beans	5 Mins	400°F 204°C	
Kale leaves	12 Mins	250°F 121°C	
Mushrooms	5 Mins	400F' 204°C	(sliced ¼-Inch)
Onions	10 Mins	400'F 204°C	(peart)
Parsnips	15 Mins	380"F 193°C	(½-inchchunks)
Peppers	15 Mins	400°F 204°C	(1-inchchunks)
Potatoes	15 Mins	400'F 204°C	(small baby, 1.5 lbs)
Potatoes	12 Mins	400°F 204°C	(1-inchchunks)
Potatoes	40 Mins	400'F 204°C	(baked whole)

Squash	12 Mins	400'F 204°C	(½-inchchunks)
Sweet Potato	30 to 35 Mins	380"F 193°C	(baked)
Tomatoe	4 Mins	400'F 204°C	(scherry)
Tomatoes	10 Mins	-18°C	(halves)
Zucchini	12 Mins	350'F 177°C	(½-inchsticks)

Pork and Lamb in the Air Fryer

Loin	55 Mins	360'F 182°C	(2 lbs.)
Pork Chops, bone In	12 Mins	400'F 204°C	(1-inch, 6.5 oz.)
Tenderloin	15 Mins	370'F 188°C	(1lb.)
Bacon	5 to 7 Mins	400'F 204°C	(regular)
Bacon	6 to10 Mins	400'F 204°C	thick cut}
Sausages	15 Mins	380"F 193°C	
Lamb LoinChops	8 to 12 Mins	400'F 204°C	(1-inch thick)
Rack of lamb	22 Mins	380"F 193°C	(1.5 - 2lbs.)

Chicken in the Air Fryer

Breast's bone	25 Mins	370'F 188°C	(1.25lbs.)
Breasts, boneless	12 Mins	380"F 193°C	(4 oz.)
Drumsticks	20 Mins	370F' 188°C	(2.5 lbs.)
Thighs, bone In	22 Mins	380"F 193°C	(2 lbs.)
Thighs, boneless	18 to 20 Mins	380"F 193°C	(1.5 lbs.)
Legs, bone In	30 Mins	380"F 193°C	(1.75lbs.)
Wings	12 Mins	400'F 204°C	(2 lbs.)
Game Hen	20 Mins	390"F 199°C	(halved- 2lbs.)
Whole Chicken	75 Mins	360'F 182°C	(6.5 lbs.)
Tenders	8 to 10 Mins	360'F 182°C	

Printed in Great Britain
by Amazon

85539300R00099